Author
Leslée Wills

Photographs
Marcel Knobil

Design
Chris Church at DRIVE

Acknowledgements
Special thanks to Marialine Verdickt from Lilt and
Claire Holder, chair of the Notting Hill Carnival Board
©1996 Creative & Commercial Communications Ltd.

Marcel Knobil is the copyright owner of all
photographs with the exception of those
attitributed to other individuals

Published by
Creative & Commercial Communications Ltd.
246/248 Great Portland Street
London W1N 5HF
Tel: 0171 388 0357
Fax: 0171 388 0370

All rights reserved

No part of this publication may be reproduced or transmitted in any
form or by any means, electronic or mechanical, including photocopying,
recording or any information storage and retrieval system relating to all or
part of the text and photographs without first obtaining permission in
writing from the publisher of this book.

Printed in Hong Kong
ISBN 0 9528153 0 3

THE OFFICIAL LILT NOTTING HILL CARNIVAL BOOK

FOREWORD BY
CLAIRE HOLDER
CHAIR OF THE NOTTING HILL CARNIVAL BOARD

WRITTEN BY
LESLEE WILLS

PHOTOGRAPHS BY
MARCEL KNOBIL

Young, old, black, white, brown: all people of the world descend upon Notting Hill as if on a pilgrimage to "the festival of life". A festival of music, dance, and colour which inspires and captivates a couple of million people for two invigorating August days.

"Carnival is we ting" as they say. But Carnival is a phenomenon which none of us really comprehend. Our academics have speculated over the years about the reasons why Carnival occurred in the first place and the reasons behind its phenomenal growth in popularity. The reasons however, essentially involve passion; the passion we feel that inspires us to labour month after month, day after day, from sunup to sundown trying to fashion that passion into the creation of Mas and into the composition of bars of music reverberating our very souls. The heavy bass, the drum beats, the peppery rhythms, the melodious thud of rubber on steel and soul searching lyrics - all evoke that passion.

Carnival means something to everyone. From an event which on the first occasion had a few hundred participants, Carnival now boasts two million revellers and enjoys support from Lilt. What used to be simply the Notting Hill Carnival is now the Lilt Notting Hill Carnival. This partnership with Lilt has been a positive step in the evolution of Carnival: it's no longer a secondary sub-culture. It's now a mainstream event.

The Lilt Notting Hill Carnival is the celebration of freedom and culture; its birth, its growth, its arts and practices and its general evolution and development all reaffirm the right of everyone to be free men and women, the right to self-determination.

Carnival's future is secure as a cultural event. The force and passion behind the Carnival manifest themselves in a spontaneous revelry amongst all those that attend. So while it started as an exclusively Caribbean festival, the Carnival now also embraces a whole range of Britain's diverse cultures which is recognised nationally and internationally. Its success and strength are grounded in the culture of diversity.

So, what is Carnival about? Carnival is about MAS; Carnival is about PAN; Carnival is about RIDDIM; Carnival is music to the SOUL.

Carnival is an event for the people and by the people. MAS is the acronym for MASQUERADE, PAN is the acronym for STEELPAN and RIDDIM is the beat that vibrates in your soul to make you sweet.

It is a fusion of unrelenting dance; potent colour; pulsating sounds and enticing aromas. Enjoyed by everyone. That is Carnival!

foreword — By Claire Holder, chair of the Notting Hill Carnival Board

history

Thirty years ago when the first bunch of die-hard carnivalists took to the streets of Notting Hill they could never have conceived that they had provided the inspiration for what was to become the largest street festival in Europe.

That festival is now known by millions throughout the world as the Lilt Notting Hill Carnival, the annual event that takes place in the Grove, Ladbroke Grove in Notting Hill, West London within the Royal Borough of Kensington and Chelsea; a borough that boasts residents from diverse cultural groups and from many walks of life.

In 1964, an invitation from a Notting Hill social worker to a group of steel panmen to come and play at the Notting Hill Festival, sowed the seeds of the modern day Lilt Notting Hill Carnival. From the moment the first steel panmen played on the streets, the West Indian community claimed the event as theirs, it was "the celebration and commemoration of their freedom from slavery" as enjoyed back home. The haunting clarity of the tenor pan playing "Yellow Bird", "Rum and Coca-Cola", "Miss Mary Ann" and other Caribbean folk songs engendered a longing for home.

Photo courtesy of Lawrence Noel

Carnival became known as the Caribbean festival in Notting Hill, organised by people from the Caribbean for the people from the Caribbean.

This modest start ignited the energy and creativity of the community. Born out of their sense of alienation, many argue that the Carnival also became an act of political and psychological defiance too. Carnival's cultural strength was tied to its ability to challenge or absorb attempts to attack its existence. Notting Hill's Carnival history is a determined expression of cultural continuity and survival.

The racial and cultural composition of these West Indians is as diverse as world culture itself. Caribbean people hail from Africa, South India, Carib, English Spanish, French Chinese and Syrian origins.

Photo courtesy of Caribbean Times

history

Their spirituality embraces Vodun, Obeah, Rastafarianism, Santeria, Pocamnia, Shango as well as Hindu, Catholicism, Islam, Methodism, and many other forms of Christianity. With such a heritage, it is no wonder that the Carnival erupts with such a diversity of colours, flavours, sounds and movements.

Carnival, derived from the Latin "carne vale" translates as "farewell the flesh" or "enjoyment". It is thought to have been a Roman Catholic inspired convention set two days before Lent with the same basic features as today's festival. Feasting, masqueing, jesting, costumes, dancing, role reversals, satire, street theatre and sexual license were its many very active ingredients.

Carnival, in most countries, takes place in February or March. In Notting Hill, Carnival takes place in August, the warmest time of the year when one can dare predict a ray of sunshine and warmth which is reflected in the moods of the people who come to Carnival.

Even without the benefit of advertising, somehow word spread, and more and more people became victims of the Carnival spell. By 1974 the number of people attending the event reached 100,000. Just one year later more than double that figure were dancing through the streets. People travelled from all over the country, and soon enthusiasts were arriving from throughout the globe.

By the late 1970's and early 80's the Carnival became a vehicle for political, not just cultural, assertion. Police attempts to constrain and control it followed several years of riot incidents (mainly outside the costume routes). Media overkill and highly exaggerated viewpoints eventually melted by the 1990's.

As more and more people of all cultures have become entranced by the Carnival over the last decade, so it has taken on the multicultural perspective that has become its trademark. And as harmony has eclipsed conflict, the event has grown at a phenomenal rate.

Photo courtesy of Caribbean Times

After thirty years, costumes, music and dance at Notting Hill still thrill, shock, stun, enrapture and 'exorcise'. The costumes sheer scale and engineering skill is a testimony to form and a tribute to generations of carnival crafts.

The Lilt Notting Hill Carnival now comprises 100 Mas bands, 15 steelbands, 45 sound systems, 25 mobile or Soca sound systems and 12 Calypsonians. They wend their way through the streets of Notting Hill dancing for twelve hours along a route of 3 miles, sometimes stopping to pose for a photograph, eat a roti or put their feet up.

The journey is long and it's arduous but oh "so satisfying".

history

Photo courtesy of Caribbean Times

While the Pan-man beats his pan, the DJ scratches his tune and the Mas-man struts his stuff, the Calypsonian will remind us, lest we forget, Carnival is a street-festival of arts. "The Road Make To Walk on Carnival Day."

The traditional music of the Carnival is Calypso, a form of social commentary set to the beat of music. The subject matter of a Calypso is as diverse as society itself. Subjects in the past have ranged from warnings to children that they must go "to school and learn well, otherwise later on in life yer go catch real hell" to commentary on the occasion when the intruder was found in the Queen's bedroom in 1980. Themes can be political and serious, amusing and whimsical, but never without satire.

Few can resist moving to the sounds of Soca which has added a new tempo to the Calypso beat, designed not just to make you listen to the commentary but to also dance and jump to it - "How yer feelin, Hot! Hot! Hot!".

Carnival is not Carnival without "Pan", "Steelpan music". A steelpan is an oil drum that has been cut, burnt, shaped and tuned and that will, on completion, produce all the notes on the musical scale. A steelpan is capable of playing any tune, from Mozart to Elton John, from Calypso to Bob Marley.

Steelpan is the national instrument of Trinidad and Tobago, and quite surprisingly, it was a post World War II invention which came about when the American sailors abandoned empty oil drums on local beaches. Inventive young men took these drums and hammered them into tune.

Steelpans come together as bands, sectioned in such a way as to produce the full range of instruments available in traditional European orchestras. Thus a steelband will often be referred to as a "Steel Orchestra" with its own musical arranger and conductor.

Steelbands appear on floats at Carnival, forty or fifty musicians, boys and girls, young and old, playing pan in harmony after months of rehearsals.

Added to this traditional music is the influence of Reggae music brought to Carnival in the 1970's by Jamaican DJs like "Lord Gelly" and "Sir Coxsone" - a different beat, a new expression of music and language.

When you hear the roar and feel the ground beginning to quiver you are, in all likelihood, getting close to Rap, Ragga, House or Jungle.

music and dance

These are recent additions to Carnival, as DJs vie with each other to attract crowds by playing popular tunes from whatever culture.

"Scratching" a record and "doing a mix" is about playing three or four records in sequence, blending the music in such a way so that the listener will think it is one continuous record. On occasions you will hear tunes like "Murder She Wrote" underplayed by "Save The Last Dance For Me" blended with "Mr Lover Man" and interspersed with the odd scratch and dub. CHECK IT OUT! SCENE! The language of the DJ while he plays his music creates a style that infuses the crowd and combines with the busyness and the heartbeat of Carnival.

So the crowds respond to the beat. Dance movements like "the Bogle", "the Donkey", "the Wine" infect the listener. "Chipping" is common to all Carnival revellers. This is when you shuffle to the beat and move your hips slightly and suggestively to show that the music has hit your soul. The young and energetic will engage in trendy footwork, doing dances that are acrobatic in nature and are not for the faint-hearted. It was at Carnival that "Breakdancing" was first displayed in the UK. They compete for small prizes and are just happy that they can perform on a platform in front of 3,000 people. Wicked!

There was a time in Carnival when brass instruments like the trumpet, trombone and saxophone ruled supreme on the road, but these have been eclipsed by the advent of the sound system with amplified sound. Occasionally, one can hear the performance of a live band on a truck in keeping with this tradition.

Not every sound in Carnival has been manufactured on record. Carnival revellers are encouraged to make their own music with the use of make-shift instruments like a bottle and spoon, a whistle, two empty cans, a horn, a dustbin lid, two sticks, "de iron" and of course, a drum.

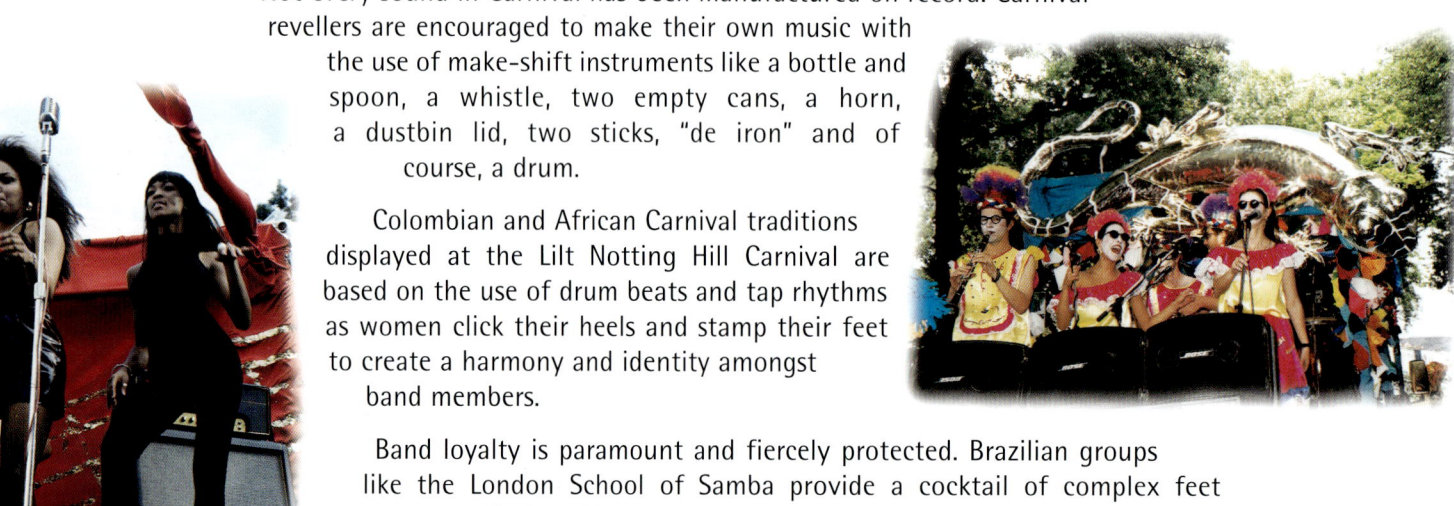

Colombian and African Carnival traditions displayed at the Lilt Notting Hill Carnival are based on the use of drum beats and tap rhythms as women click their heels and stamp their feet to create a harmony and identity amongst band members.

Band loyalty is paramount and fiercely protected. Brazilian groups like the London School of Samba provide a cocktail of complex feet movements displayed by scantily dressed women.

"Bawdy", "satirical" and "provocative" are the only appropriate words to describe evolving trends in dance and music at Carnival. That is what the revellers go for, and that is certainly what they get.

music and dance

music and dance

Booming sounds burst from mountains of massive speakers, each surrounded by thousands of sweat ridden dancers paying homage.

A sound system can be likened to a discotheque set up either in the streets or on a mobile float at Carnival. Soca, Rap, Reggae, Soul, Jungle, Zouk, House, emanate from speakers. Music designed to rock your soul and make you vibrate to the beat. It is loud, raucous and raunchy and in many ways, it is an extension of a culture which encourages you to lose your mind and personality in a frenzy of dance and movement.

Forty-five static sound systems and twenty-five mobile/Soca sound systems provide the music of Carnival. The static sound systems are spread within the three-mile Carnival route and the mobile sound systems wend their way through the streets with the procession. The music is emitted from the huge bank of speakers tethered to specially decorated lorries, with the DJs on board shouting "jump and wave and misbehave". Nobody is allowed to stand still. Everybody is encouraged to wine, to gyrate, to move their feet and shake their waist to the rhythm of the beat.

Static Sound Systems thrive on being on the margin of society and they emphasise the satire of their notoriety in their names and their rhythms. Killer Watt; Rappattack; 4 Play; Confusion; Master Mind; Rampage; Paddington Terror; names that amuse, say who they are, what they are about and that "we are here. Ignore us if you dare".

Static sound systems became part of Carnival in the 1970's much to the chagrin of the costume bands. Costume bands resented the systems because they were on route and would play competing music to make people stop and dance, rather than follow the procession. A compromise was reached and static systems retreated to the streets off the Carnival route. Their followers are mainly young and energetic. They dance from the moment the first note is played until the end of the day: hot, sweaty and high on rhythms.

Even though static sound systems are so popular, they have an uneasy relationship with the residents some of whom consider them to be too loud and resent the "invasion" of their streets by crowds coming to groove to the beats. "It shouldn't be allowed" they say "It should be in a park like a pop concert". Not so, respond the supporters, static sound systems are a part of Carnival, and Carnival is a festival of arts on the streets.

On average 3,000 people dance around each site, mainly young, funky and energetic types, they are quite satisfied to stand next to huge mountains of speakers encouraging listeners to "Check out" the latest dance step - "Lose yourself in de riddim of de beat".

sound systems

The elaborate costumes of the Carnival create an exotic pantomime, a breath-taking Caribbean Disneyworld, a kaleidoscope of dreams and rose-tinted flash-backs.

Masquerade is the mainstay of Carnival. Stand on the Carnival route and you will be passed by unimaginable creations from bands such as Trinbago, Mahogany and Masquerade 2000. Human flowers of immense scale; men in horrifying make-up; African warriors in dramatic masks; wild Indians flaunting multicoloured feathers; ostentatious butterflies; sea creatures displaying the beauty of marine life. The costumes continue non-stop throughout the day and the crowds are treated to an ongoing flow of sumptuous, glittering and magnificent images.

Through masquerade, one is allowed to hide one's true personality behind the beauty or the gruesomeness of the Mas.

The tradition began in the days of slavery when the slaves, black people, were not allowed to walk the streets after dark unless they were accompanied by their white masters. When the laws were repealed, the black people began to mock the old system in their dance and rituals on the streets. Some would dress in apparel that reflected the types of clothing whites would wear and would distort the figures in order to emphasise the ridiculousness of their social deprivations. Some would wear masques depicting the faces of white people, sometimes with huge gruesome heads to portray the evil that was in the mind. The tradition of masquerading grew out of that, each era providing ample material for satirical expression in art and design.

Particular themes are developed by different bands at the Carnival and are expressed in spectacular fashion. Awesome concepts have included "Things with Wings"; "Fruits of the Caribbean"; "Fancy Sailor"; "United Colours of Africa"; "Zulu Warrior" and "Black Foot Warrior". A number of bands specialise in a particular theme, most notably anything to do with the American Indians, who will be glorified as noble warriors in a time long since gone, just as blacks had been before the days of slavery.

The costumes are often so intricate, demanding such considerable craftsmanship that as one Carnival finishes, designers begin working upon next year's creations.

Step into a participants home in October and you will be confronted by piles of wire, heaps of cloth and an array of equipment and tools required to craft future creations.

Drawn on paper, outlining the interpretation in the form of colour and materials to be used, the designer will then carefully secret those away. Competition is keen. Sometimes he will deliberately spread the word that he is playing "English

costume

costume

Country Garden" when in truth he is playing "Tropical Rain Forest" (deception designed to confuse other competitors). Then, he will begin the process of recruiting members for the band who will help make the costumes and then wear them on the two days of Carnival.

The King and Queen are carefully chosen, the designer will want someone who can reflect the demands of the role in dance and movement on Carnival Day at the judging point. To be King or Queen of Carnival is the most prized accolade.

Costumes are made from many different types of materials. Some from recycled washing-up bottles, dried leaves, papier-mâché, plaster of paris, chicken wire etc. Others will be more expensively produced with the use of authentic materials, sequins, feathers, silks and satins, wire, cane, fibre glass with glue and paint (mostly silver and gold). Whatever the Mas maker could provide.

The effect is sensational.

A costume or Mas band is made up of five elements: the Queen, the King, the Male Individual, the Female Individual and the Section Mas. A band will have a theme and the five elements will work together to portray the different aspects of the theme. By way of example, if a band's theme is "Wildlife in Africa", the Queen will be portrayed as a lioness, the King will be a lion, the Male Individual could be portrayed as the strong and protective gorilla and the Female Individual as an elegant giraffe. The rest of the band will wear stunning costumes representing other animals portraying the kaleidoscope of African wildlife.

However, not every theme in Carnival is a reflection of this satire. Some themes are chosen because the Mas-maker just fancies the idea. He wants to make a pretty Mas, he wants to indulge his creativity. That too is also very welcome. In recent years, we have seen the advent of South American Carnival bands - the Samba King and Queen rule the day. Colourful, exciting, and dramatic.

Now more and more children are participating, exploring ideas with teachers at schools, in Carnival workshops, and at clubs. They, like the adults, are beginning to wear costumes, subjugating themselves and their personalities to the dictates of the theme. Costume themes have become more radical in concept as Mas-makers seek to capture the attention of the world media and dominate cultural politics.

Thirty years ago, about fifty people wore costumes. Now there are approximately ten thousand. Every year the numbers are growing, as the motto of the Lilt Notting Hill Carnival says: "Every Spectator is a Participant".

As any Carnival-goer can confirm, the Notting Hill two-day event is a food festival in itself.

The full range of Caribbean cuisine is available from close to 400 different stalls. Carnival has become a small business jamboree. Substantial quantities of speciality foods, as well as rum, beer, Lilt and other drinks are stashed in basements beforehand to sell from trolleys, doorways and tables outside homes, as well as from elaborately decorated stalls. Caterers from across the land also converge on the Carnival, and food is cooked on gas rings, electricity burners and coal-pots. It's hot, it's fresh and it's tasty.

Dishes include traditional Rice and Peas, the rice cooked together with the peas, which is usually "kidney beans" or "gunga beans" and "cooked down" with coconut and seasoning. Every grain must be separately infused with a combination of herbs and spices. The meat that goes with it is either "curry chicken", "curry goat" or "curry beef". Although, more recently, "vegetarian curry stew" with "melongen" (egg plant) "bargi" (spinach) or "stewed beans and pumpkins".

A tasty snack can be had in "fried plantain" a slightly sweet and savoury member of the banana family that is twice the size of the banana. Or there is the "fry bake" a mixture of flour, salt, water, butter, sugar, rolled into dough and fried. This goes well with the "saltfish buljoil" or "ackee and saltfish" made from salted cod, boiled and marinated in oil, peppers, tomatoes and other vegetables.

Probably the most popular snack at Carnival is the "Jamaican Pattie", shaped like a Cornish Pastie and made with a lightly curried dough with curried beef or curried vegetable filling.

The ultimate food of Carnival is "de rotee" or "roti" a pancake seasoned with dried dal, herbs and salt, which is cooked on a platter and then wrapped around a "dollop" (a spoonful) of meat or vegetable stew.

Caribbean drinks on sale include "mauby" made from the bark of a tree, "sorrel" made from a Caribbean flower, "Lilt", "Rum Punch", "Guinness Punch", made from Guinness swizzled with milk, rum, nutmeg, clove and egg - drunk to keep your energy level up; and "shave-ice" to cool you down.

In recent years, the widening cultural diversity of the Carnival has brought new styles of cuisine to the event. Philippino cooking, grilled prawns, chicken and kebab skewed and roasted in front of the customer; Nigerian "Souya"; Guyanese "Pepperpot"; Grenadian "Lambee", Jamaican "Jerk Pork" and the American "Hamburger" are all available.

For those who prefer fruit, coconuts, sugar cane, mangoes, Portugals, paw paws, guavas, governor plums and jelly fruit are on offer.

Carnival must be the largest open air kitchen in Britain.

It was a moment of inspiration when Lilt, one of the UK's best-loved tropical soft drinks, first became the official sponsor of the Notting Hill Carnival in 1995 (now renamed the Lilt Notting Hill Carnival). This annual festival, uniquely celebrating the fun-filled joys of the Caribbean in the heart of London, couldn't have found a better partner in Lilt - the totally tropical drink encapsulating the Caribbean zest for life.

The Lilt Notting Hill Carnival is the biggest street festival of its kind in Europe. To keep it that way, Lilt has stepped in. Claire Holder, Chair of Notting Hill Carnival Ltd describes Lilt's partnership as "a positive and complementary one which can open doors for future investment. Lilt's participation secures the public's enjoyment of the Carnival, not only by ensuring greater safety measures, but also by supporting its traditional cultural events".

Photo courtesy of John Dunbar

It's as if the street-event and the drink were made for each other. The famous Lilt logo sits comfortably with all Carnival merchandise, banners, lamppost pennants and was a welcome sight for 1995's Carnival-goers in the Lilt 'Cool Down Zones' where sprays of water refreshed the partying crowds. Further refreshment could be found in the drink itself. Close to two million funsters attended the 1995 carnival and more of them drank Lilt than any other soft drink.

Everyone knows Lilt. Since its launch by the Coca-Cola Company in the 1970's, Lilt has become the third biggest non-cola brand in the UK. Like the Carnival, the "totally tropical" drink has rapidly attracted a vast audience of admirers.

Photo courtesy of John Dunbar

Lilt has universal appeal. At the Carnival you'll find it quenching the thirst of grateful youngsters recovering from hours of energy sapping dancing, as well as satisfying the parched palates of onlooking adults. When it comes to savouring the totally tropical taste, age just doesn't matter. Why? It's simple..... there is no match to the unique taste of Lilt.

Nothing quite lives up to the Lilt taste. Totally tropical in essence, its refreshing, high-juice, fruity formula offers a distinctive combination of flavours - one common fruit, one exotic, a blend of the sweet and the sour - and although classified as a carbonate, Lilt is in fact less fizzy than its counterparts. It has half the carbonation level of the average drink.

Photo courtesy of Lilt

The traditional Lilt taste teams Pineapple and Grapefruit (a diet variant arrived in 1987), and Lilt-Lovers can now savour the tongue-tingling delights of the Mango and Mandarin formula, introduced in 1994. A can of Lilt is an ideal refresher for any time of any day - whether it's taking the tea out of the traditional tea-break, with a snack in the workplace or at school, relaxing at home or out and about... and of course, as the perfect complement to a Carnival-weekend fizzing with fiesta-spirit.

Photo courtesy of David Trollope ARPS

Lilt is currently benefiting from vibrant new packaging and an inspirational advertising campaign set in the sun-soaked Caribbean. The message is clear.

Here is a drink that can be enjoyed by anyone. It embodies the attitude to life - laid-back, cool and confident. Refreshment for people who take life in their stride.

Lilt stands for the colour and calm of the Caribbean. It evokes the sun-drenched beaches, clear blue skies and palm trees. The tropical ease which fantasy is made of.

But Lilt has bite as well as thirst-quenching body. Switch onto the Lilt experience, harness the mind, let that moment of inspiration take over...

Photo courtesy of David Trollope ARPS

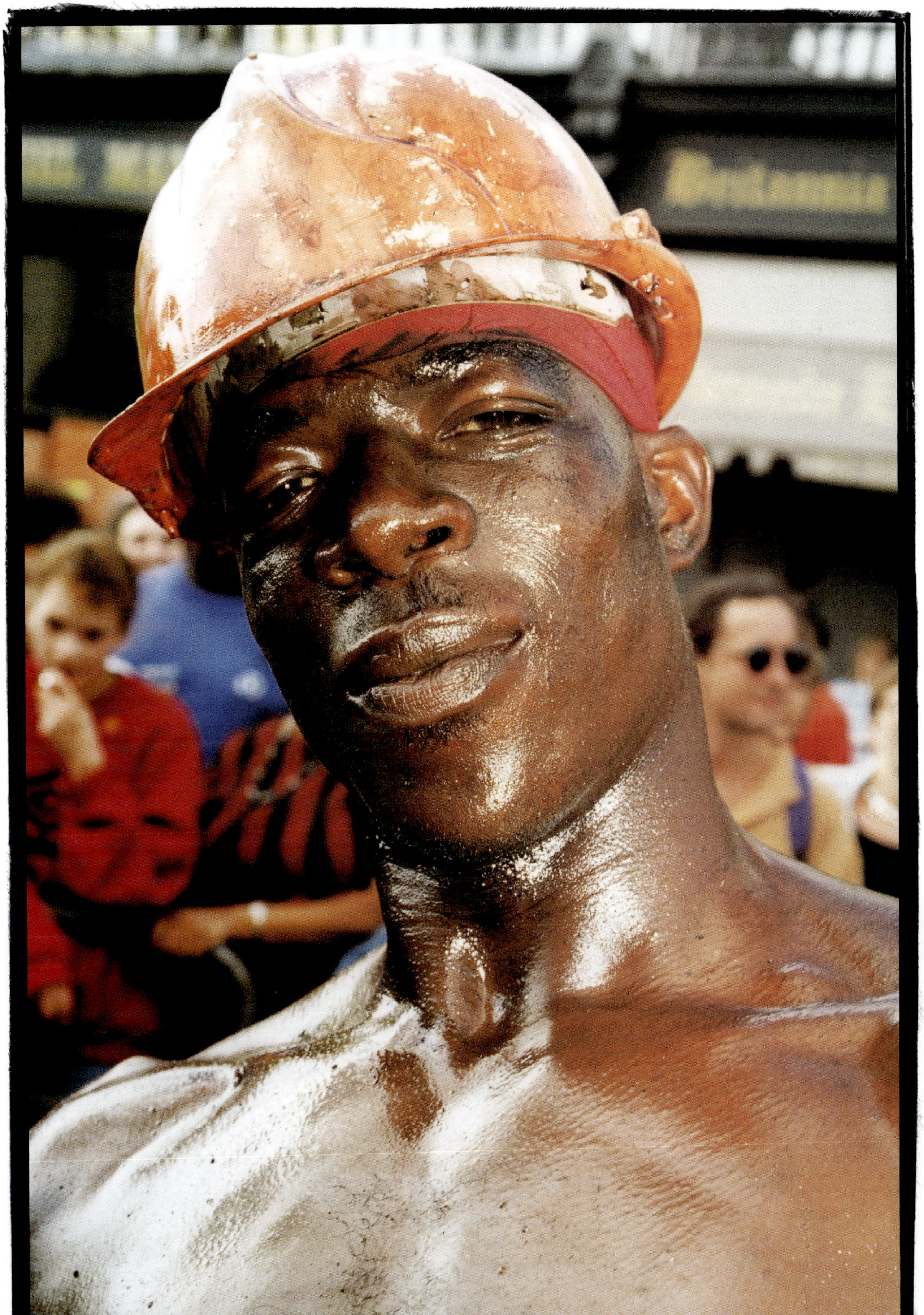

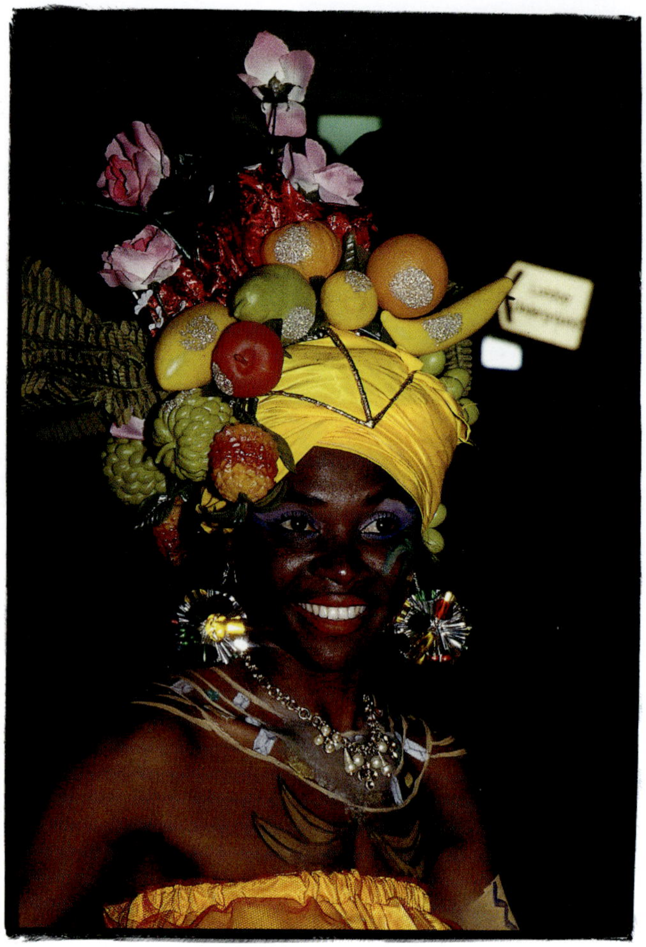
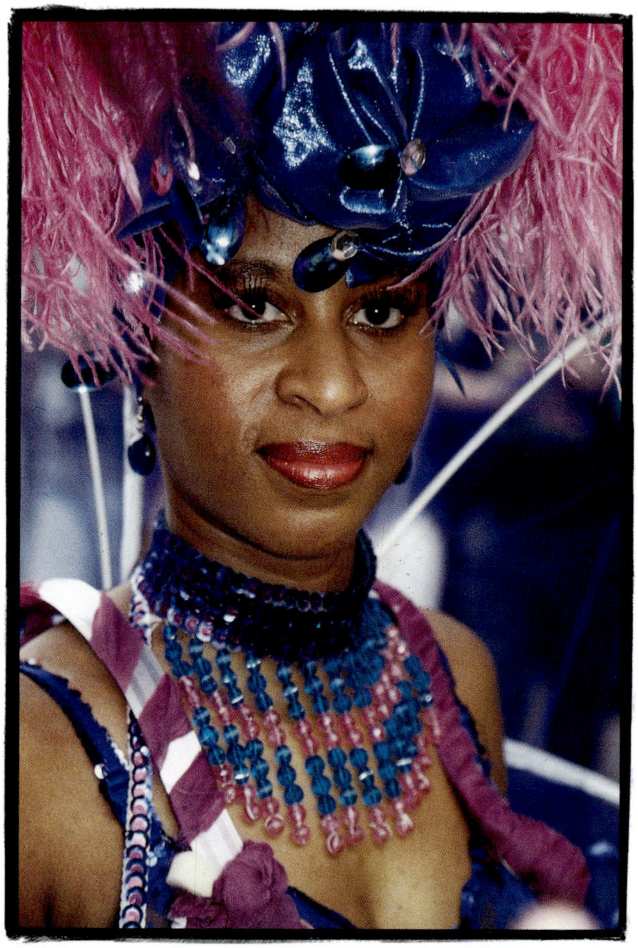

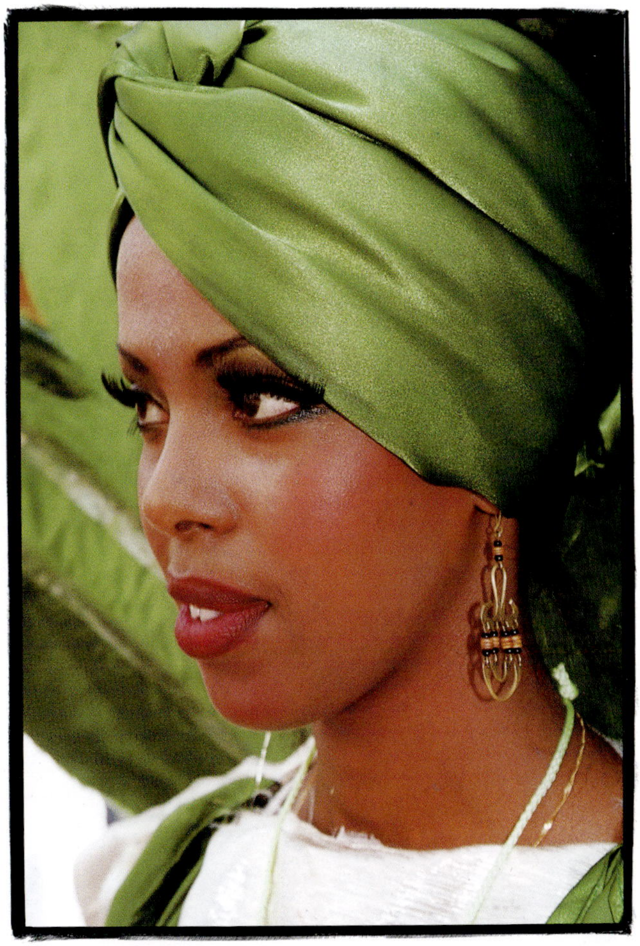

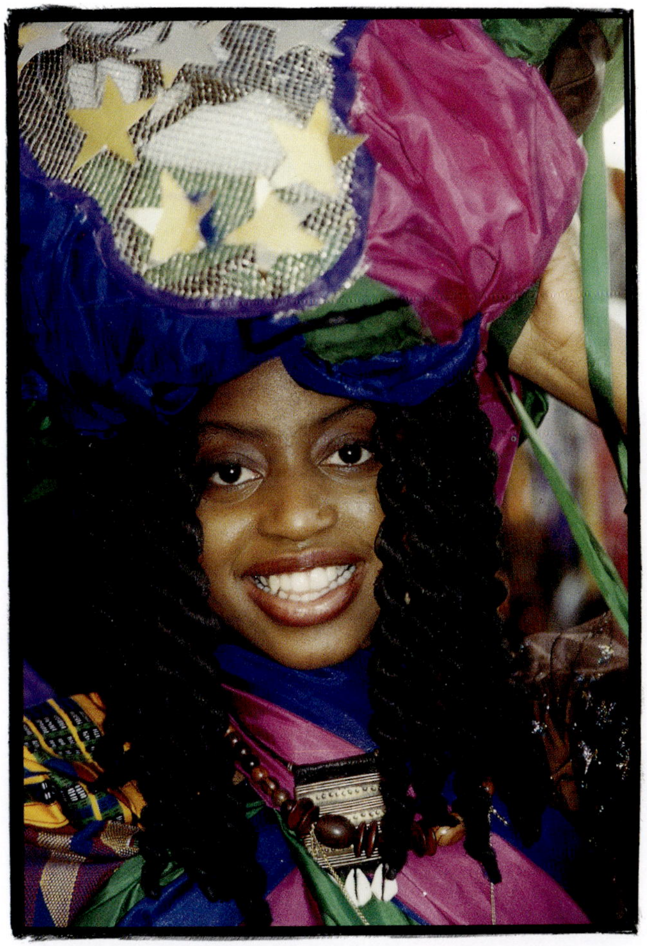

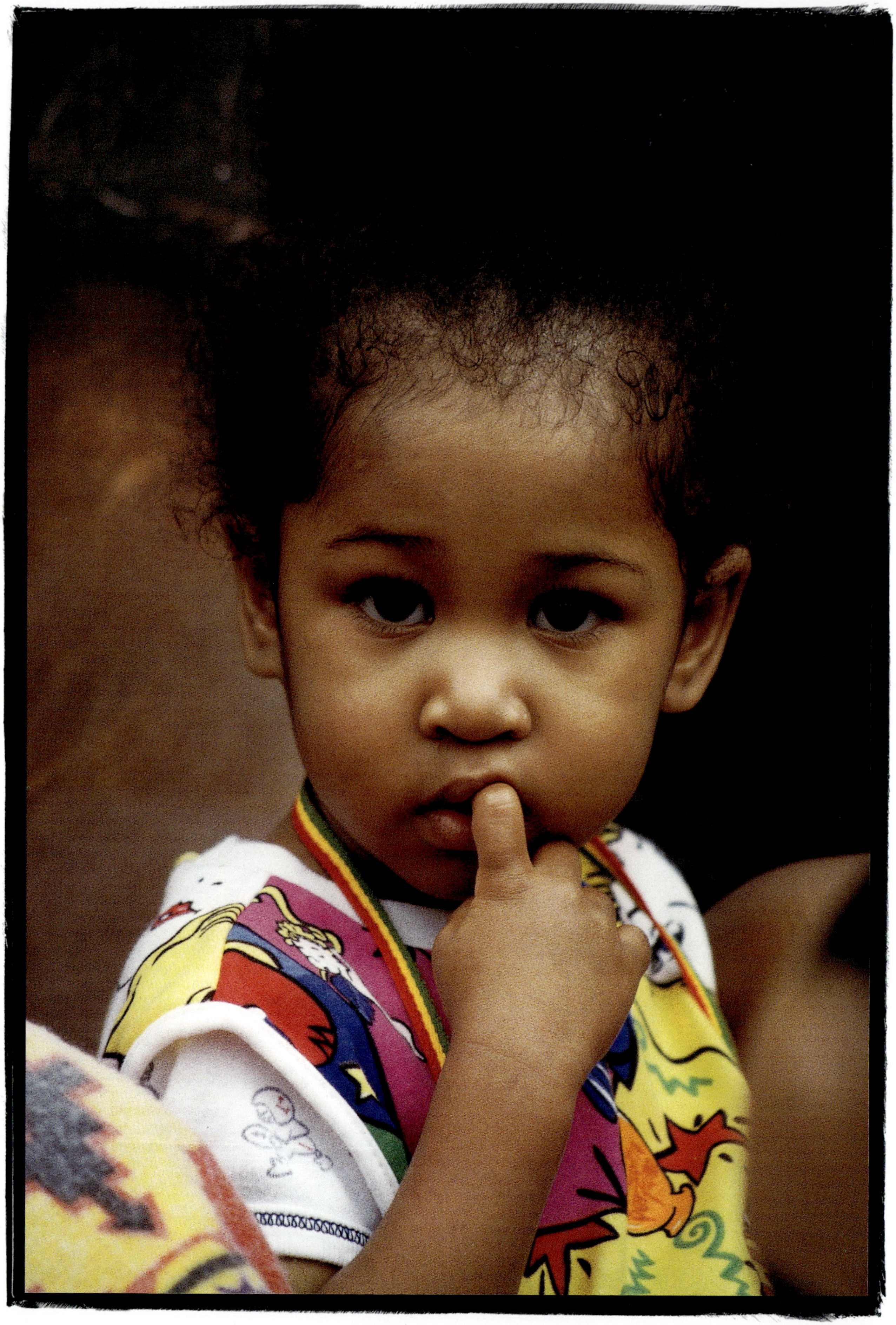

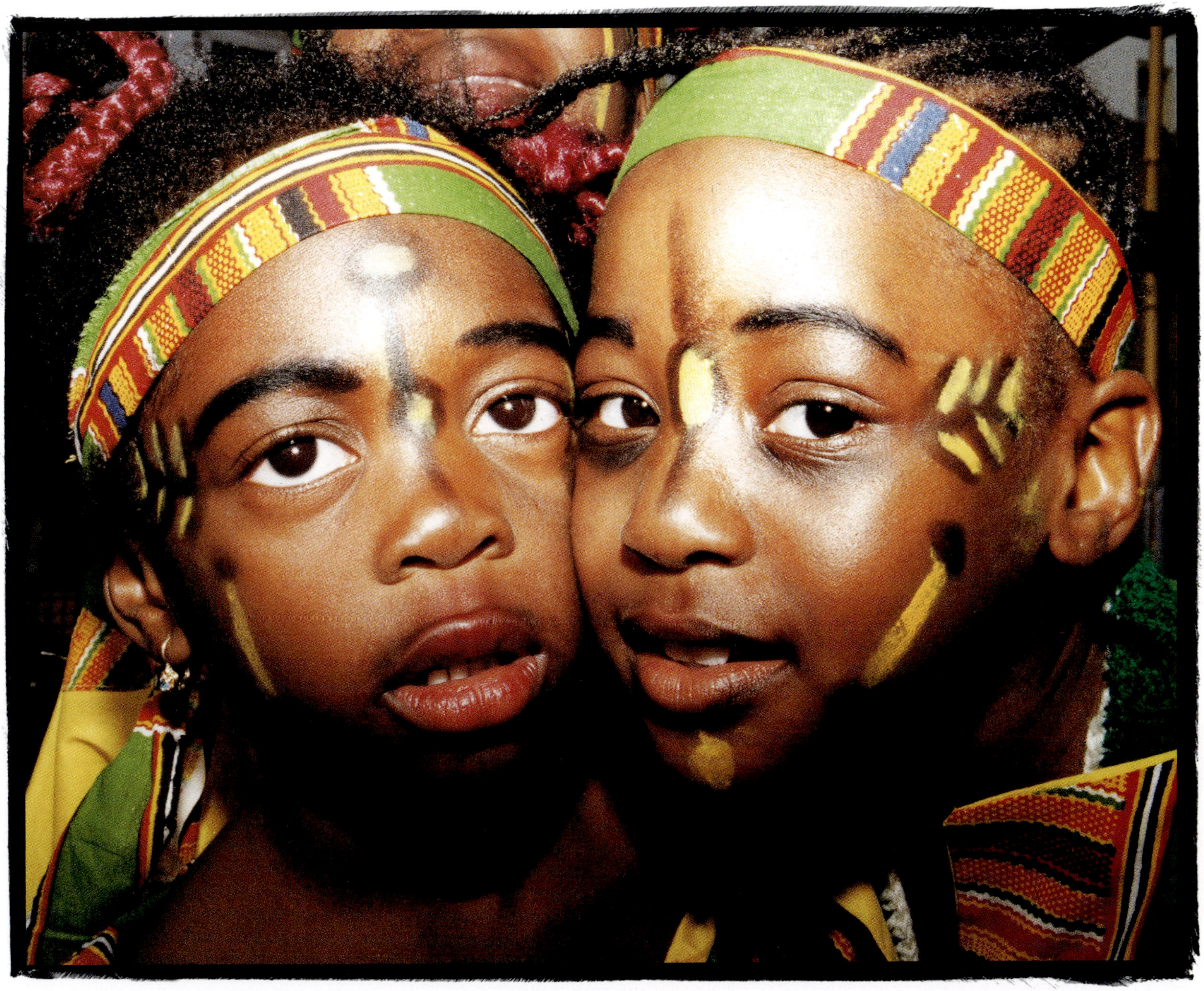

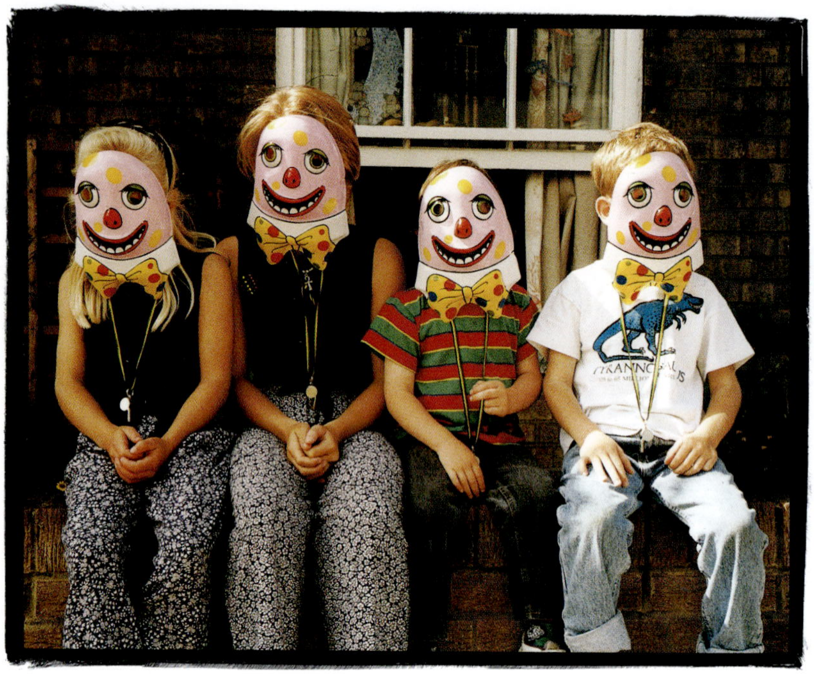

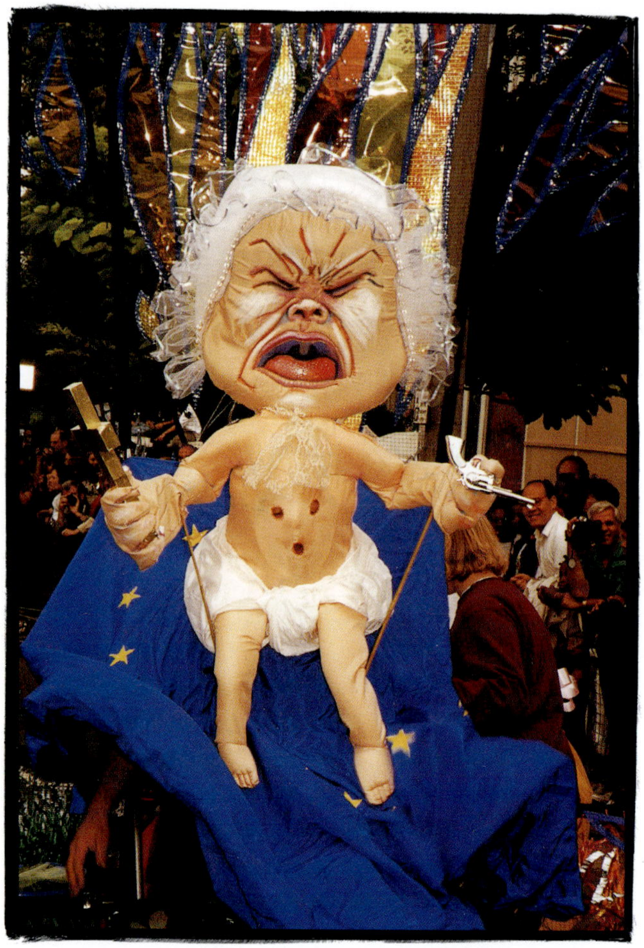

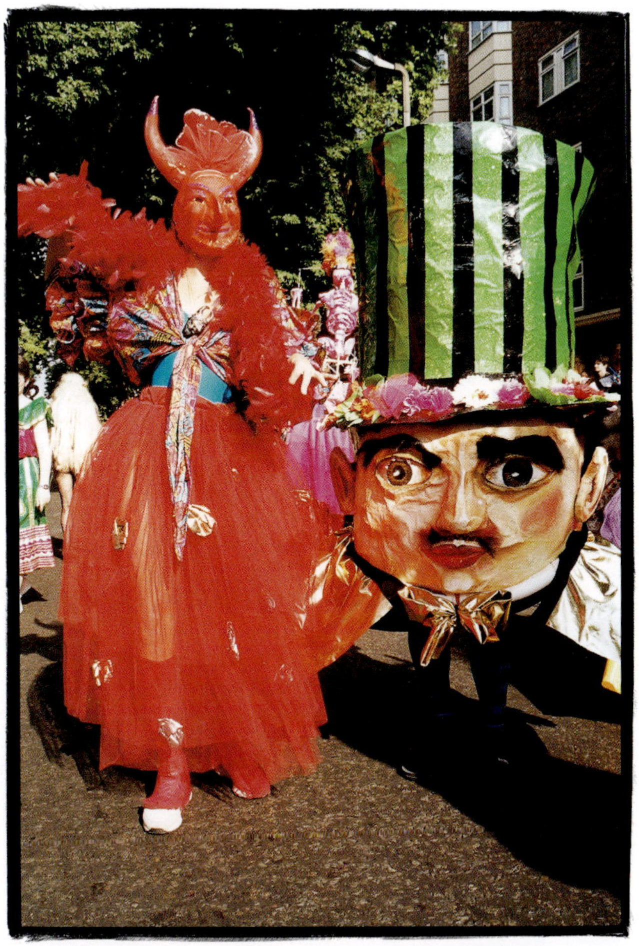

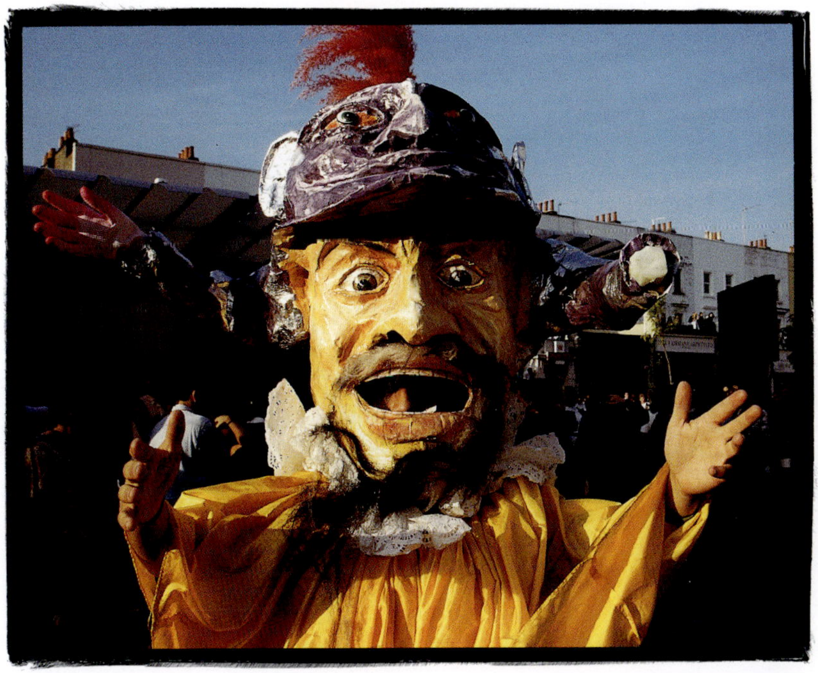

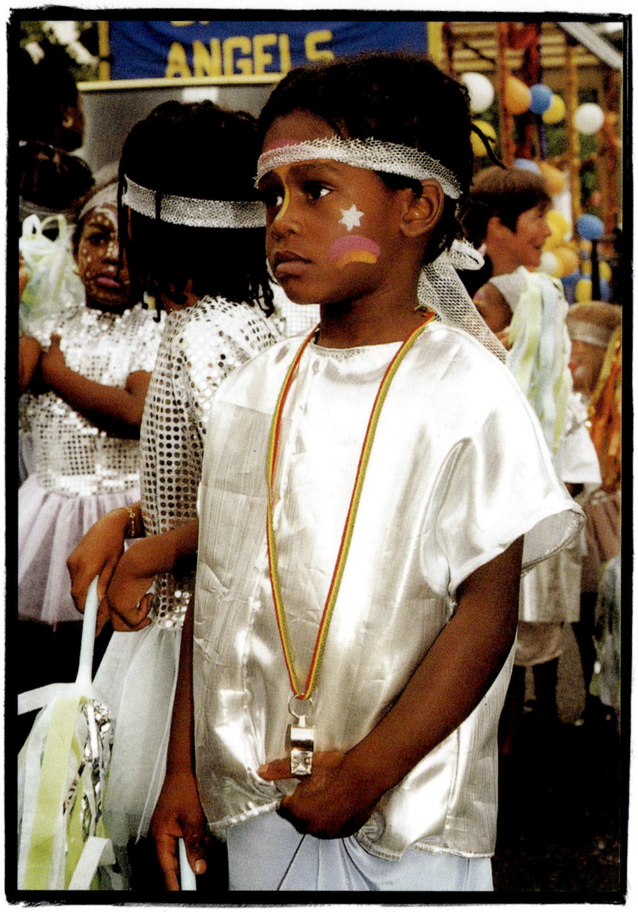
ANGELS

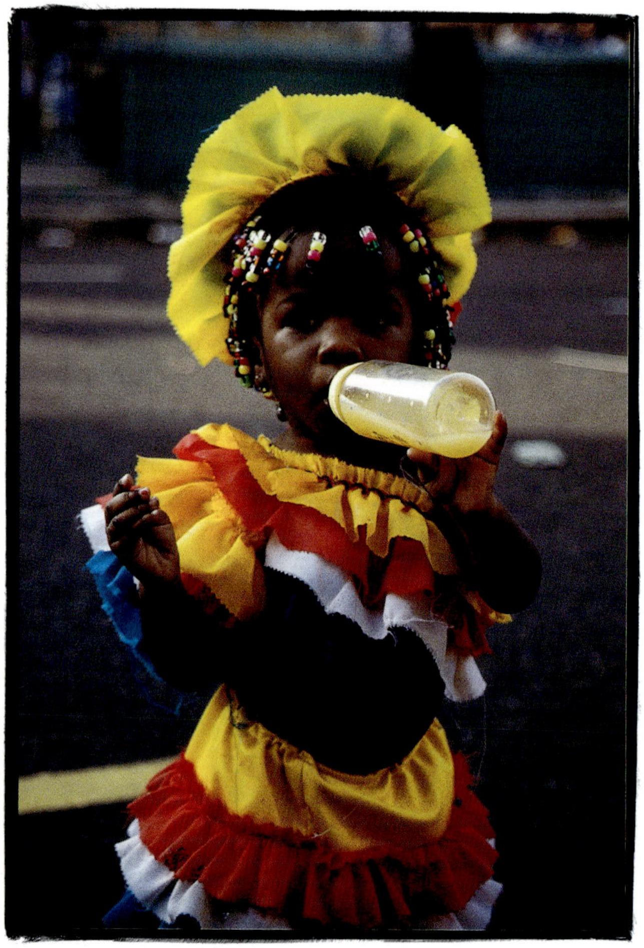

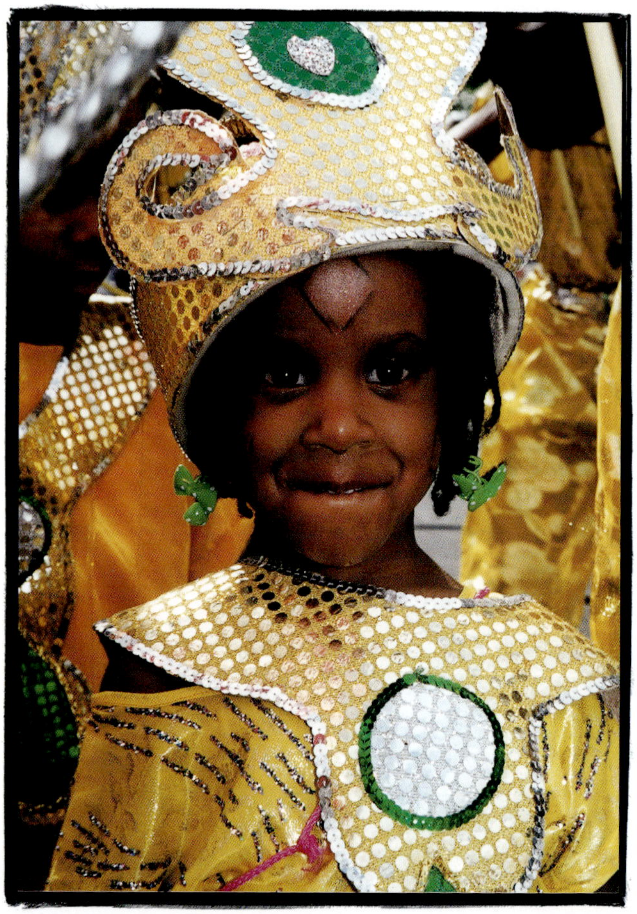

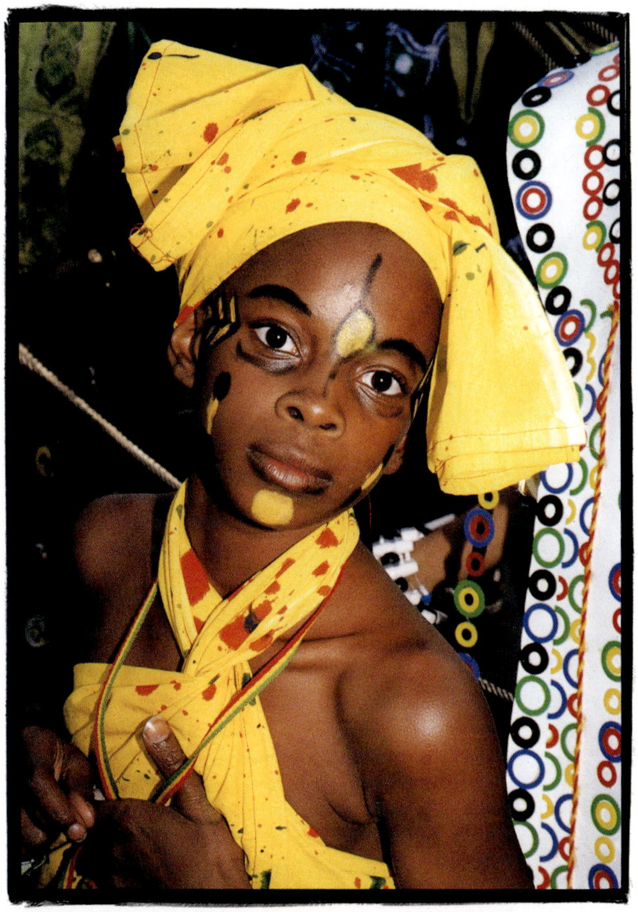
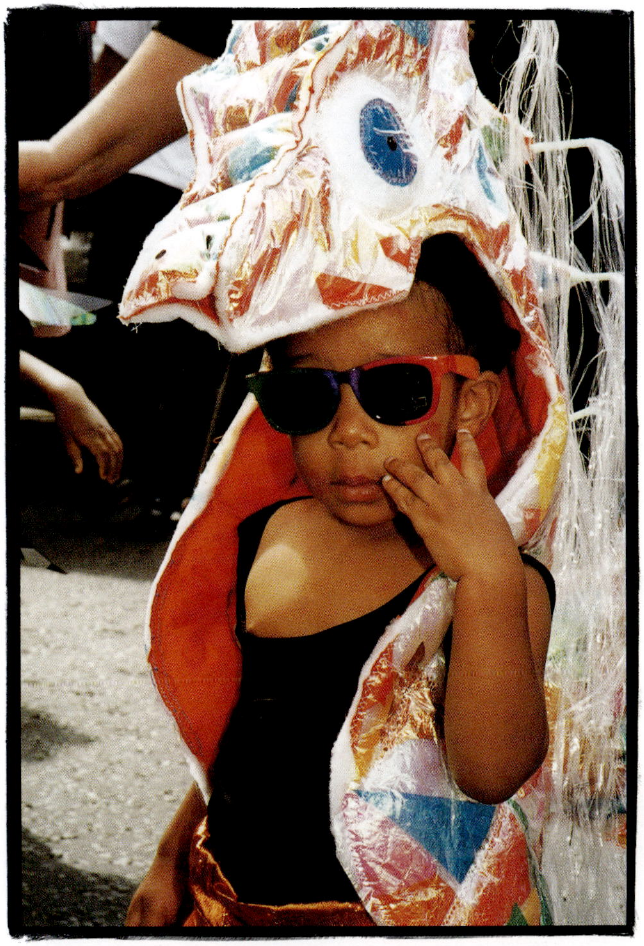
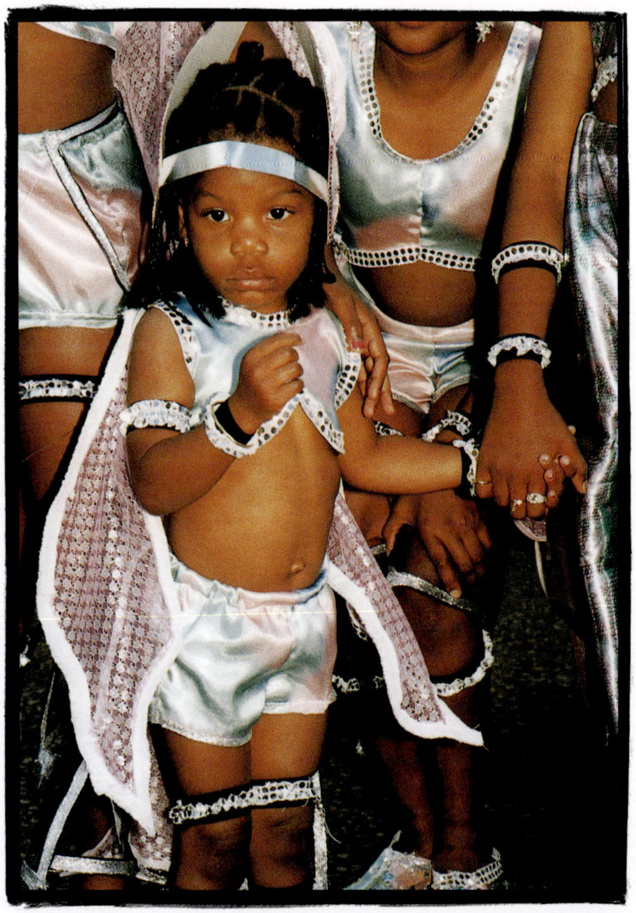

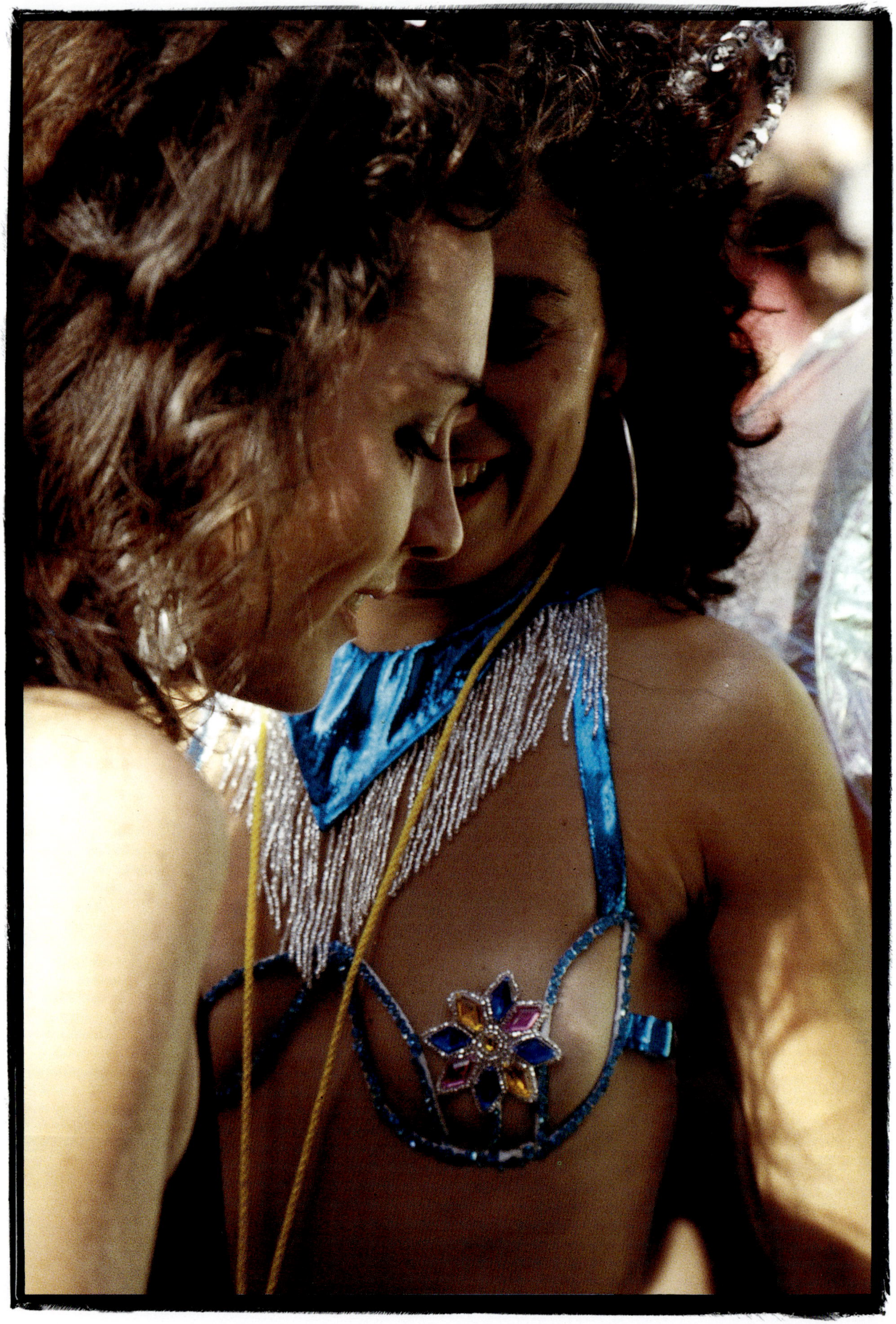

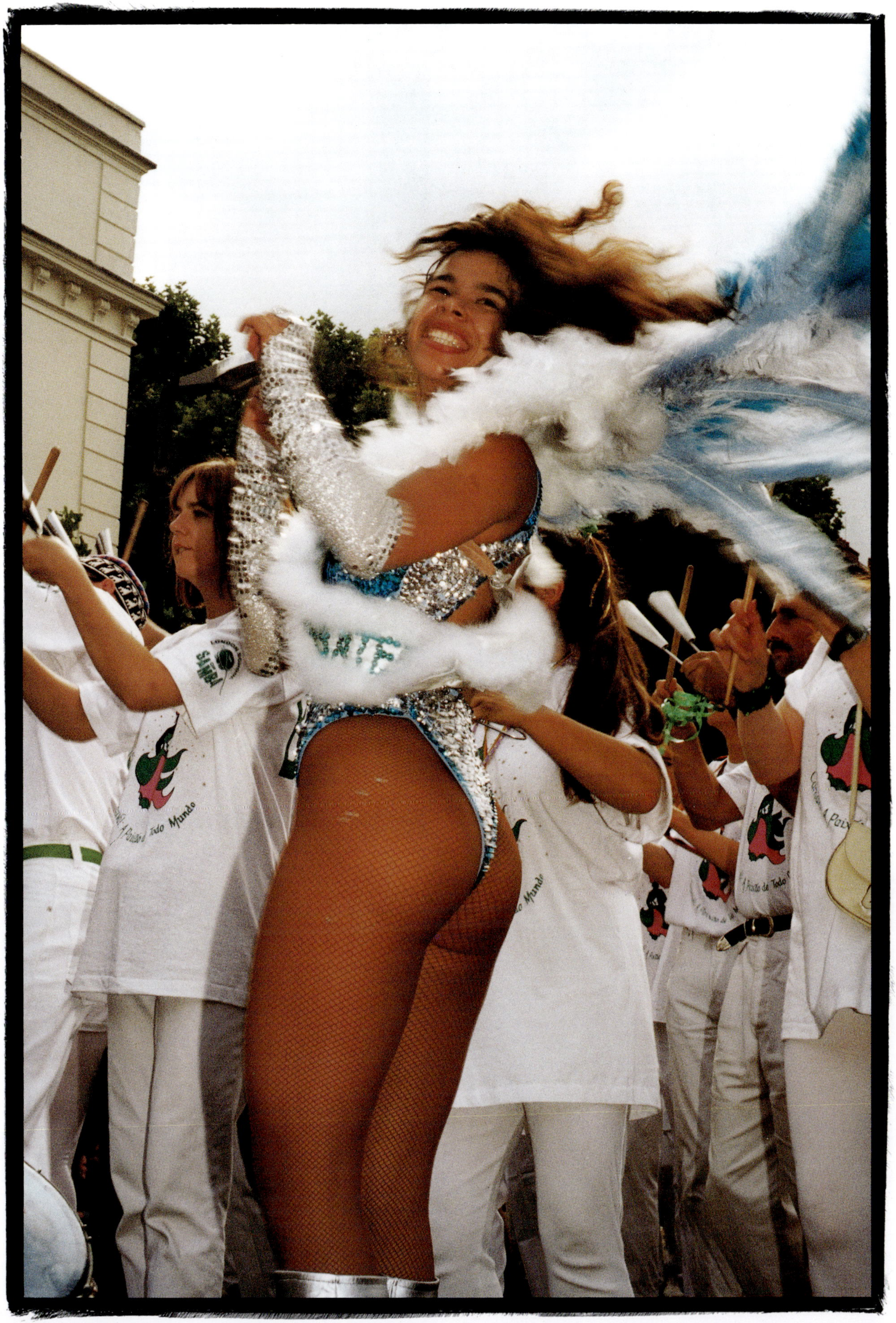

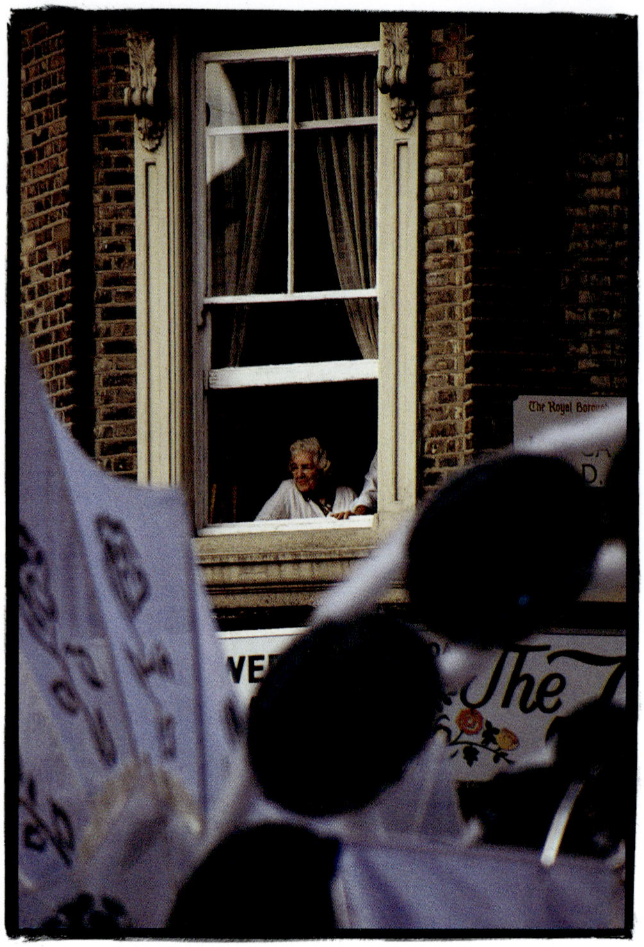
The Royal
The

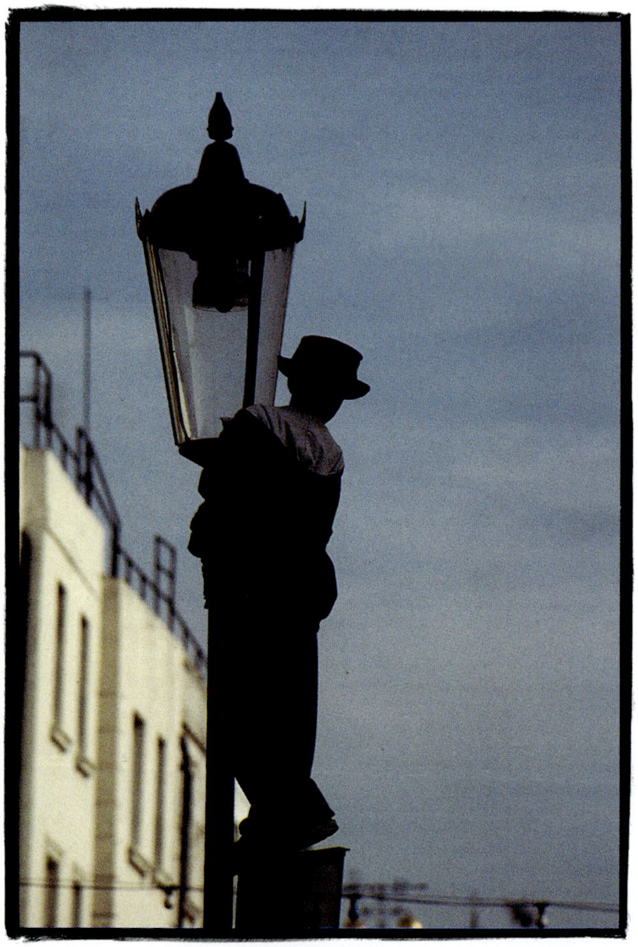

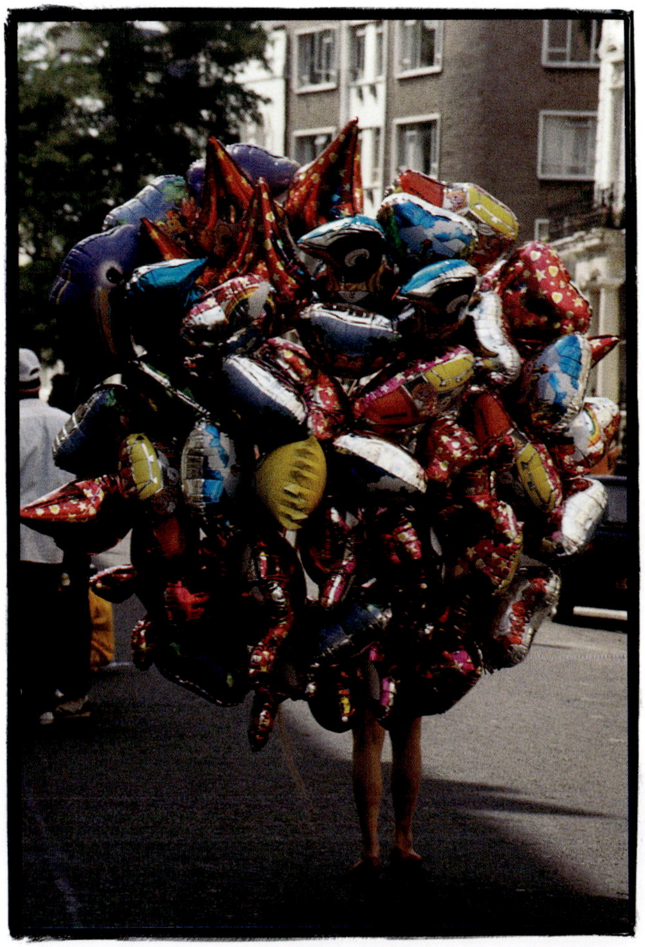

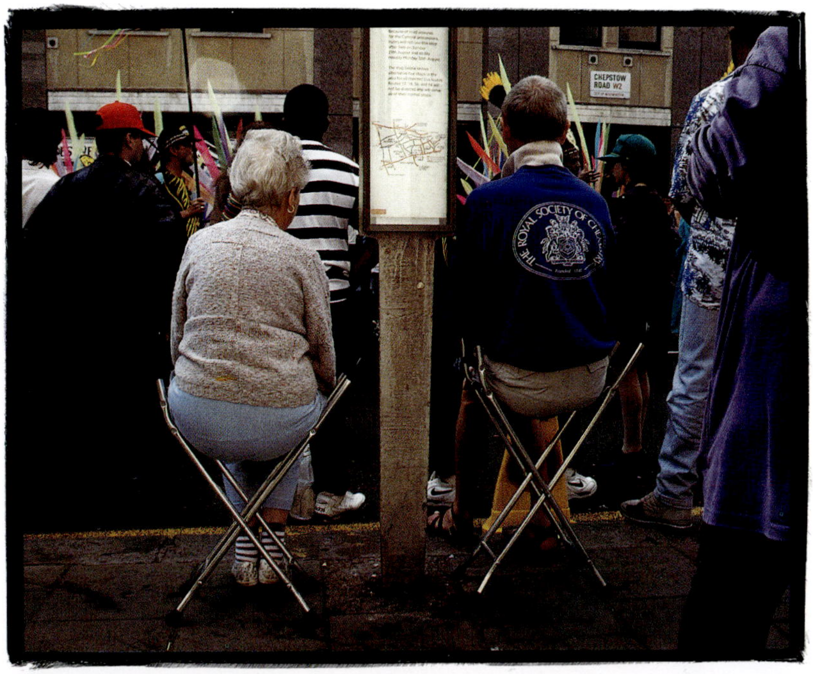
CHEPSTOW
ROAD W2

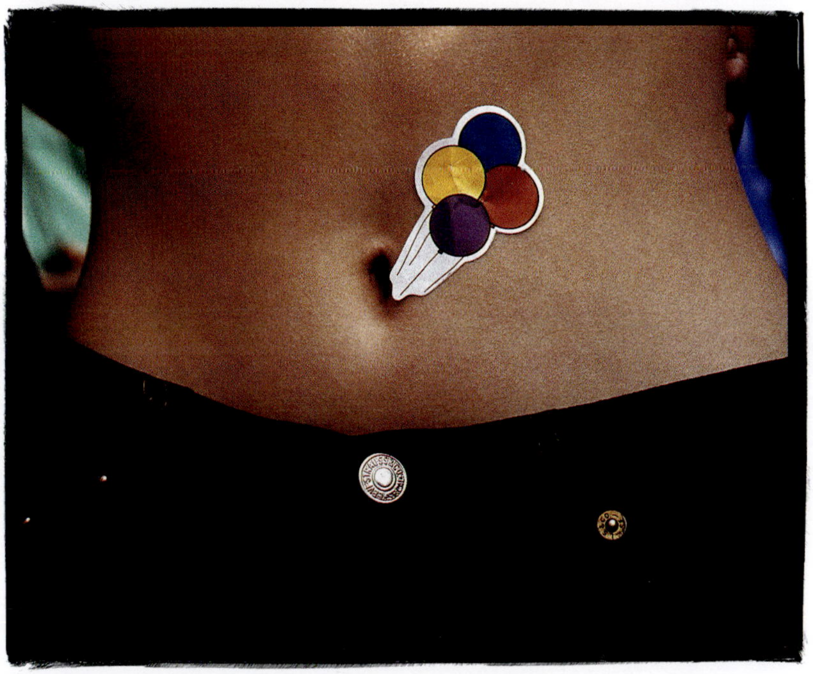

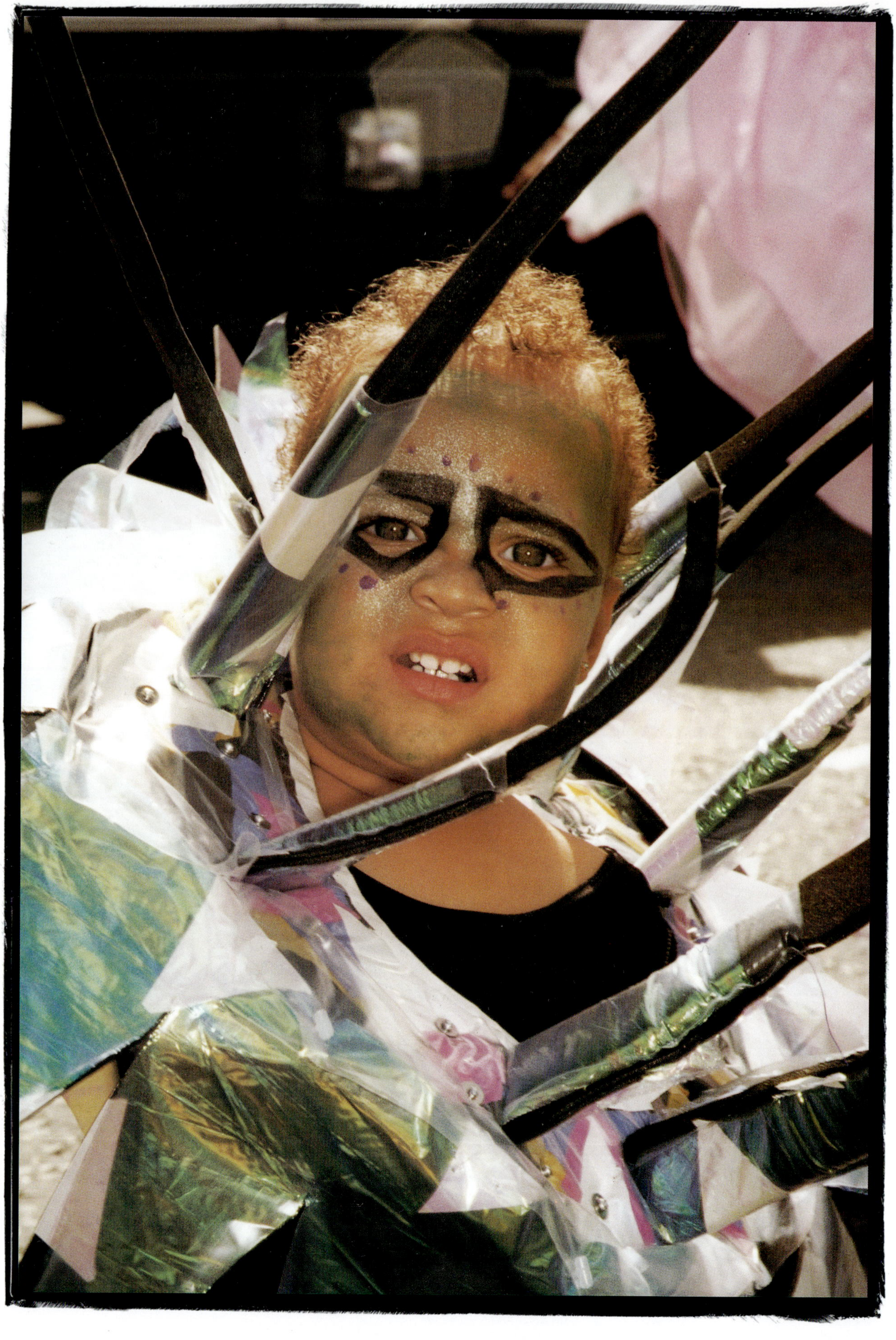

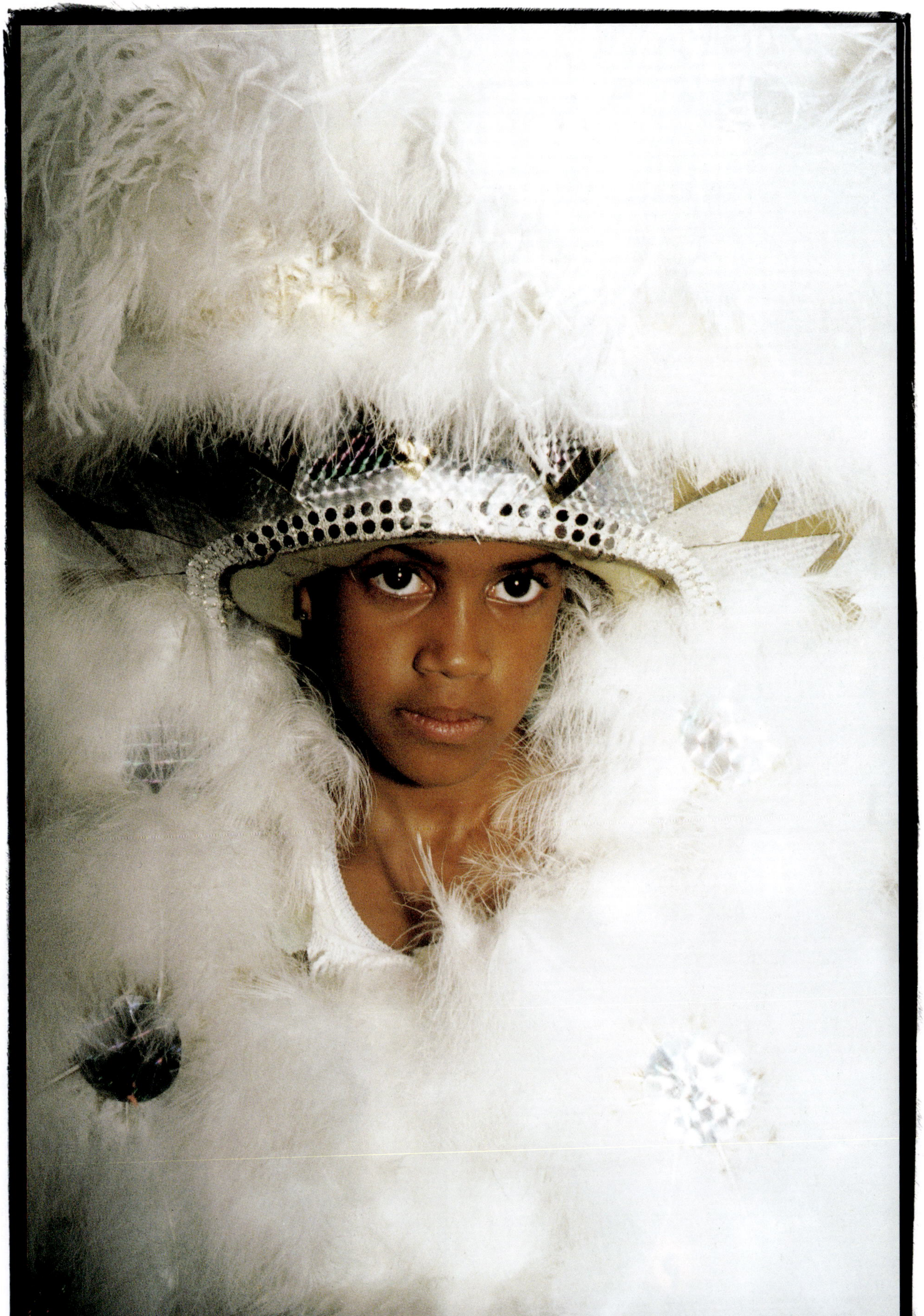

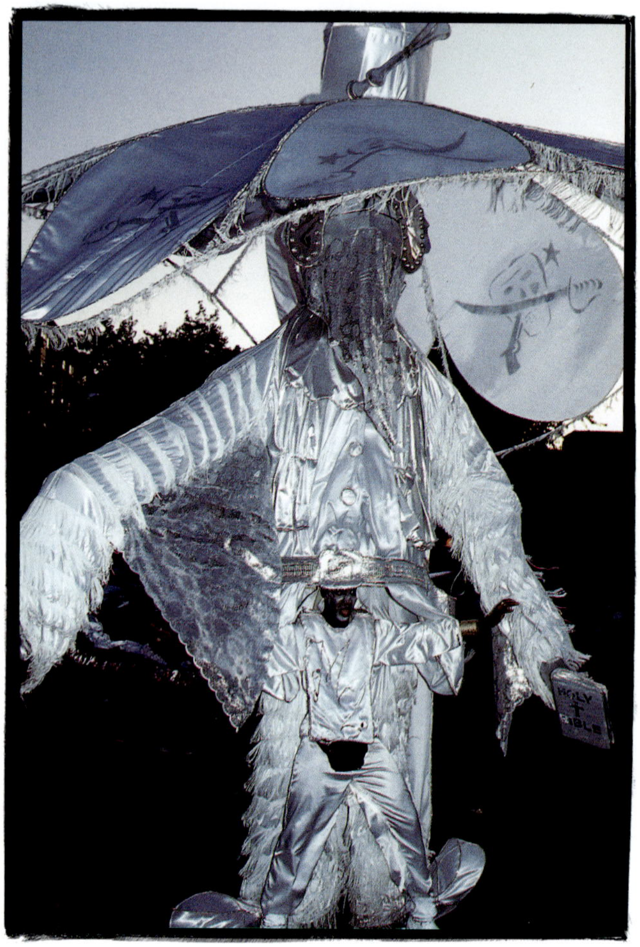

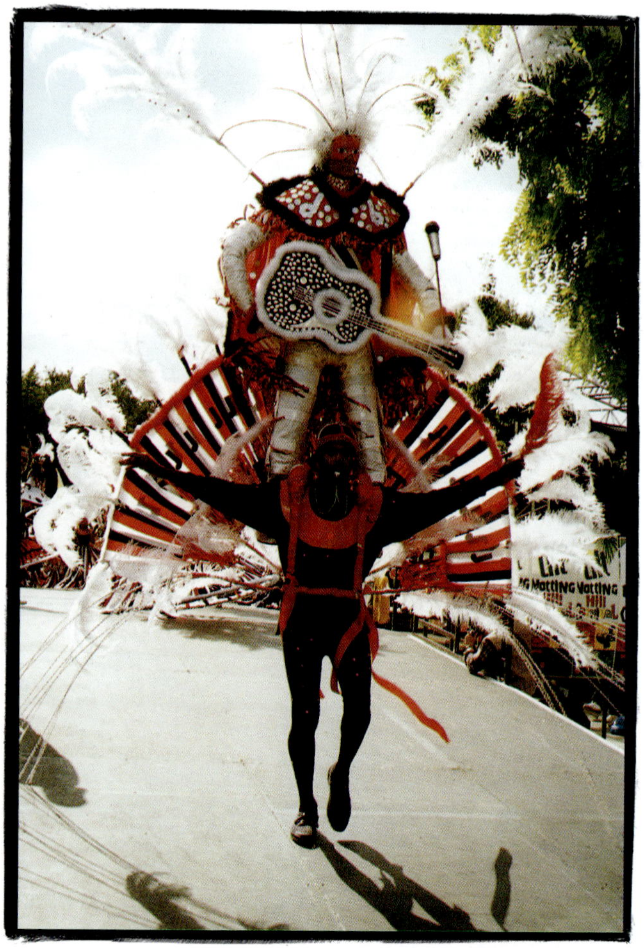

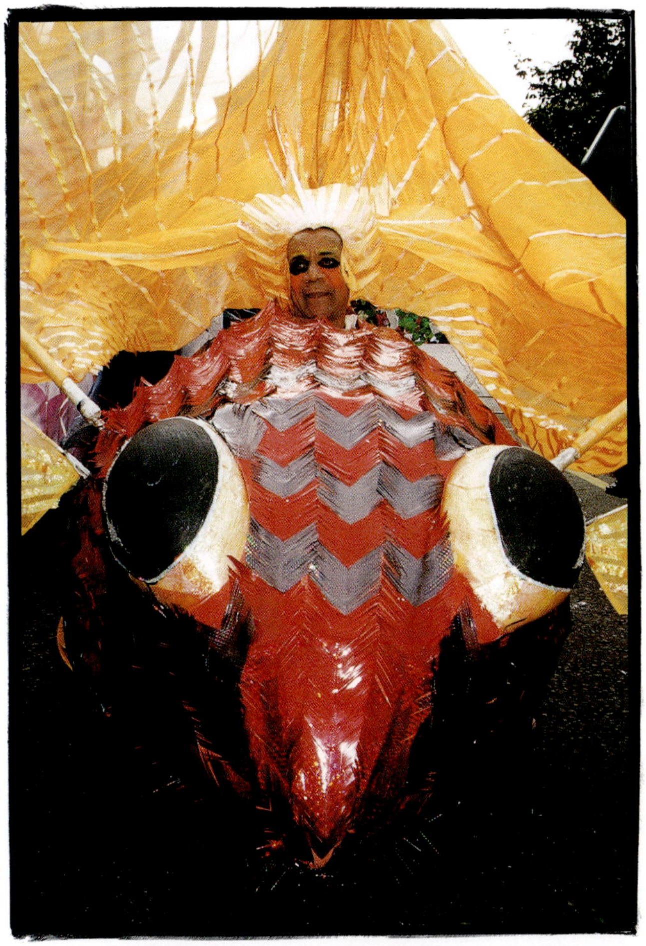

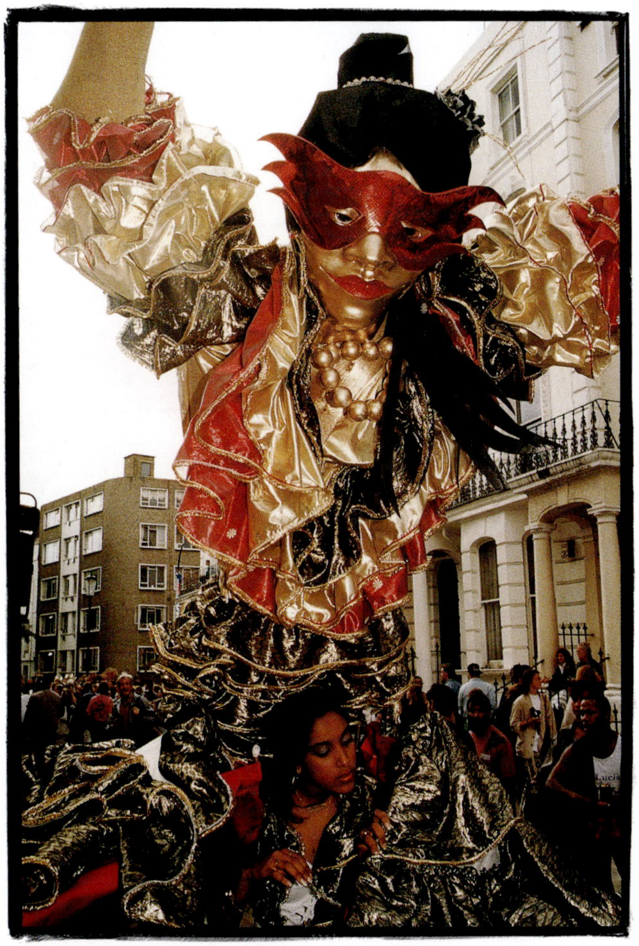

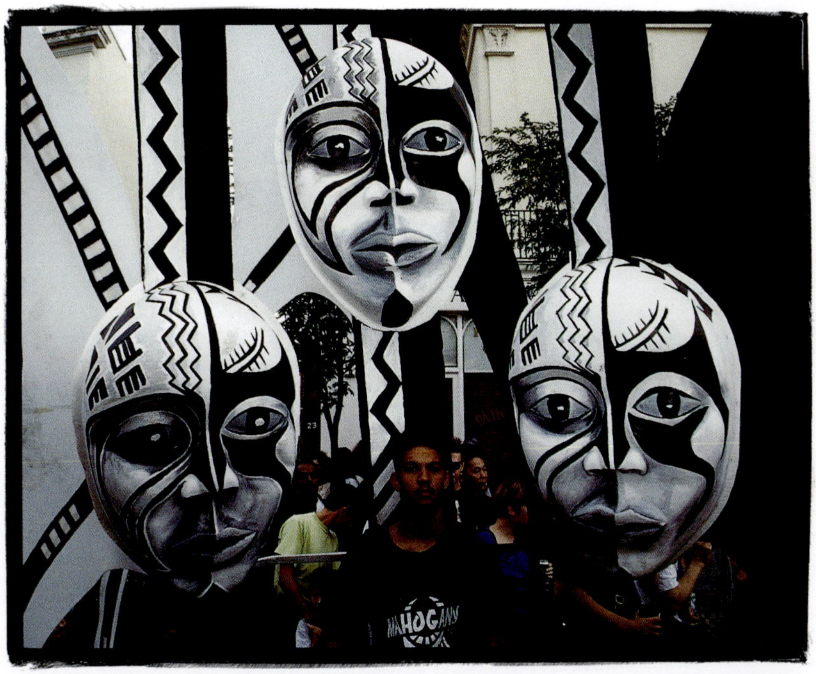

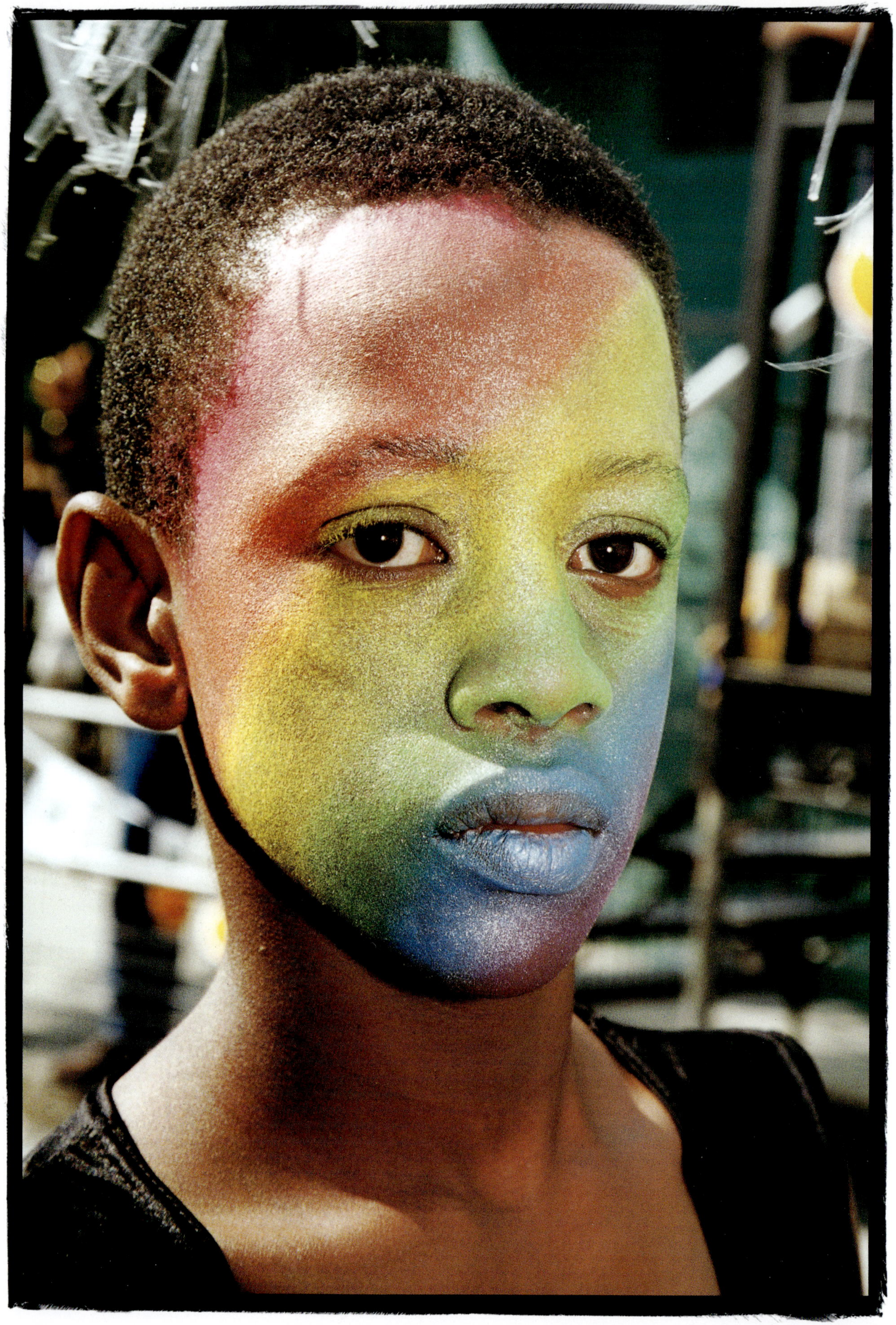

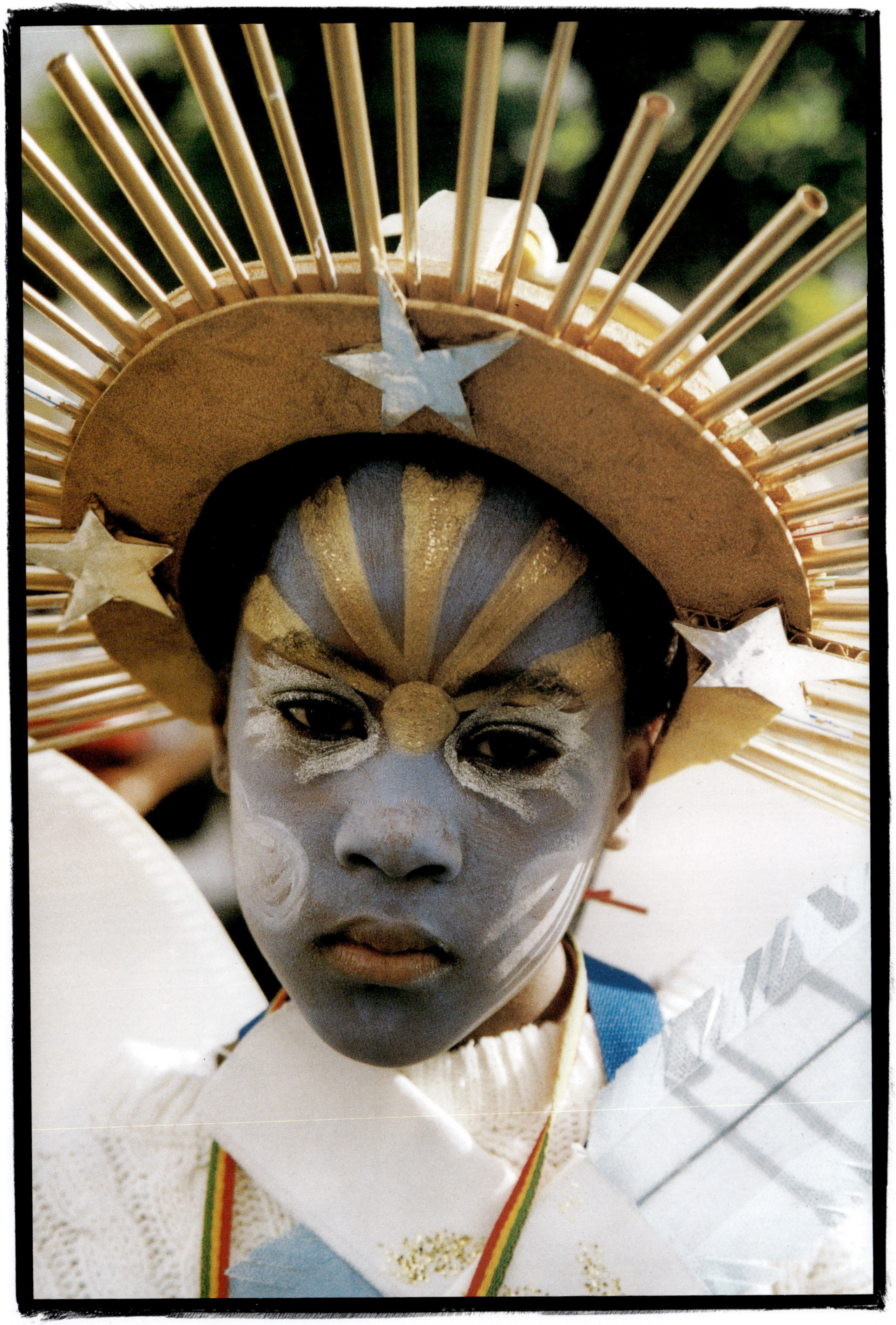

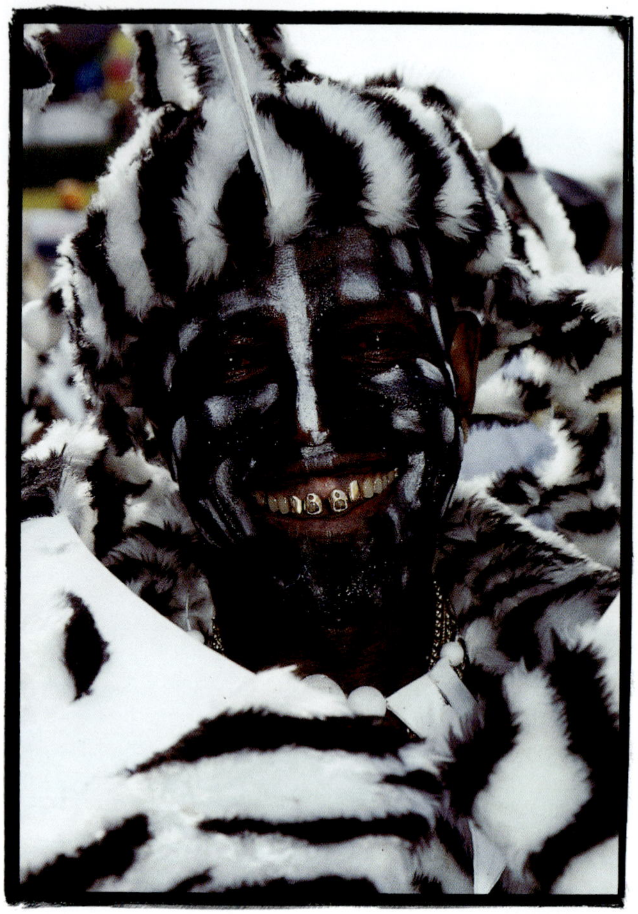

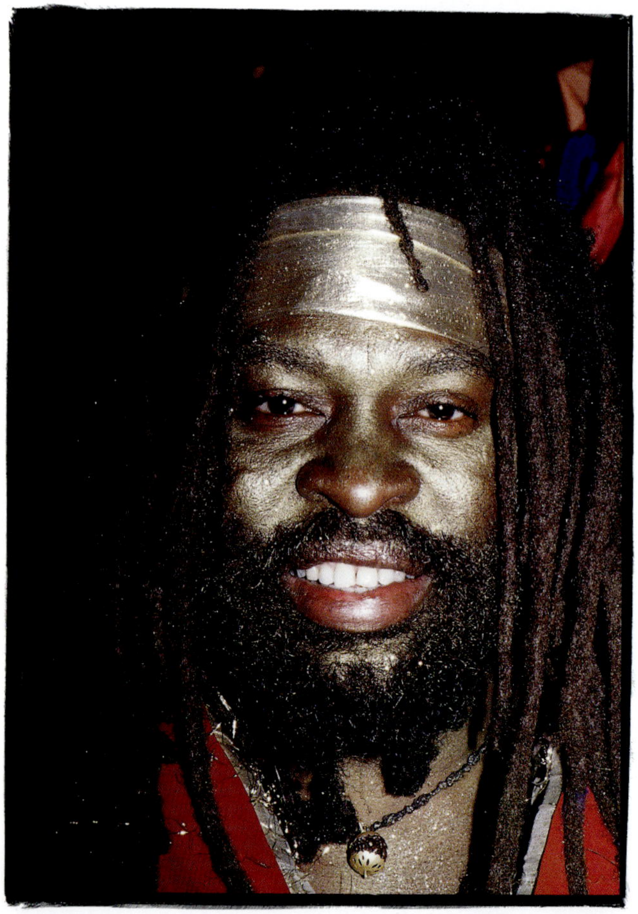

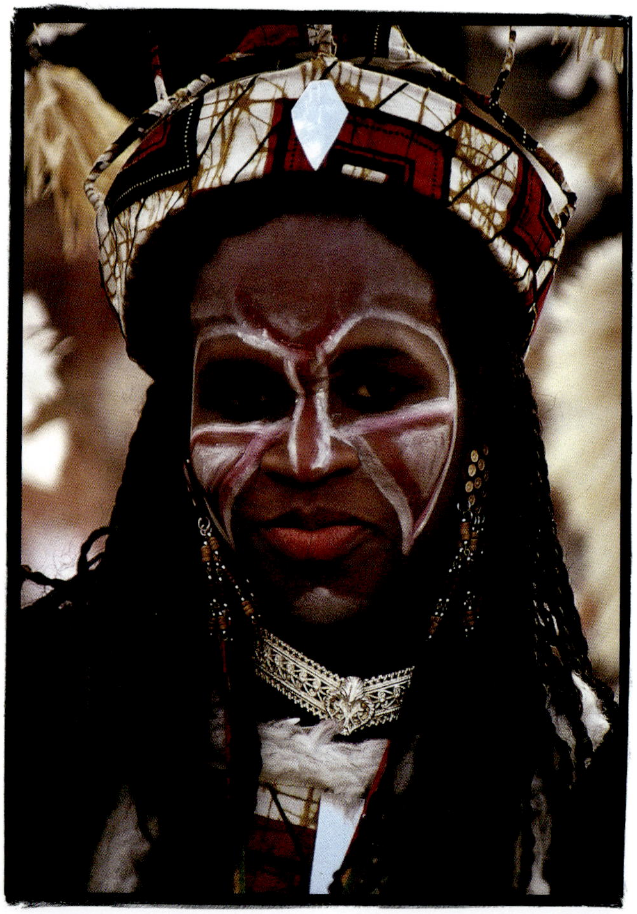

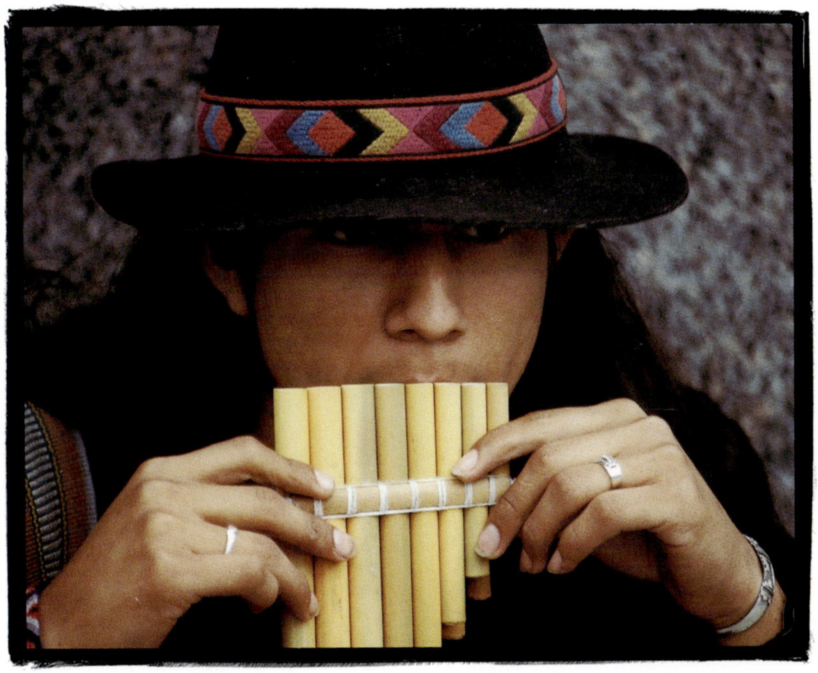

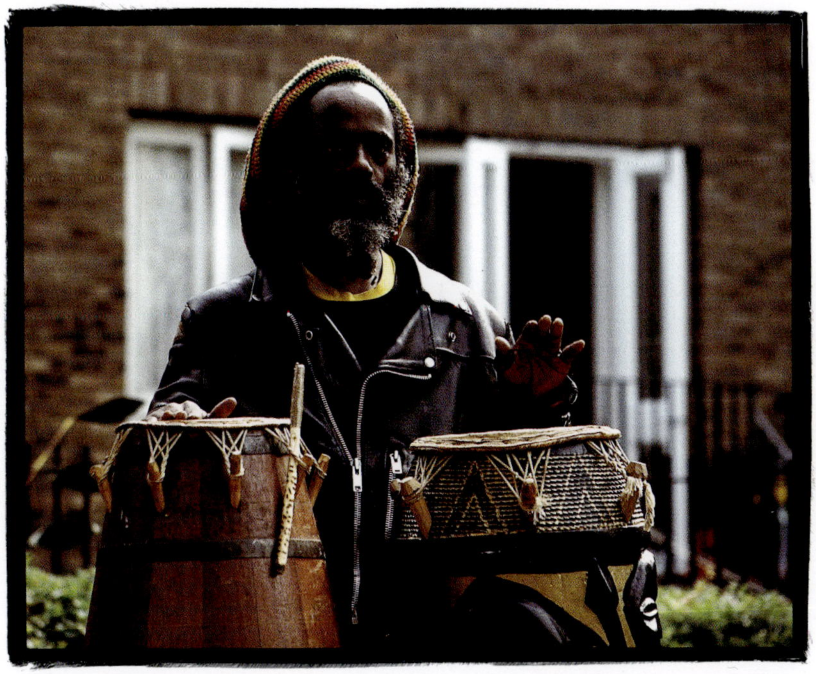

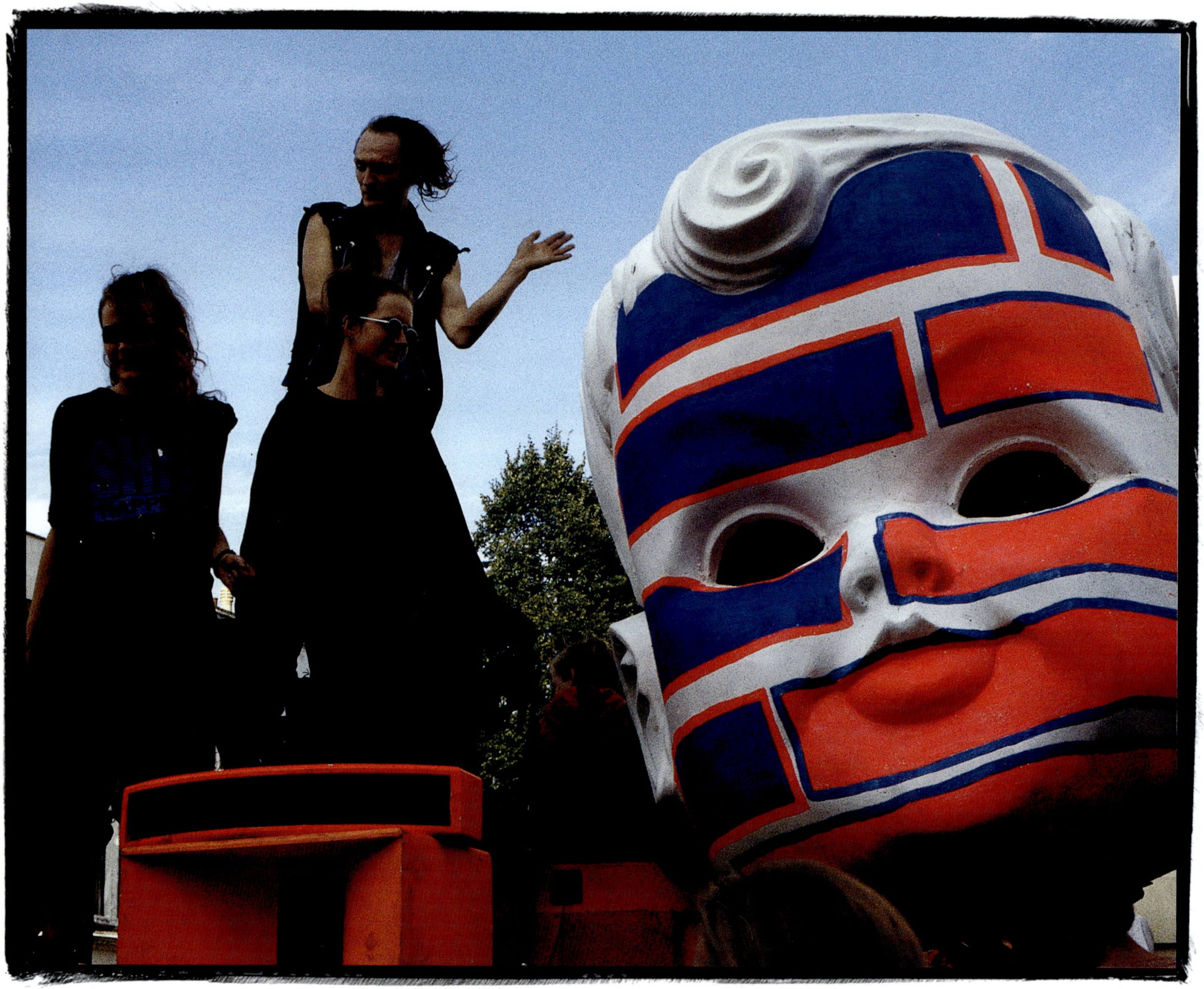

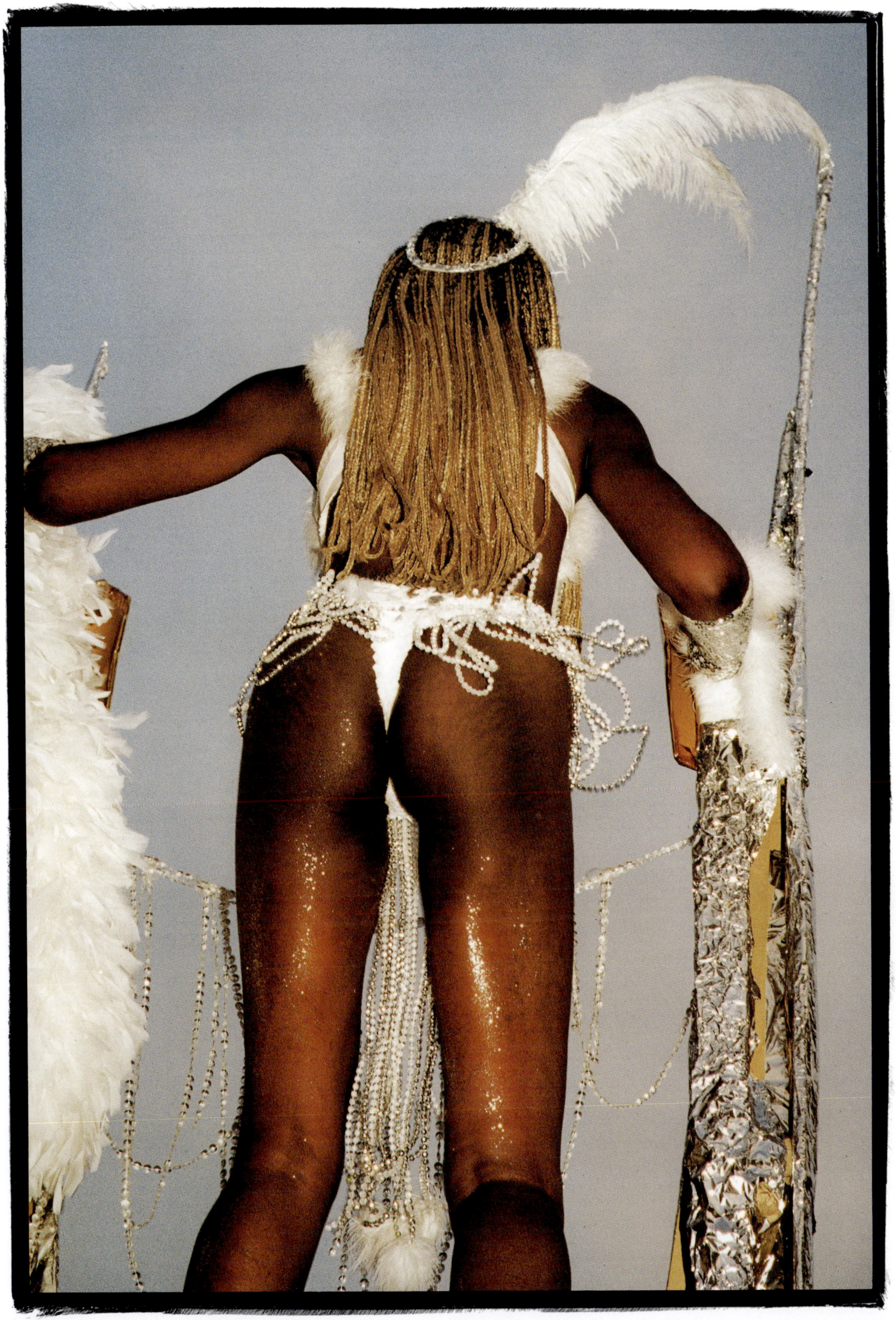

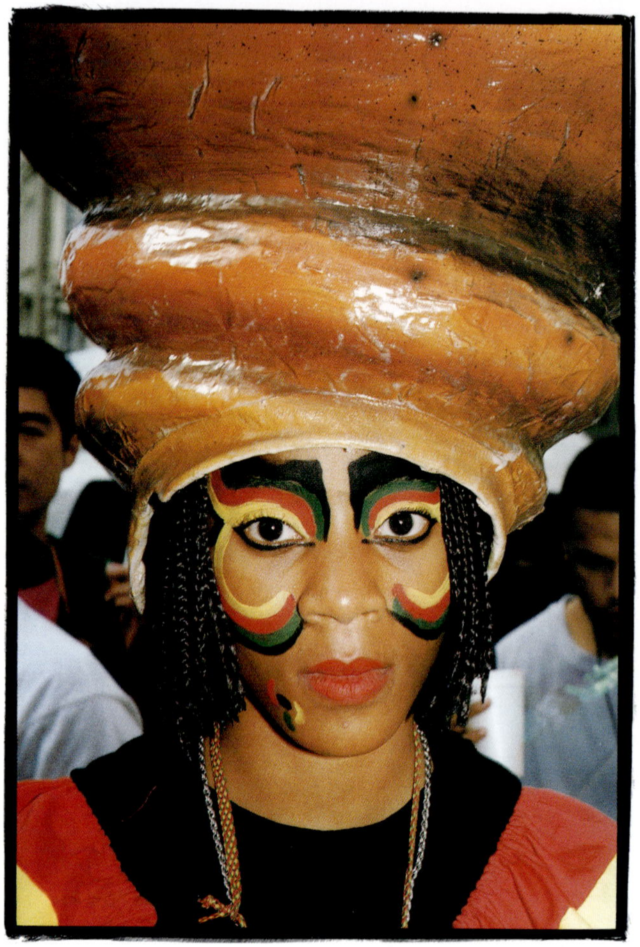

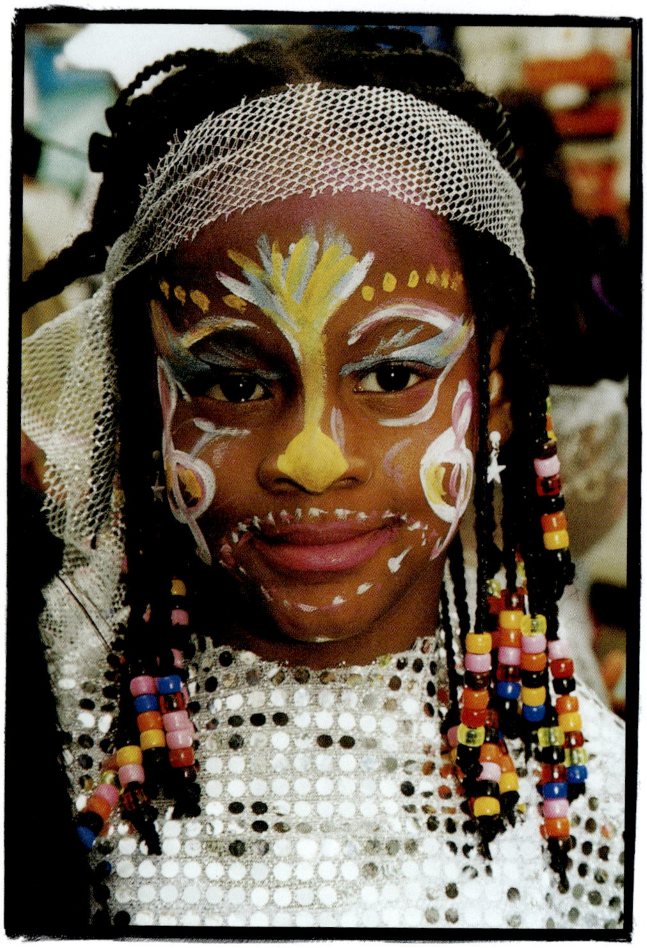

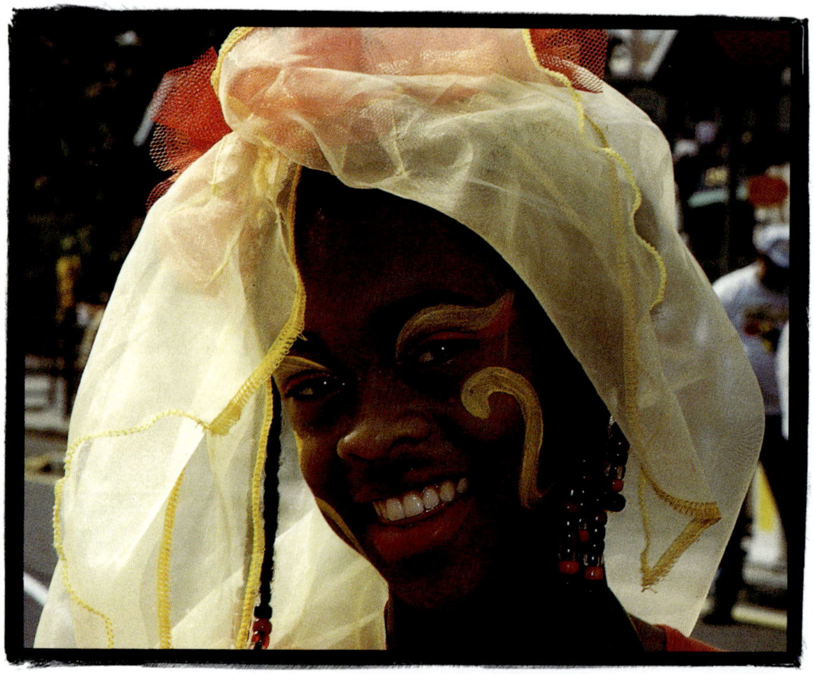

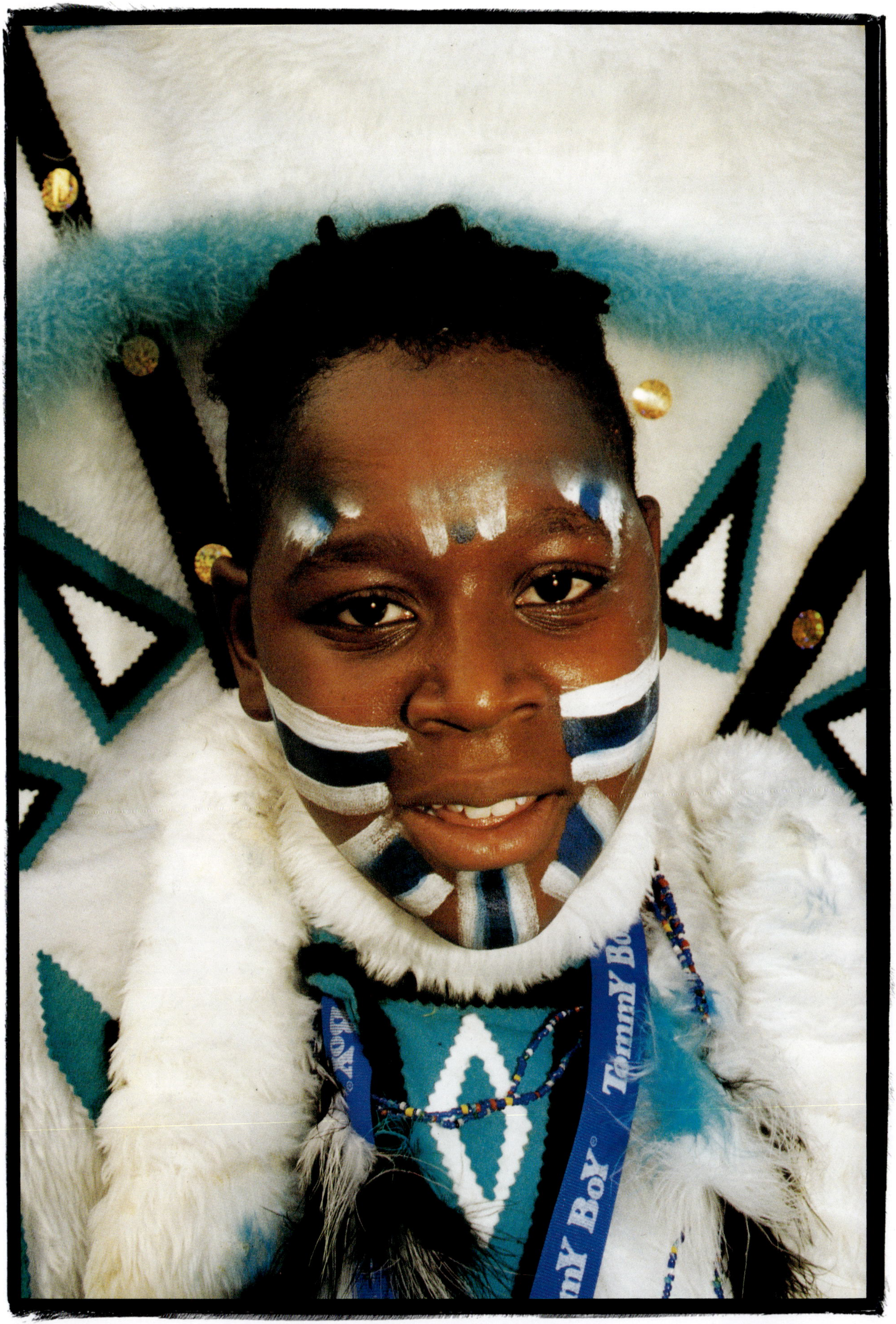
TommY BoY
TommY BoY

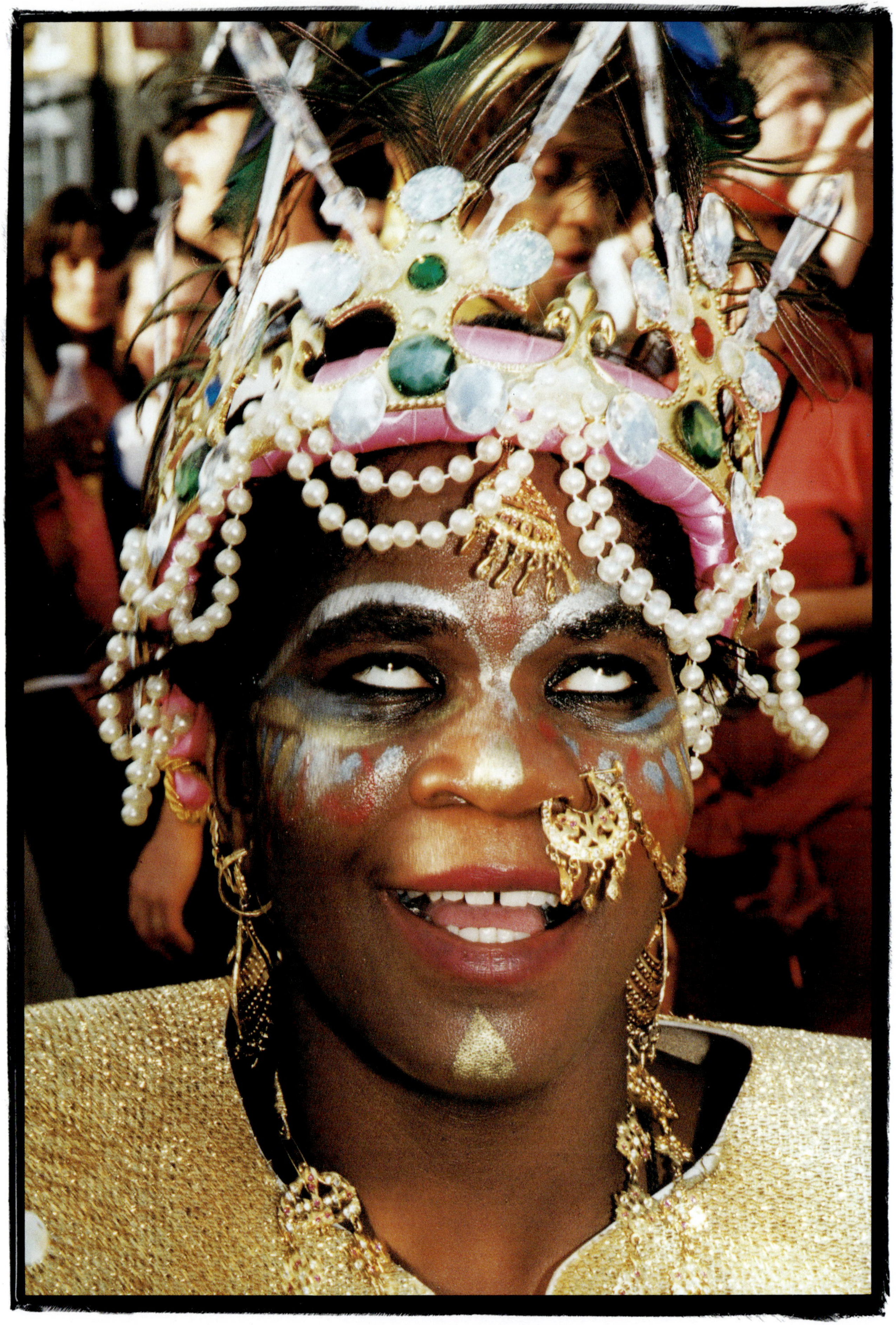

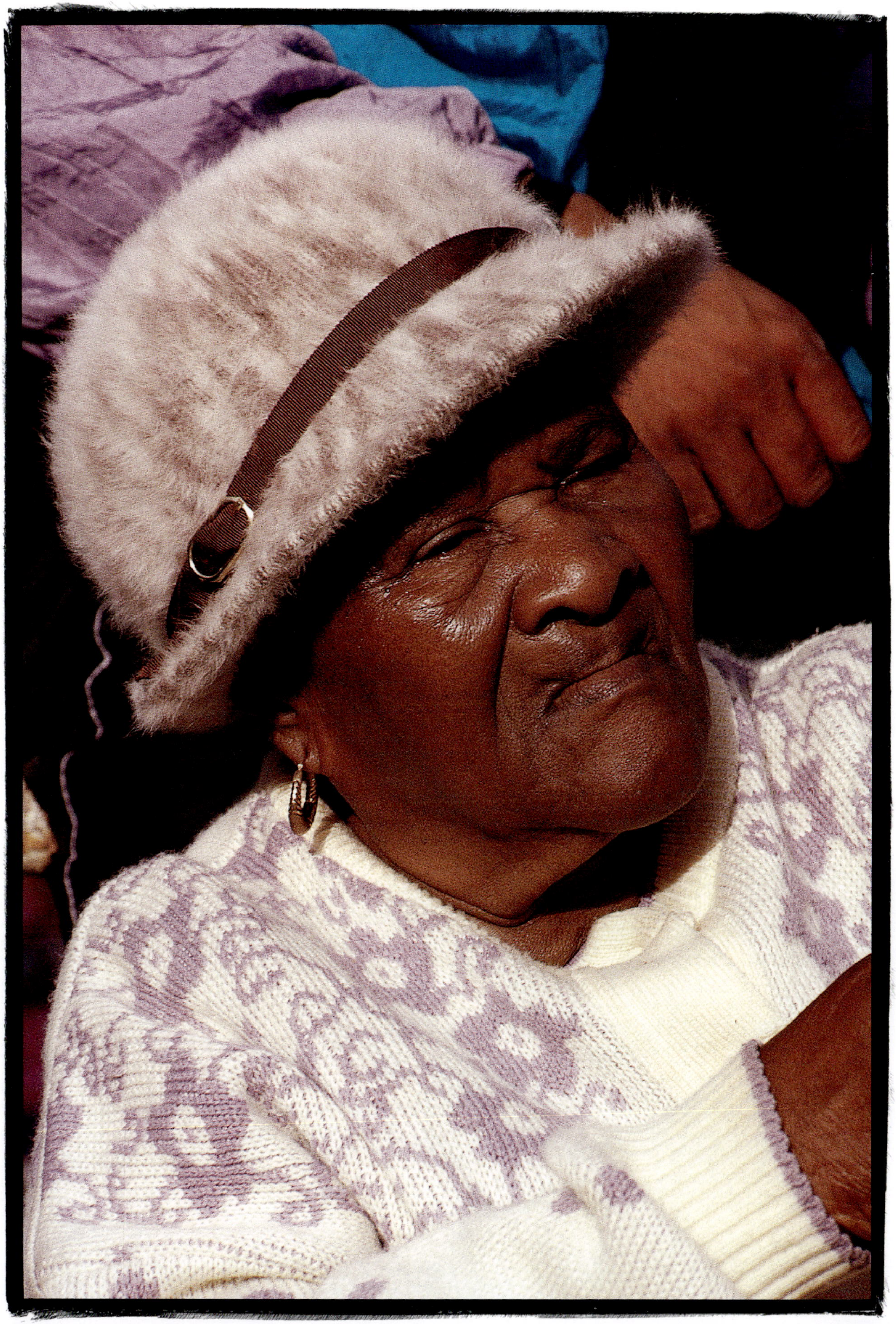

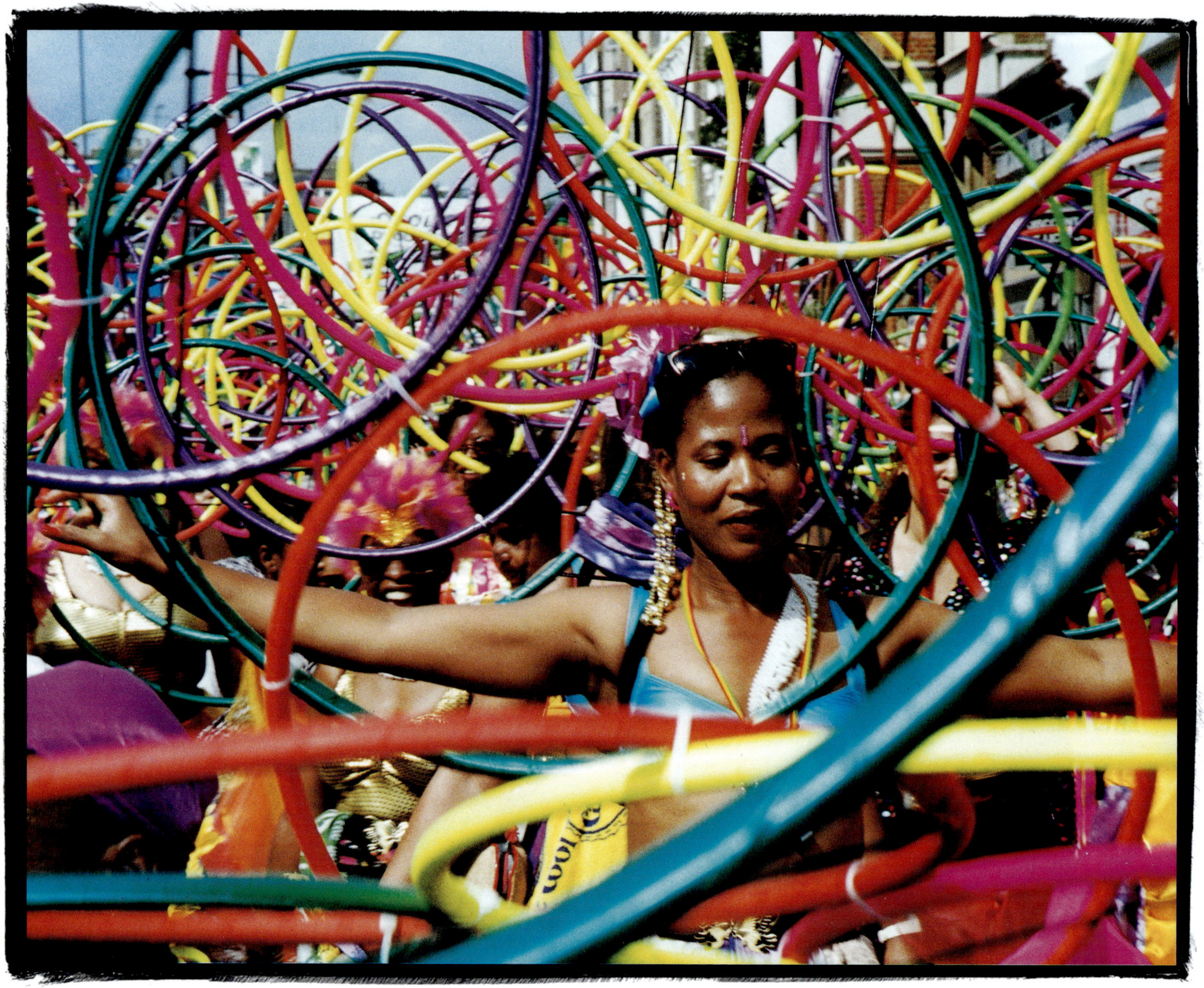

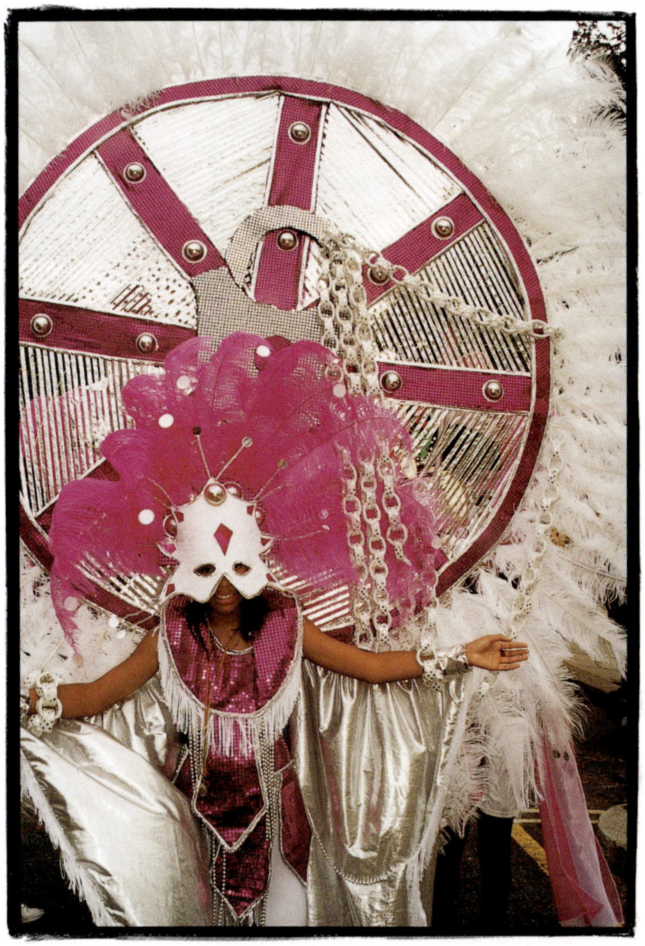

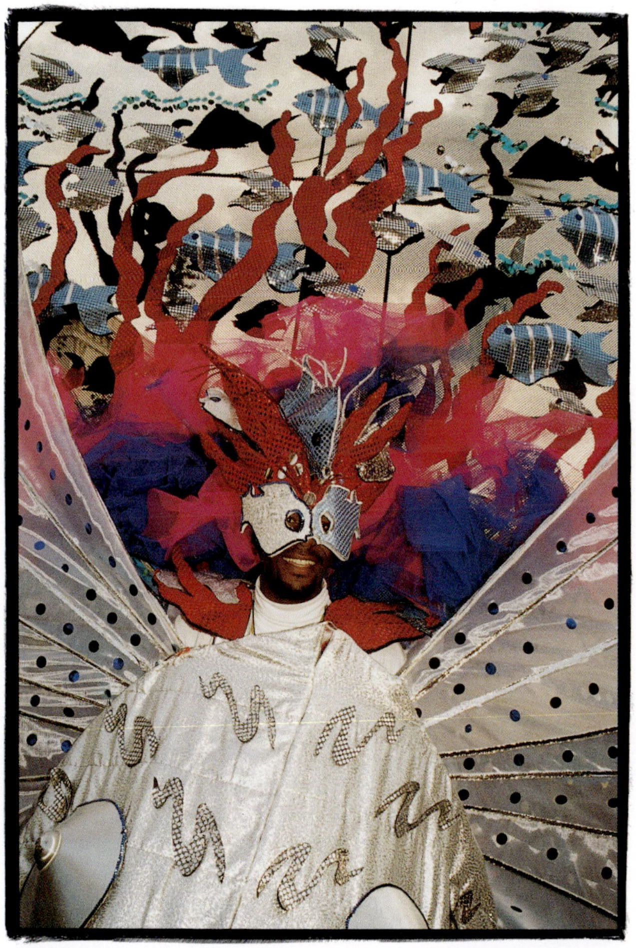

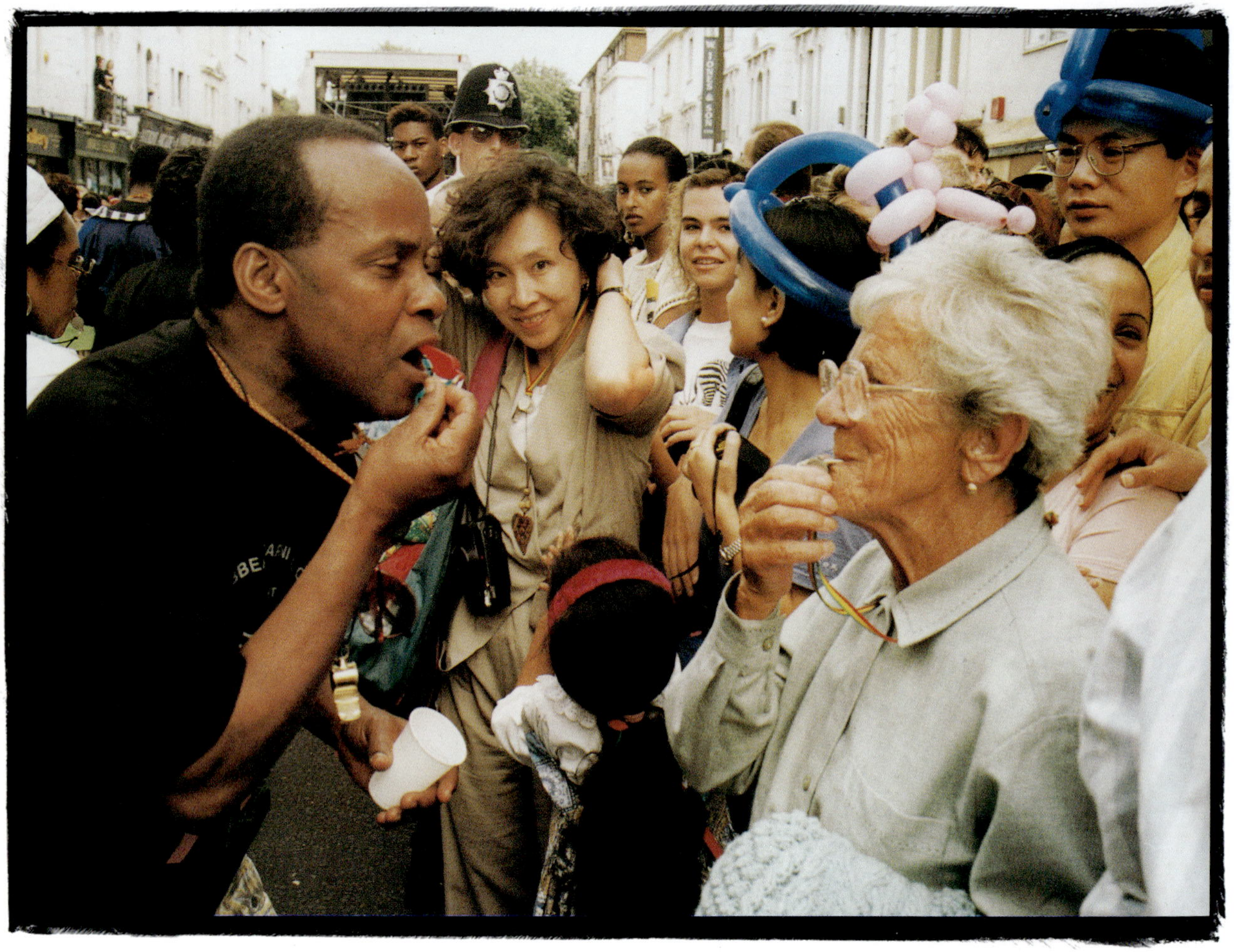

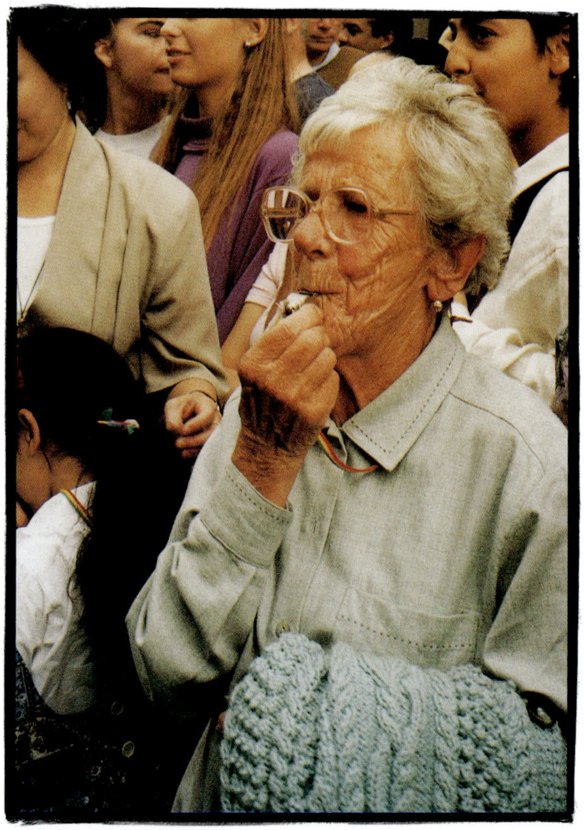

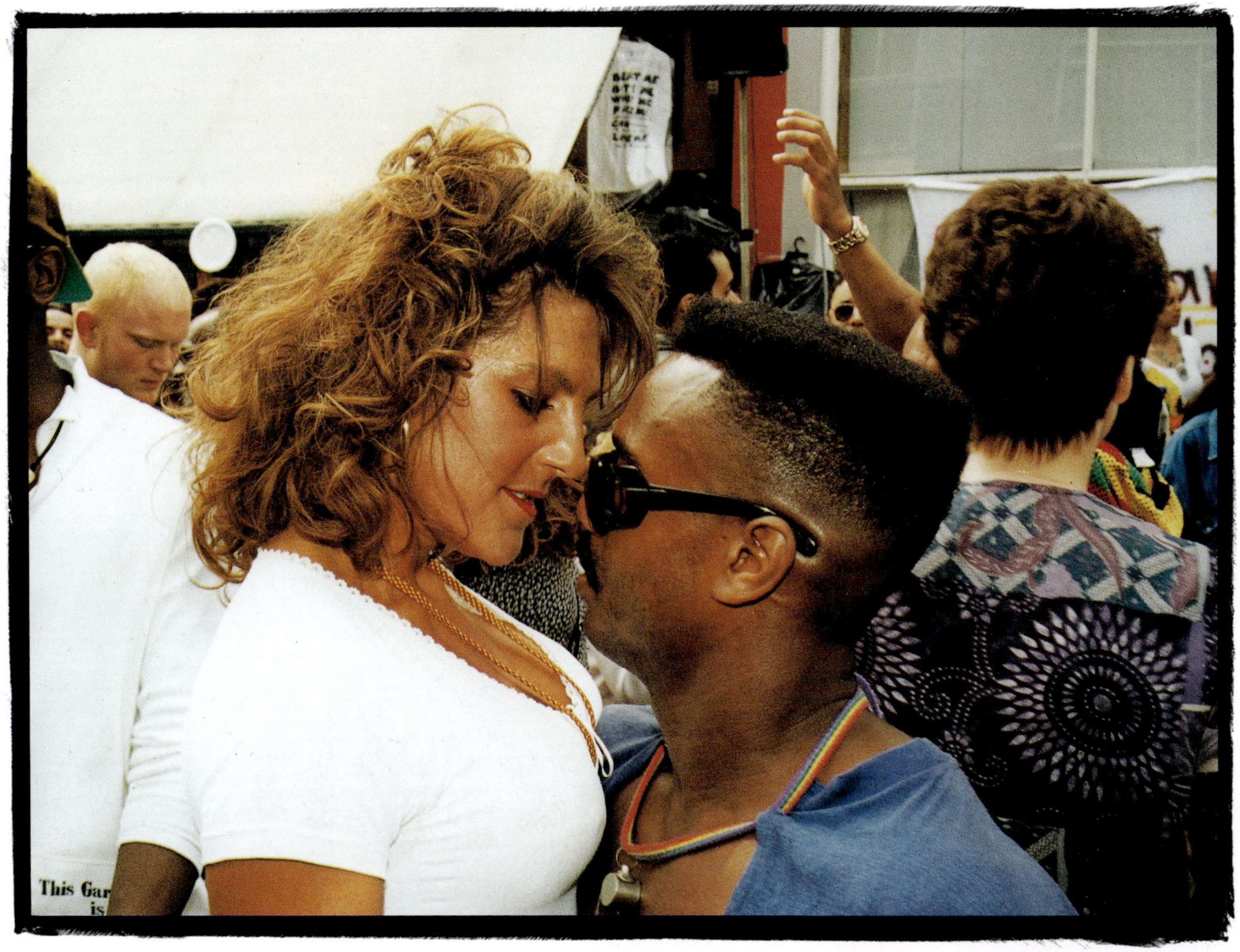

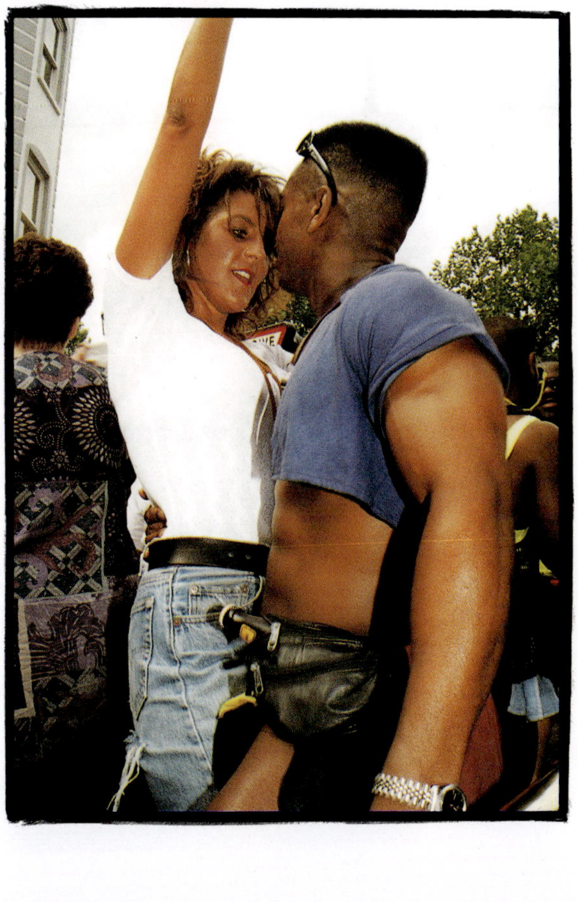

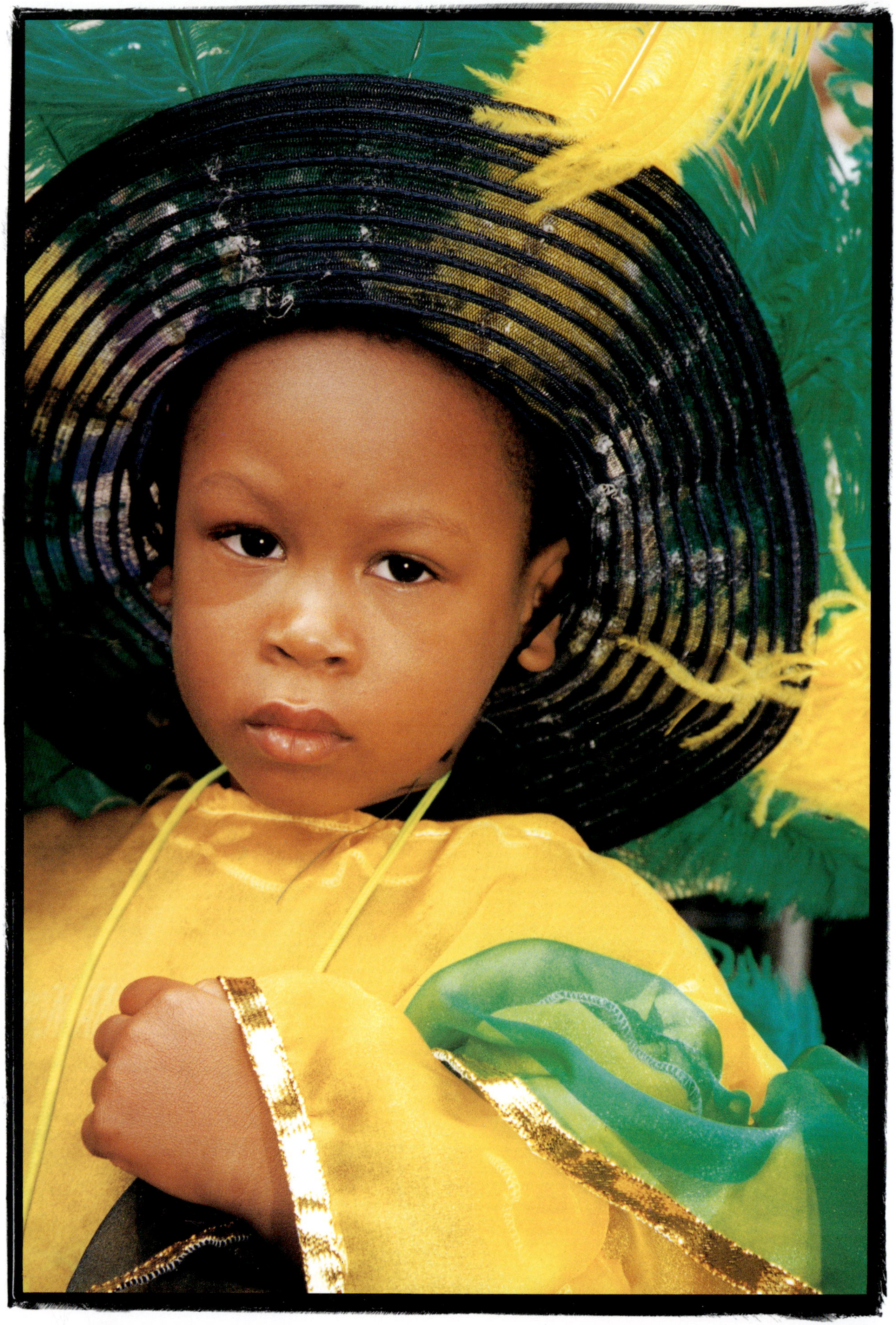

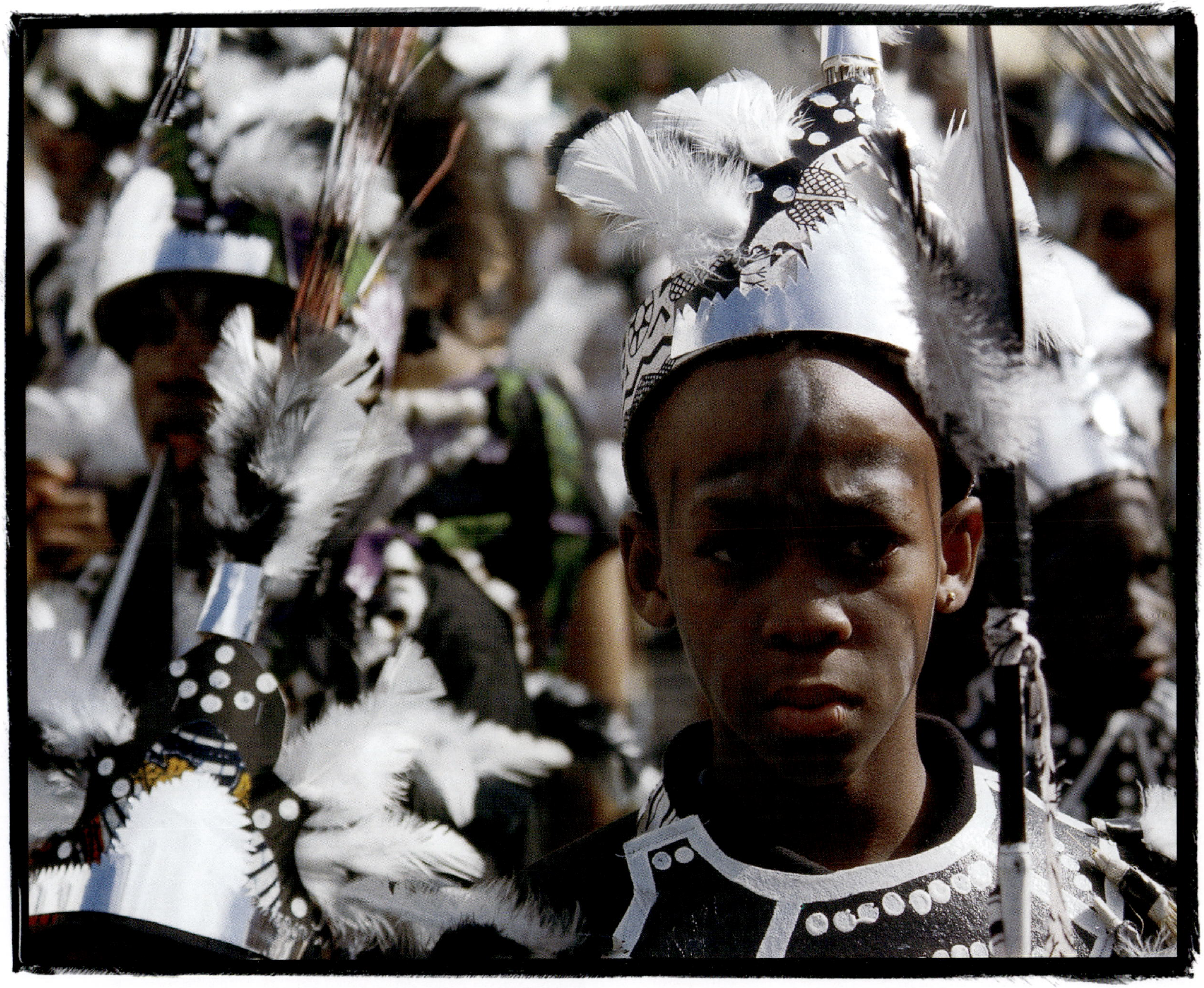

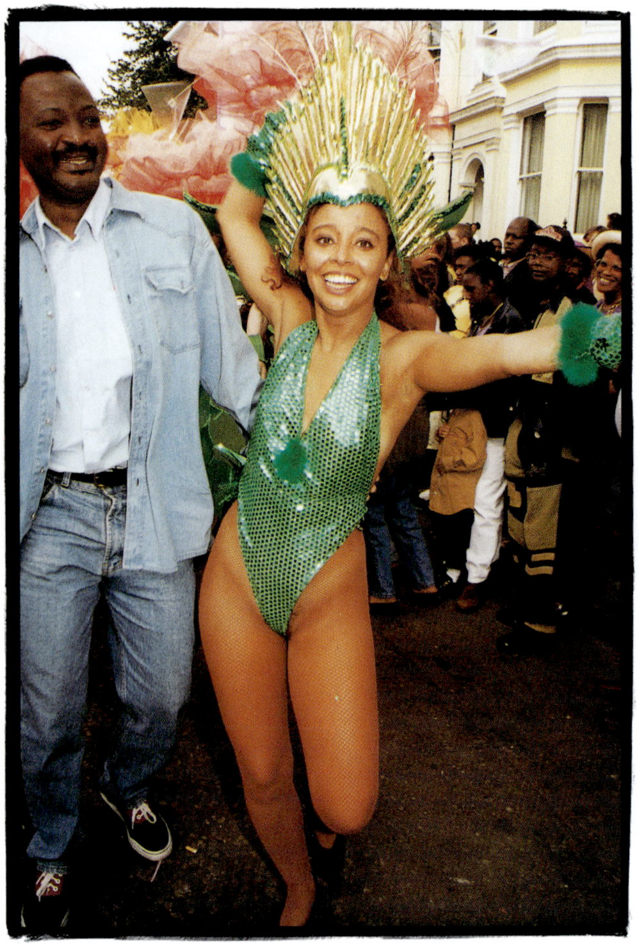

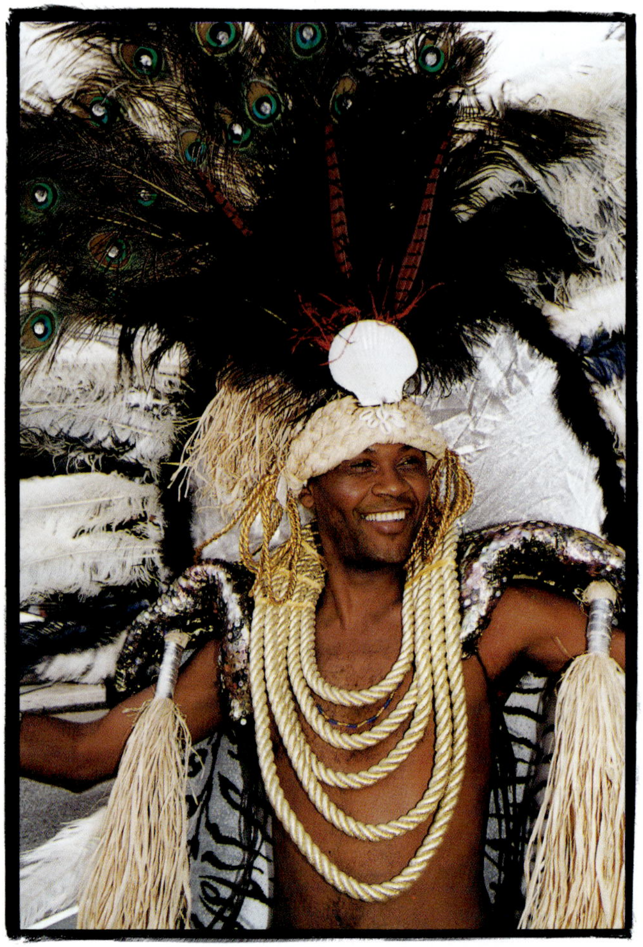

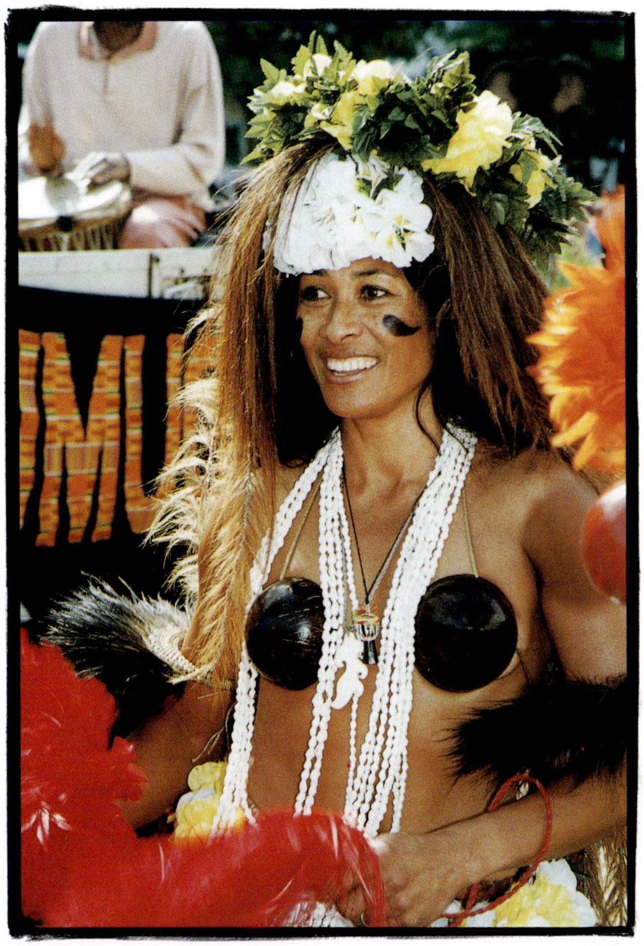

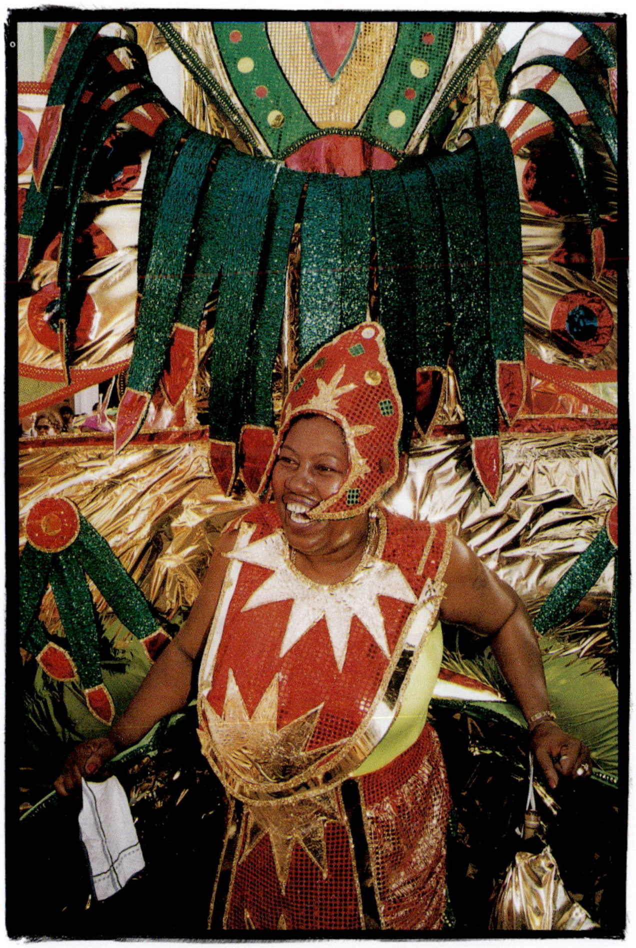

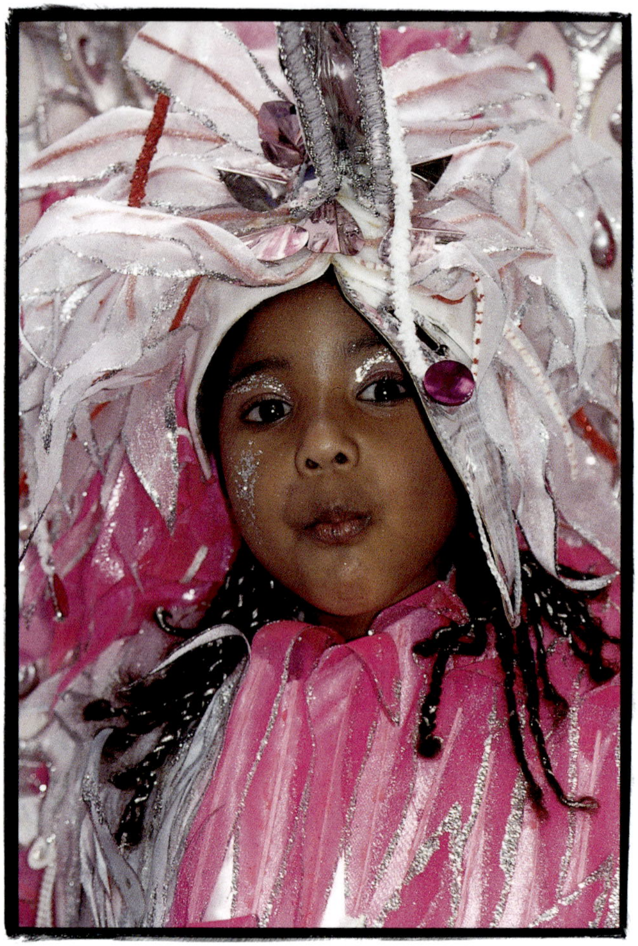

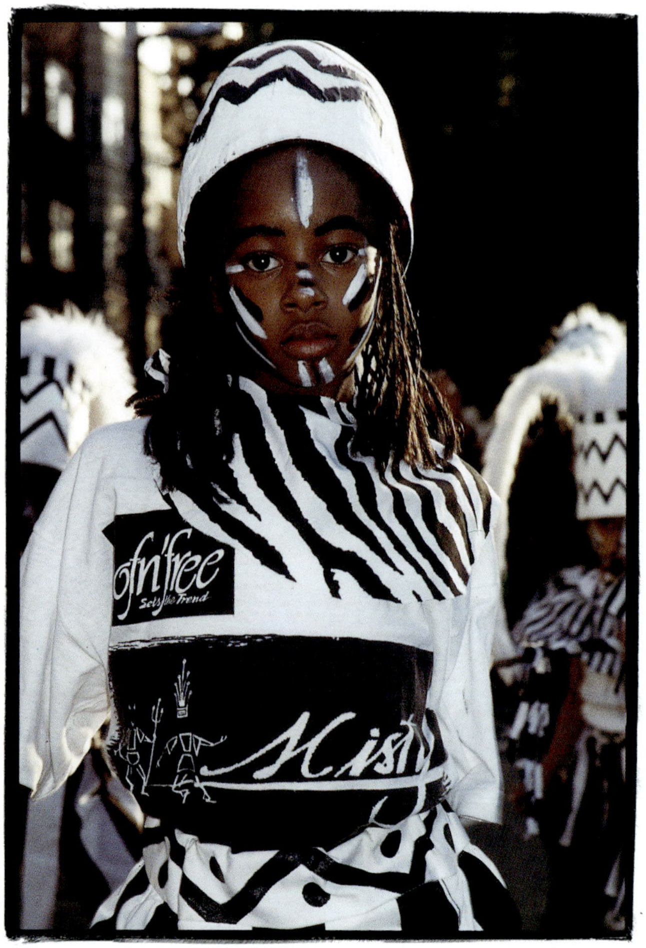
ofn'free

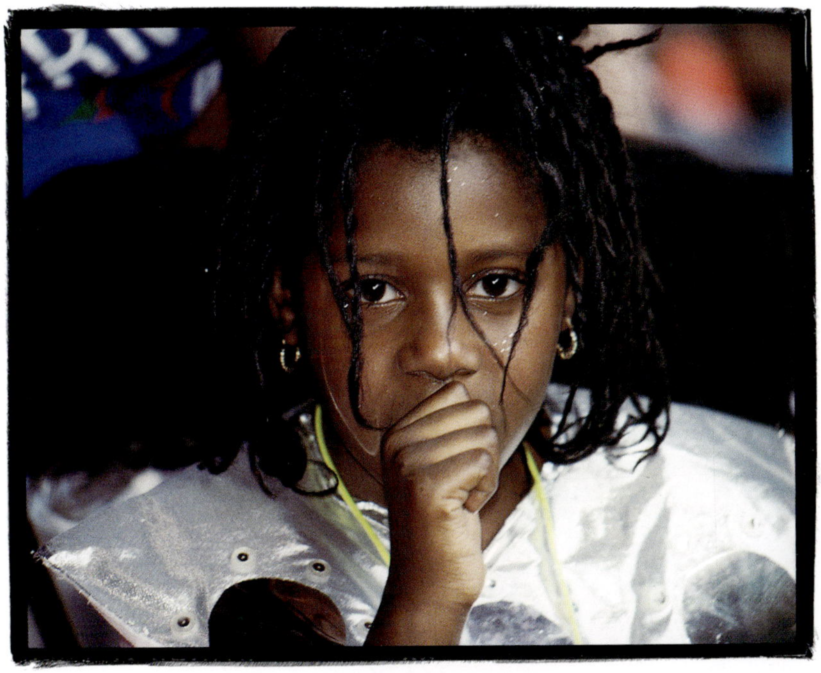

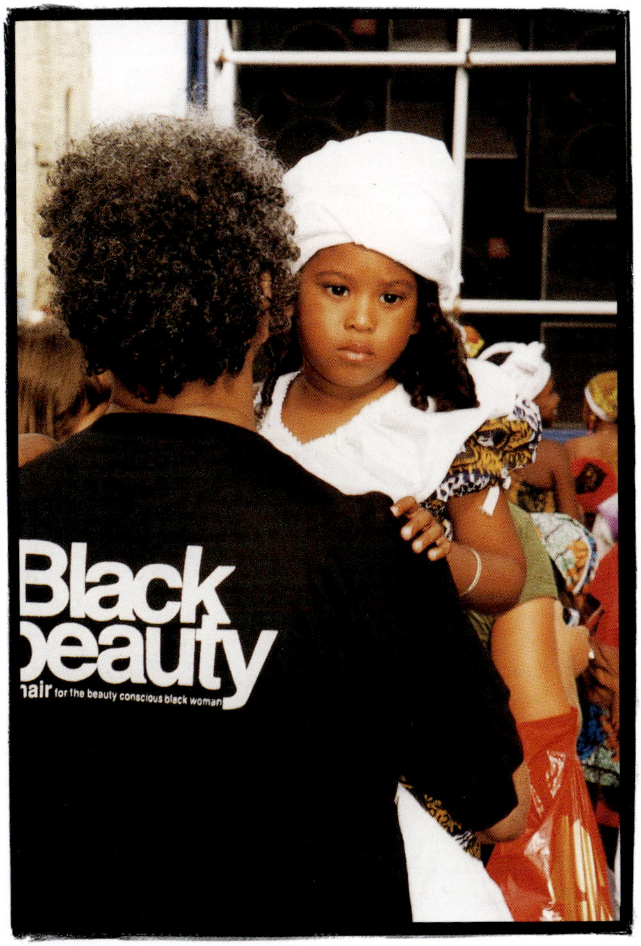
Black
for the beauty conscious black woman

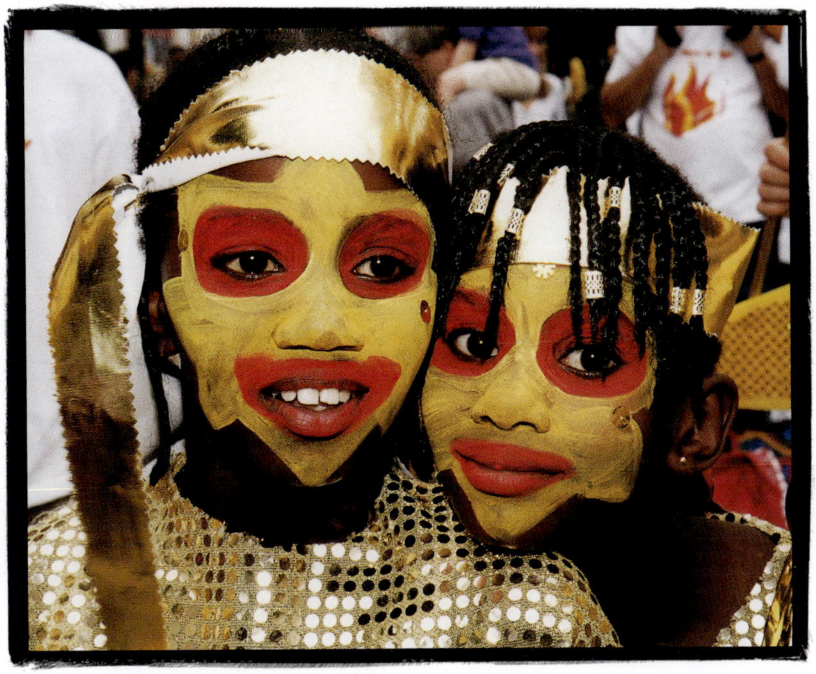

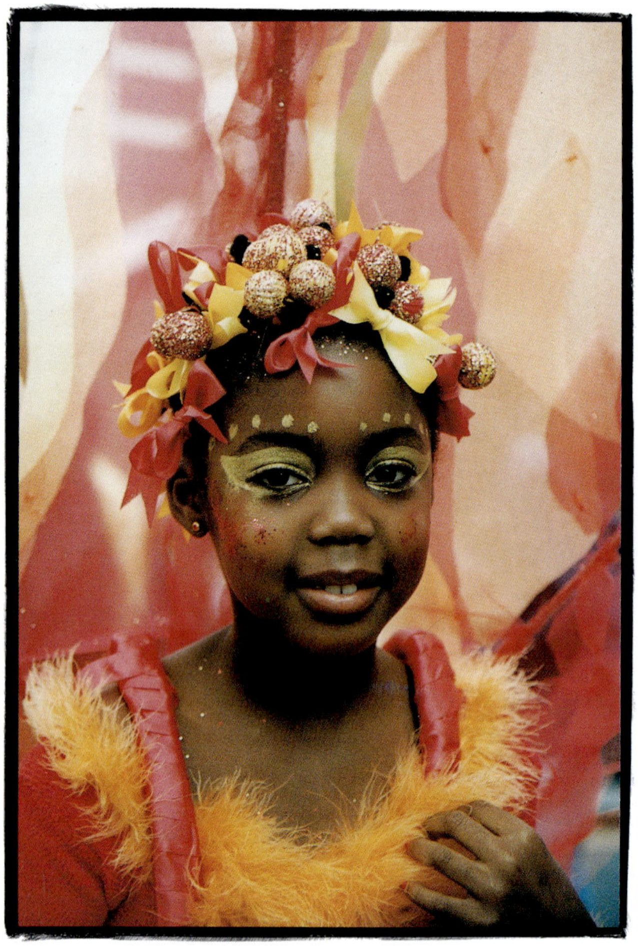

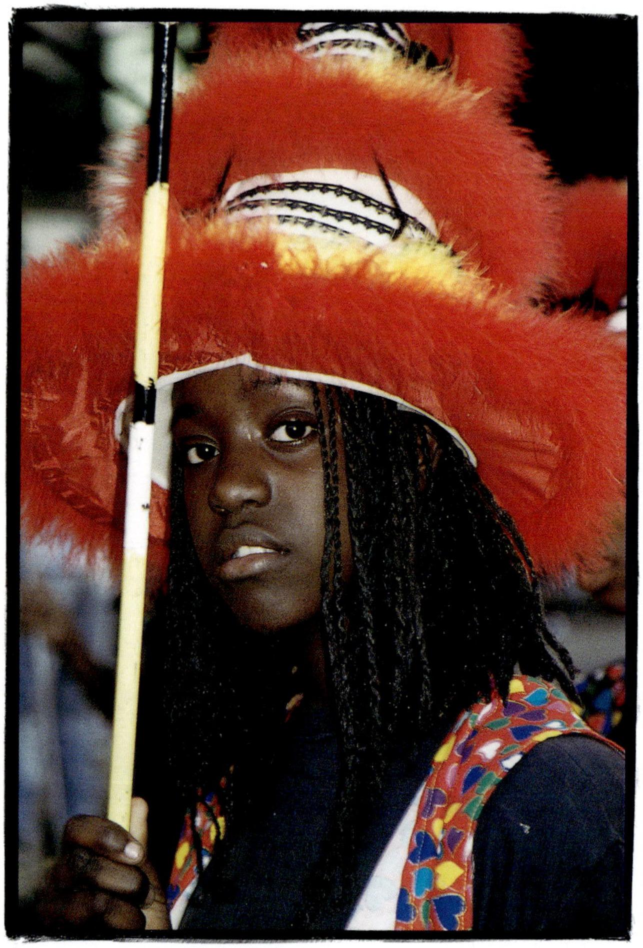

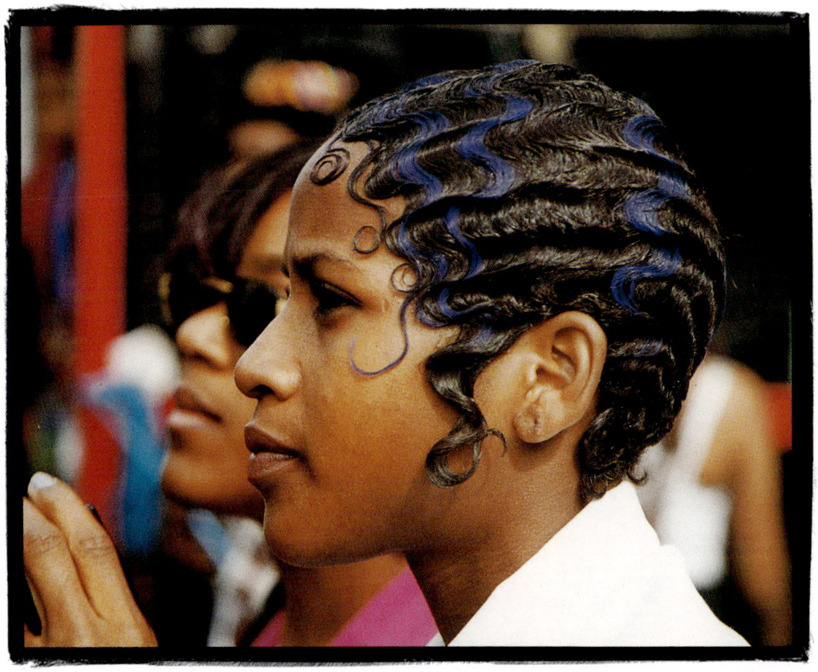

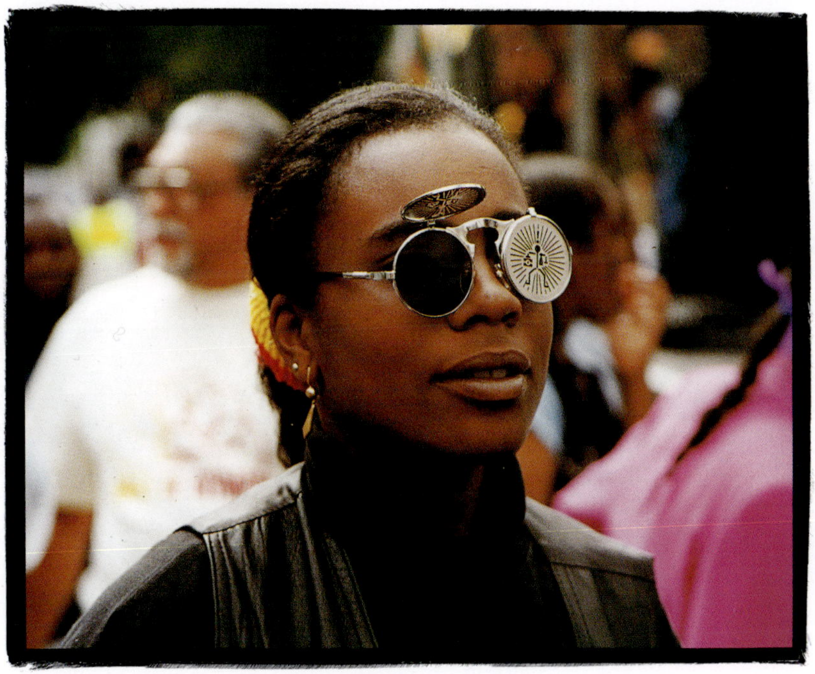

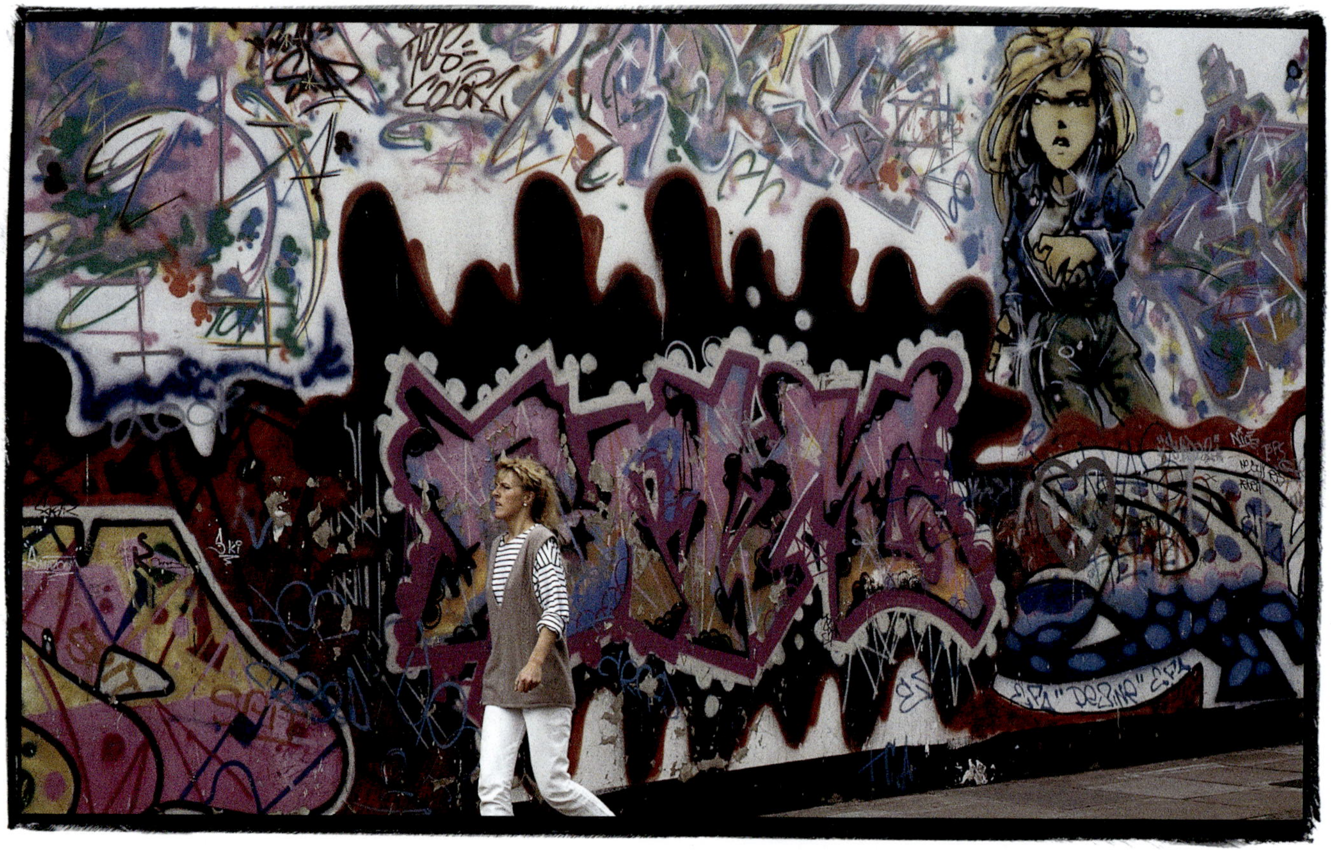

hair on, but where's
the Comfort in that.
SOUTHERN COMFORT
THE BIG EASY

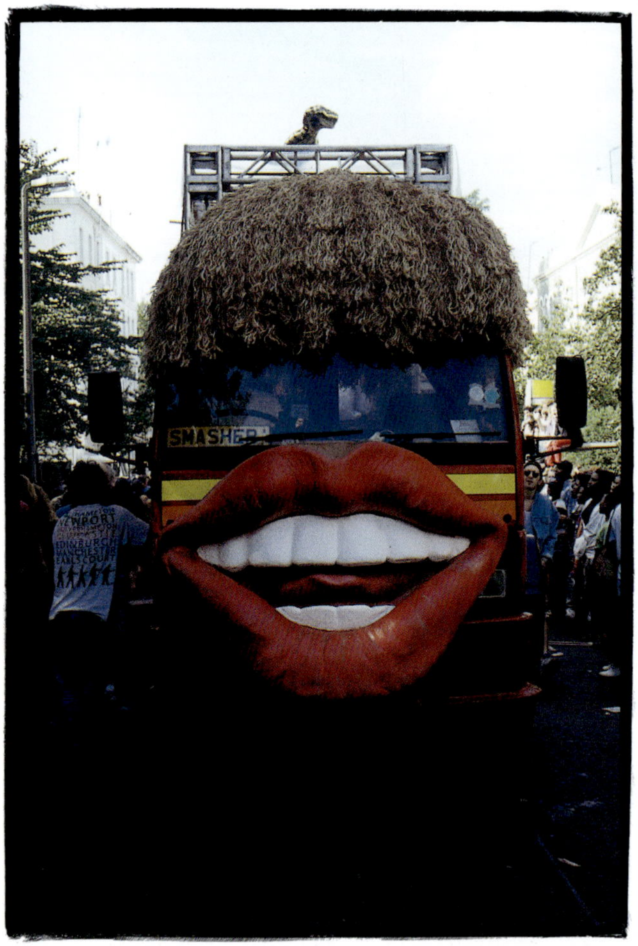
SMASHER

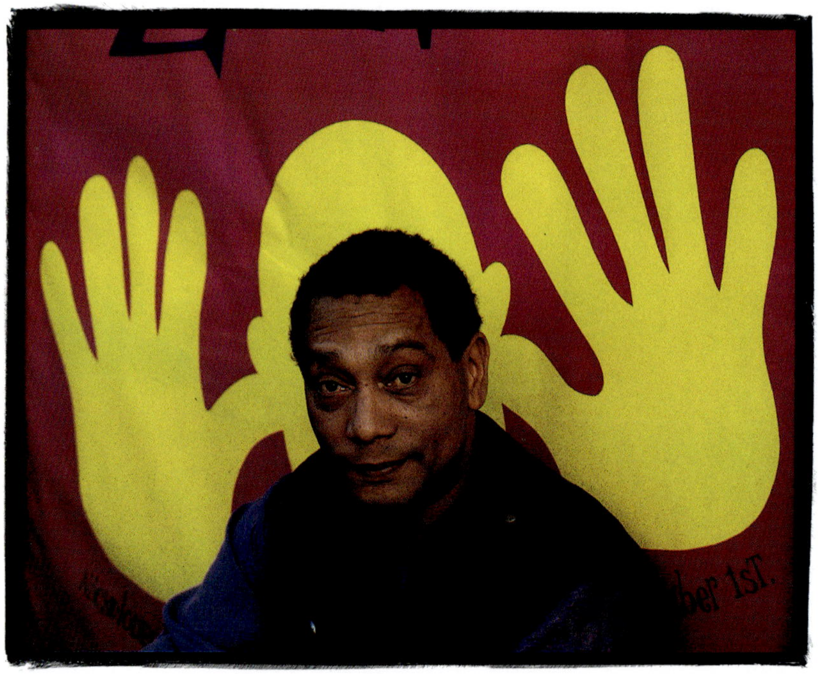

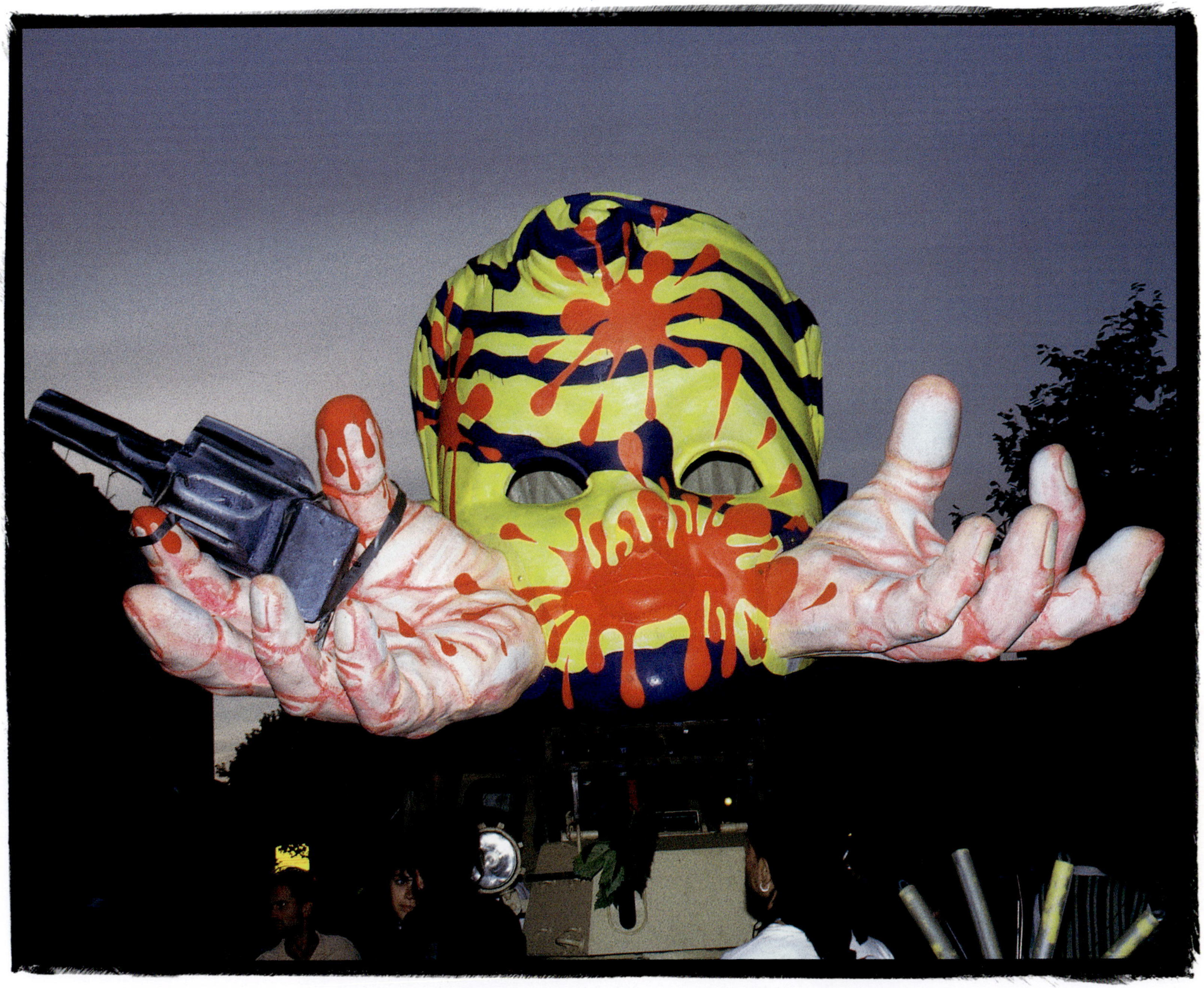

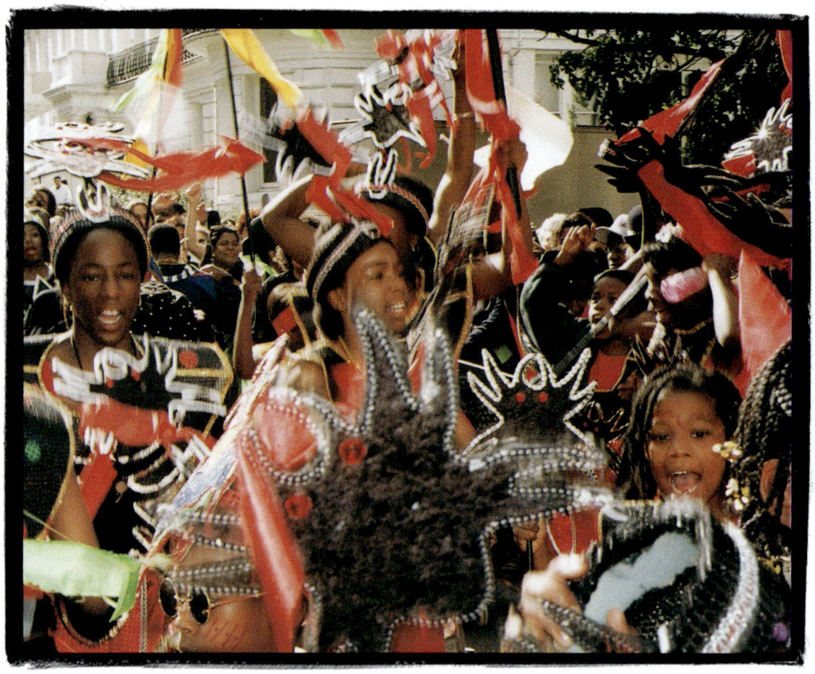

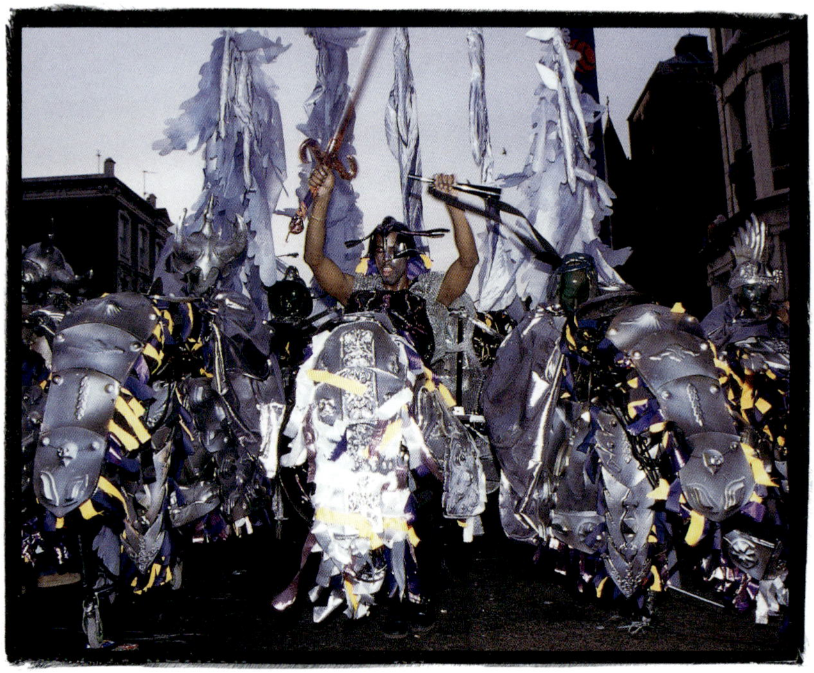

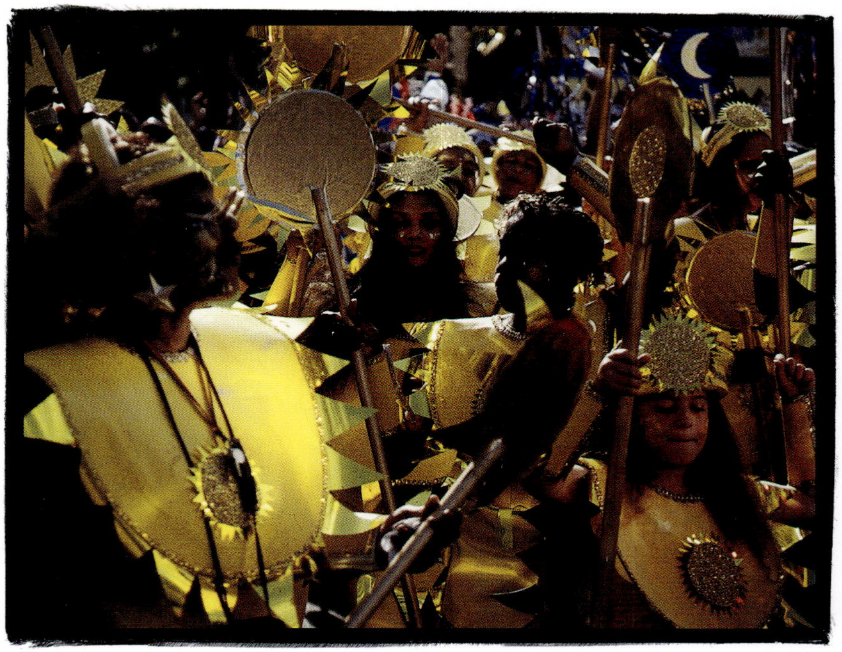

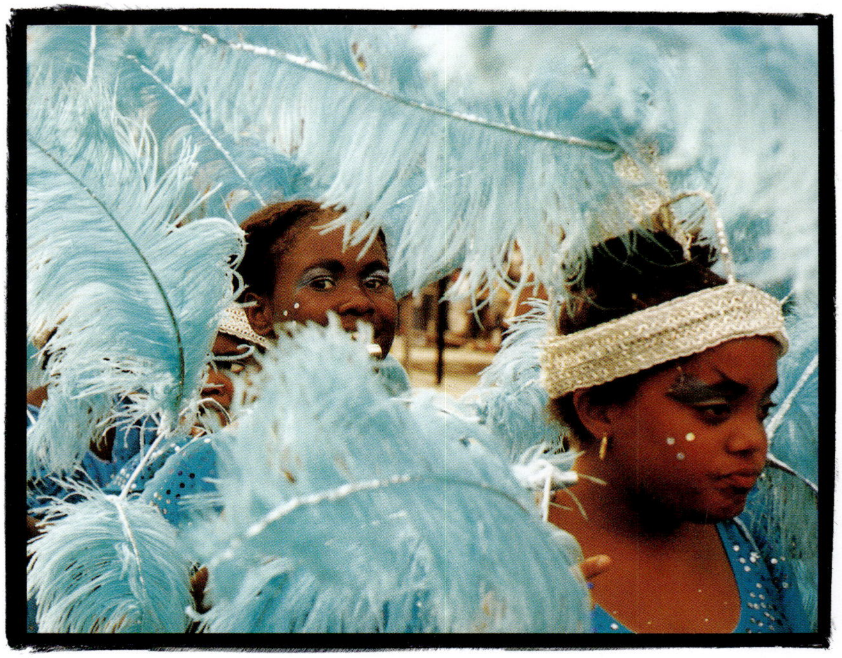

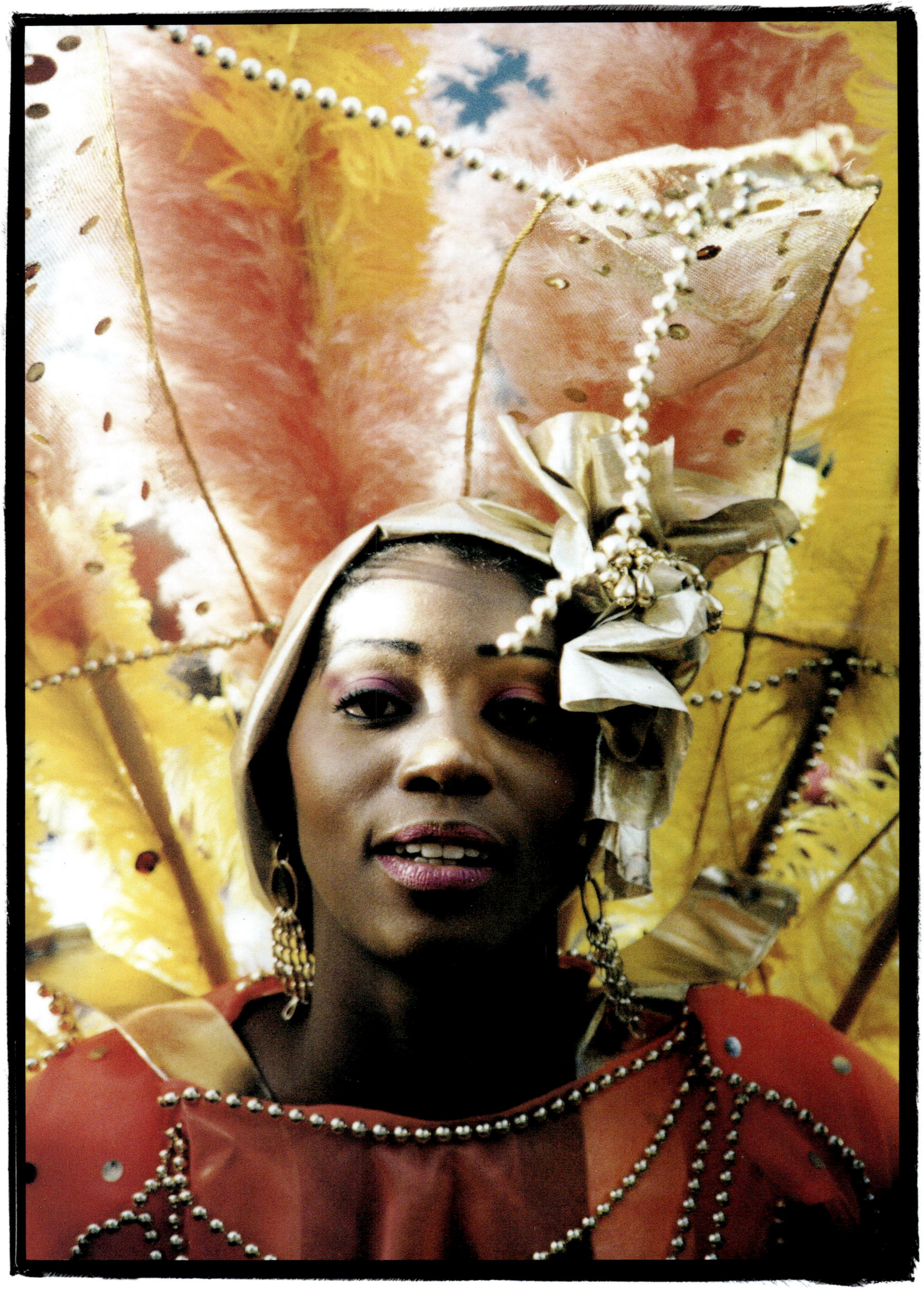

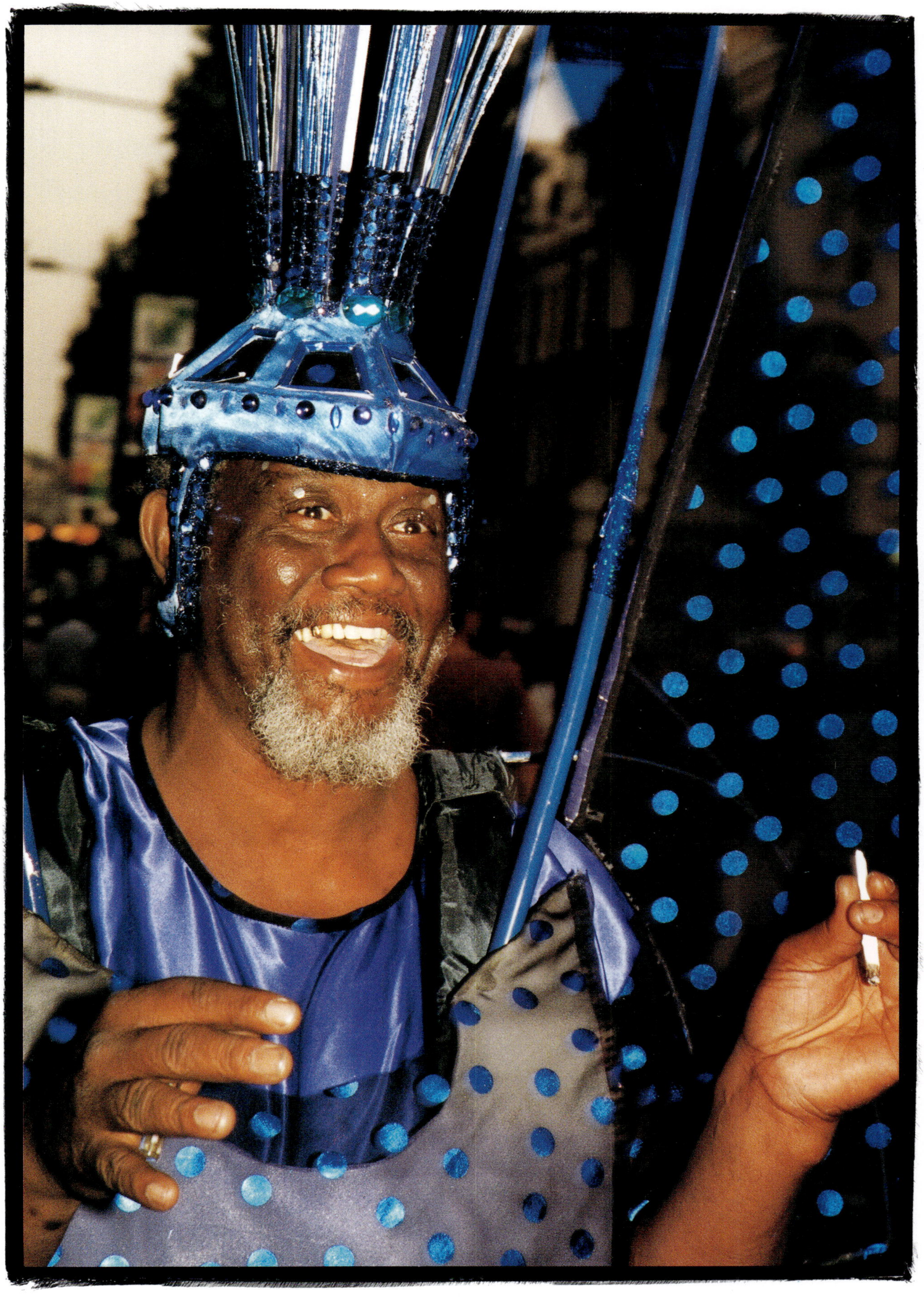

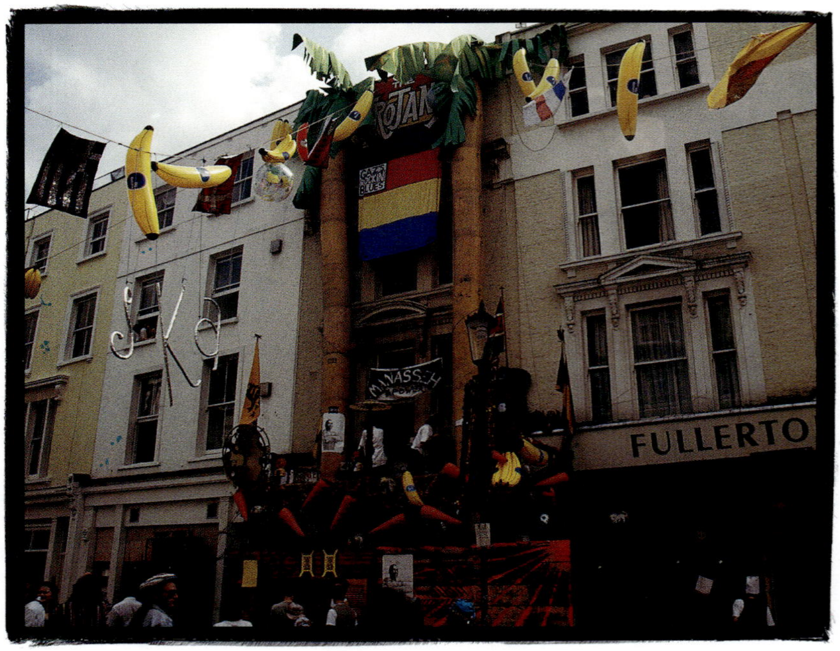
FULLERTO

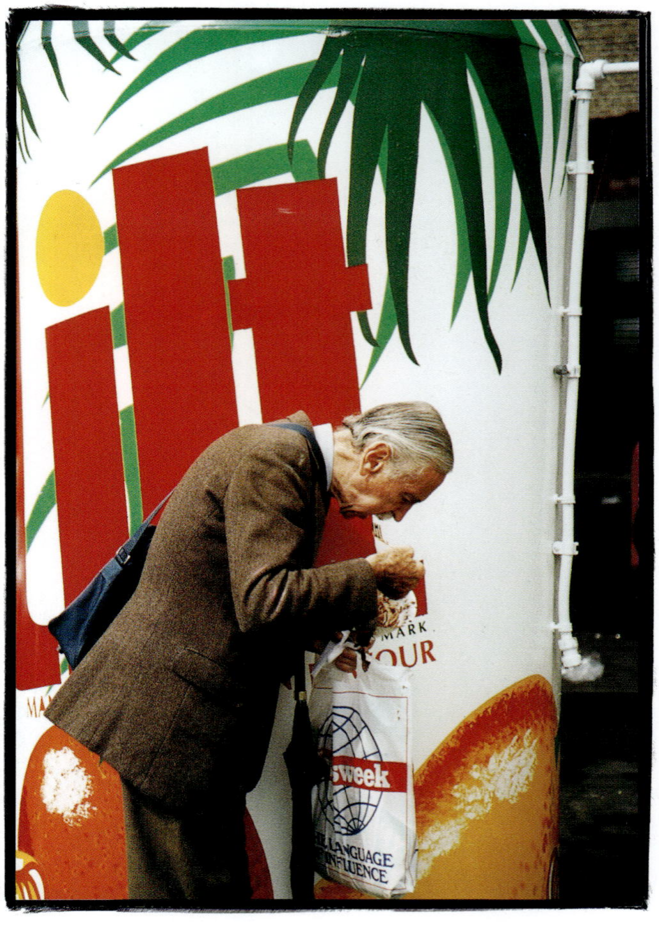
MARK
OUR
week
LANGUAGE
INFLUENCE

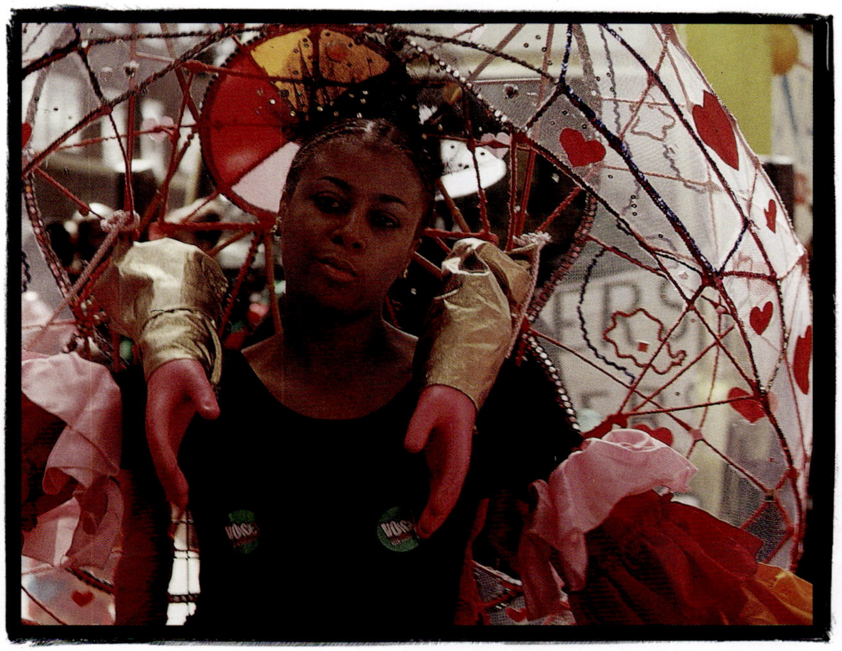

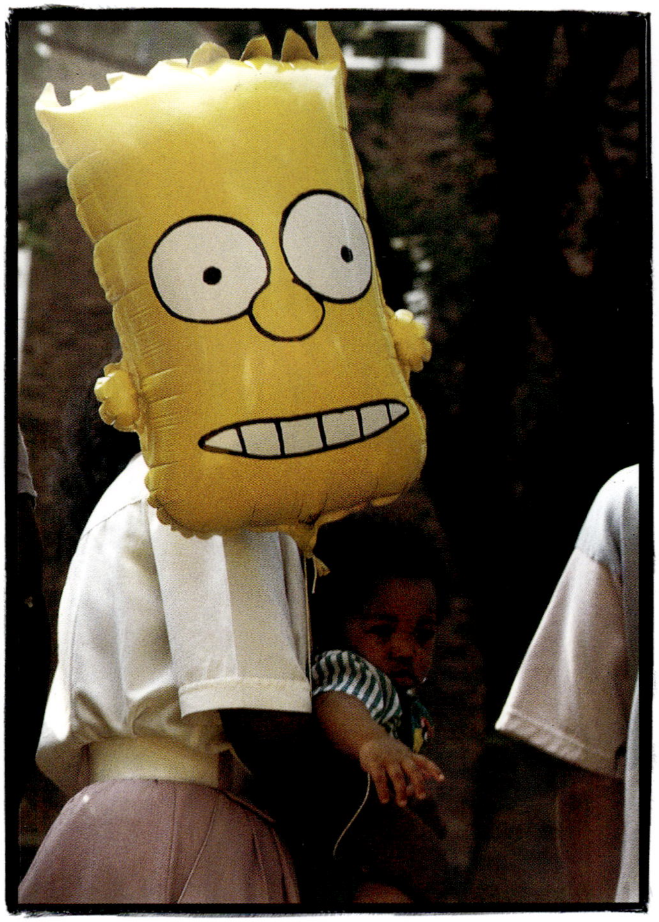

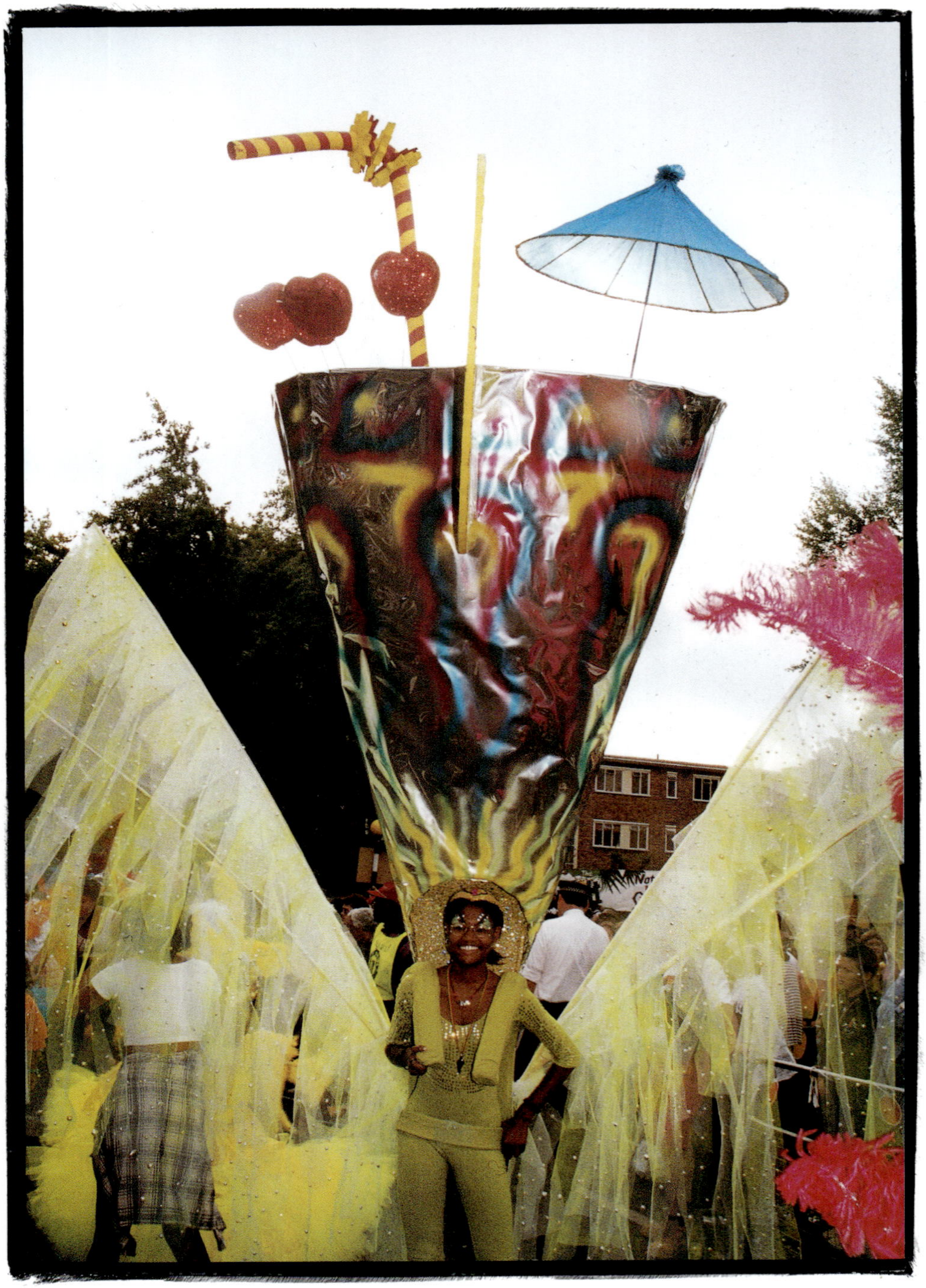

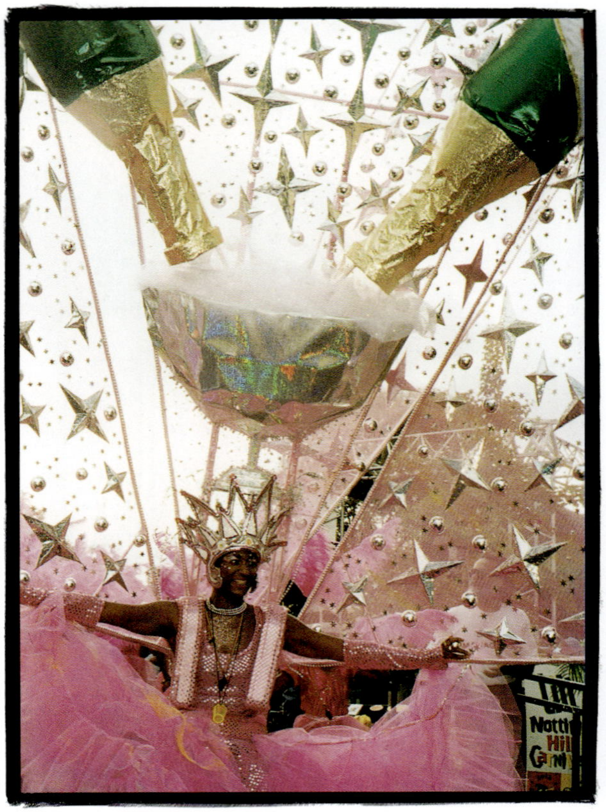

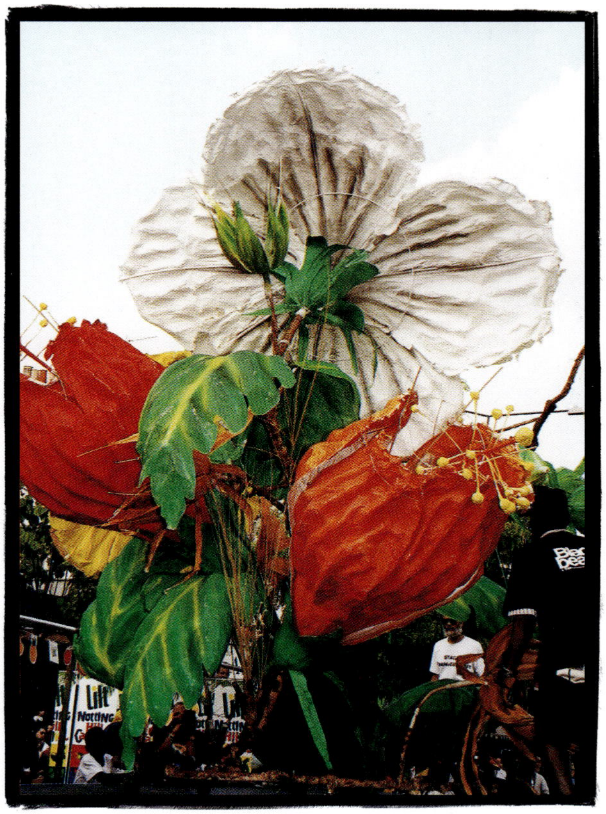

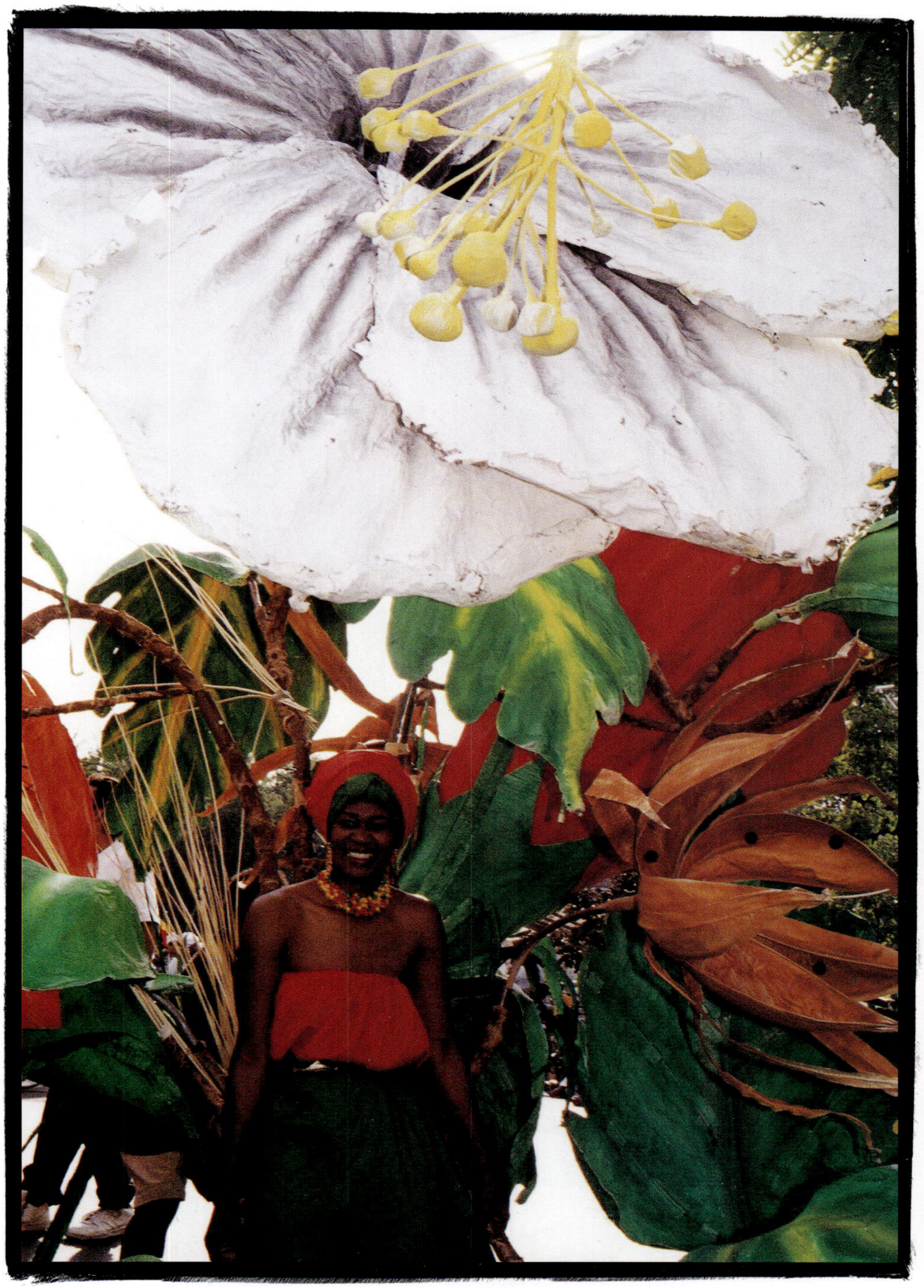

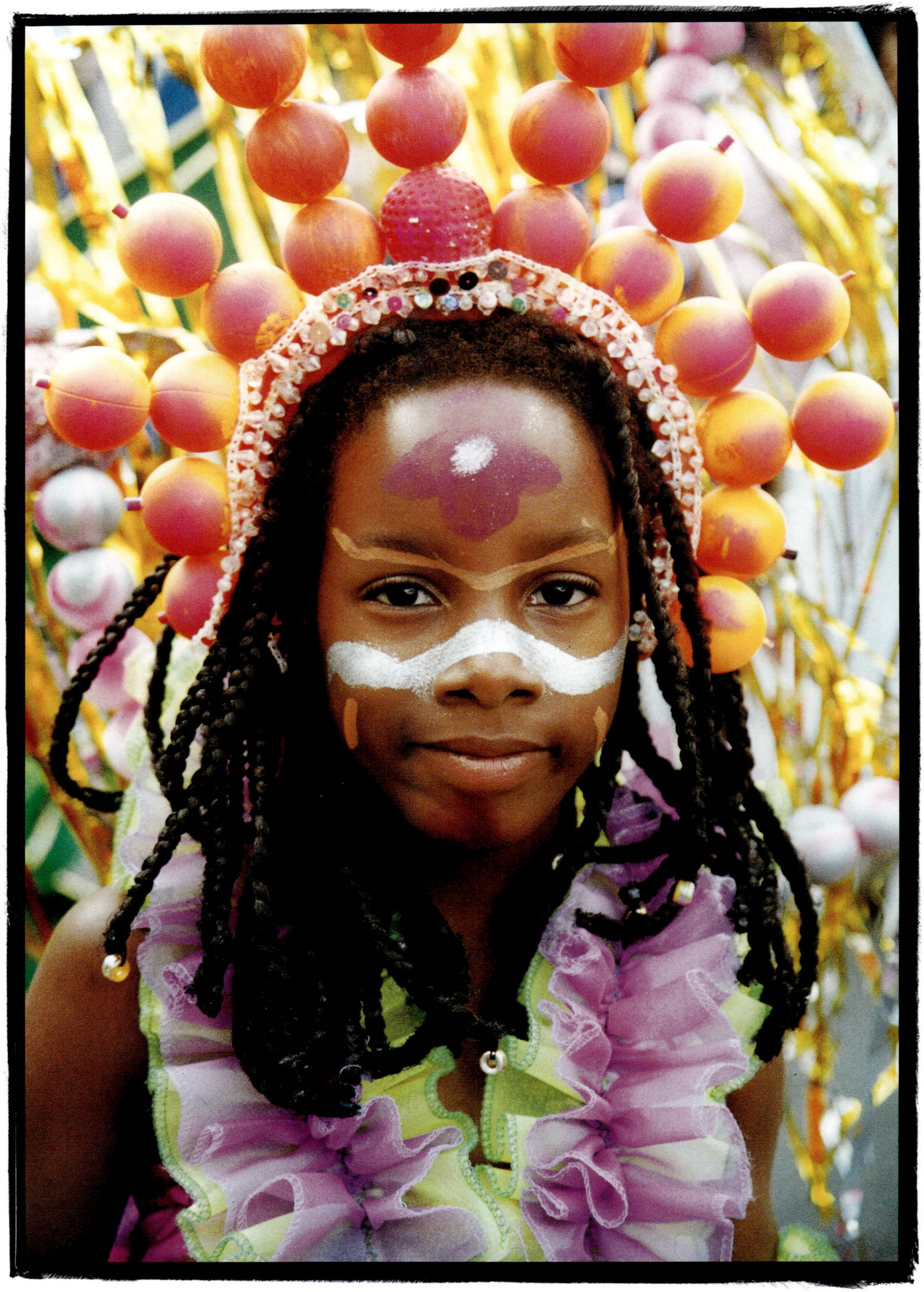

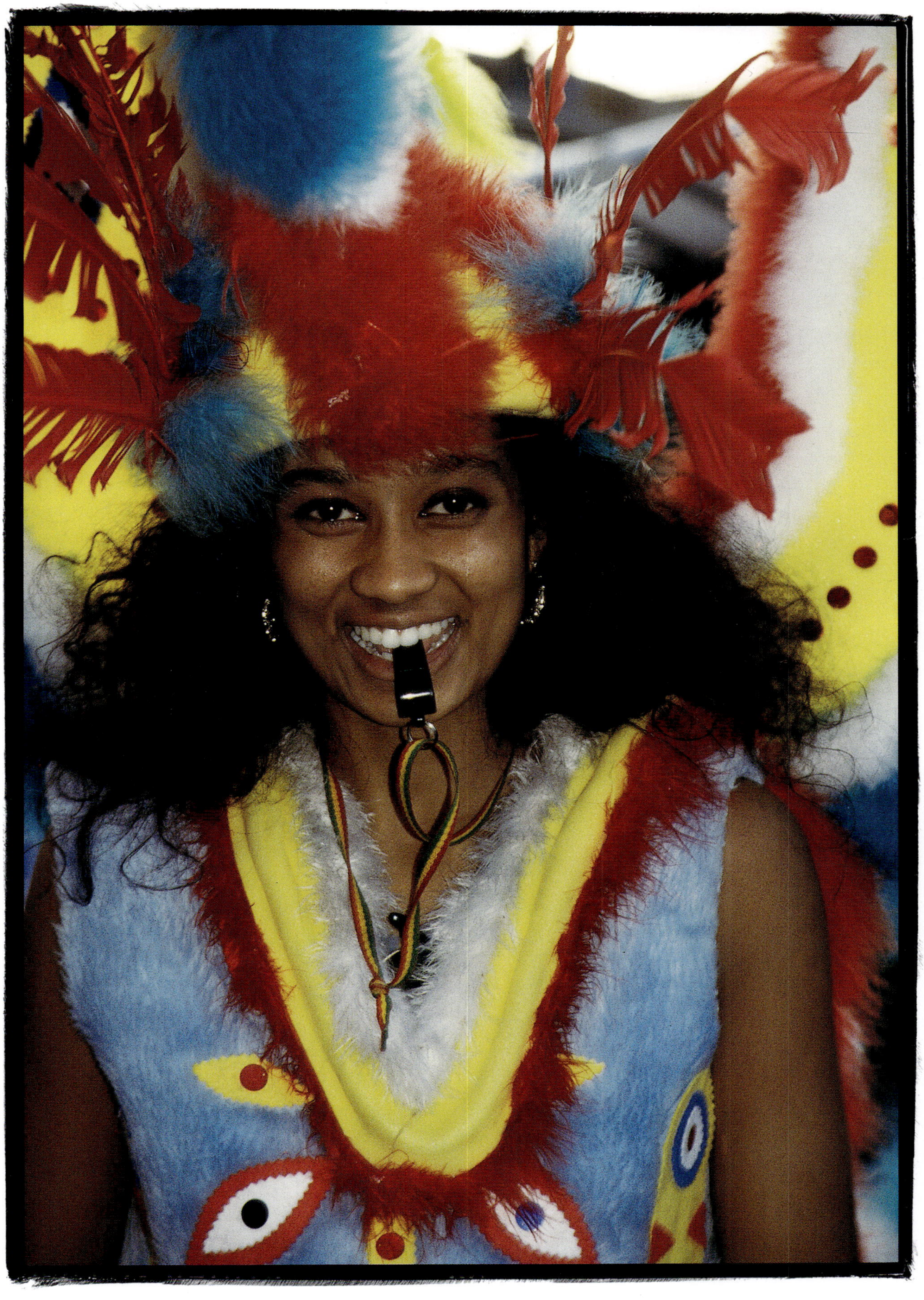

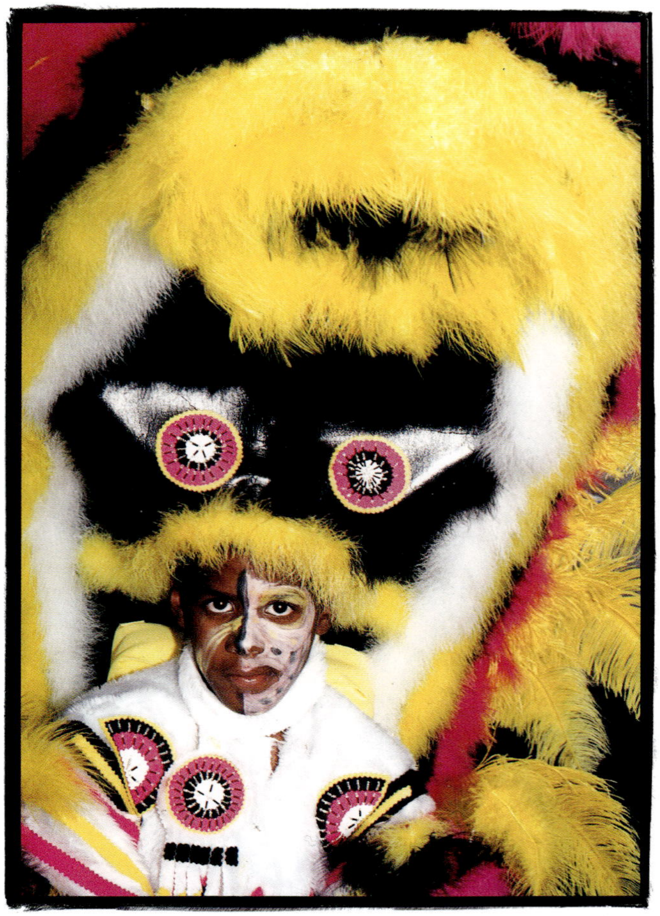

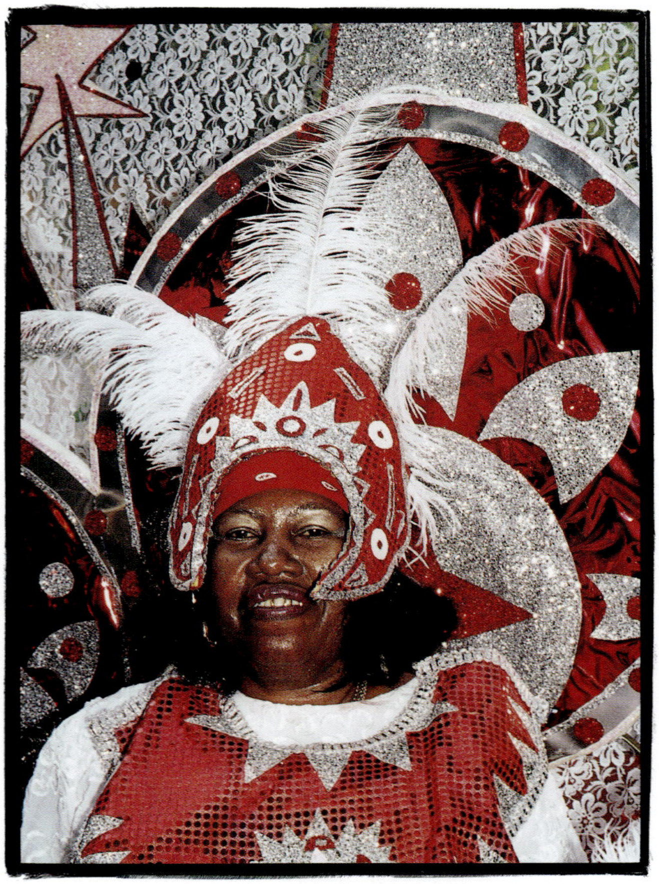

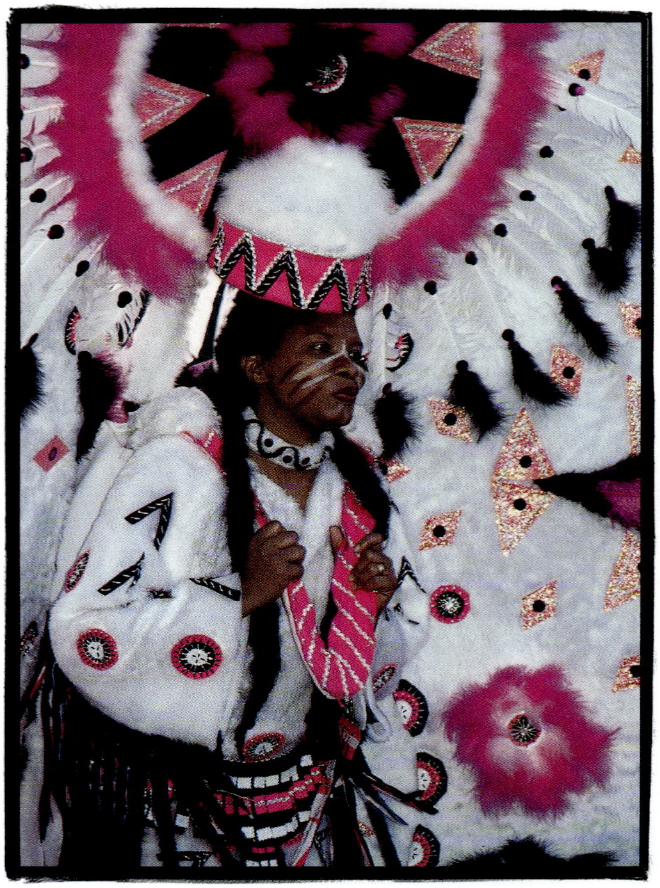

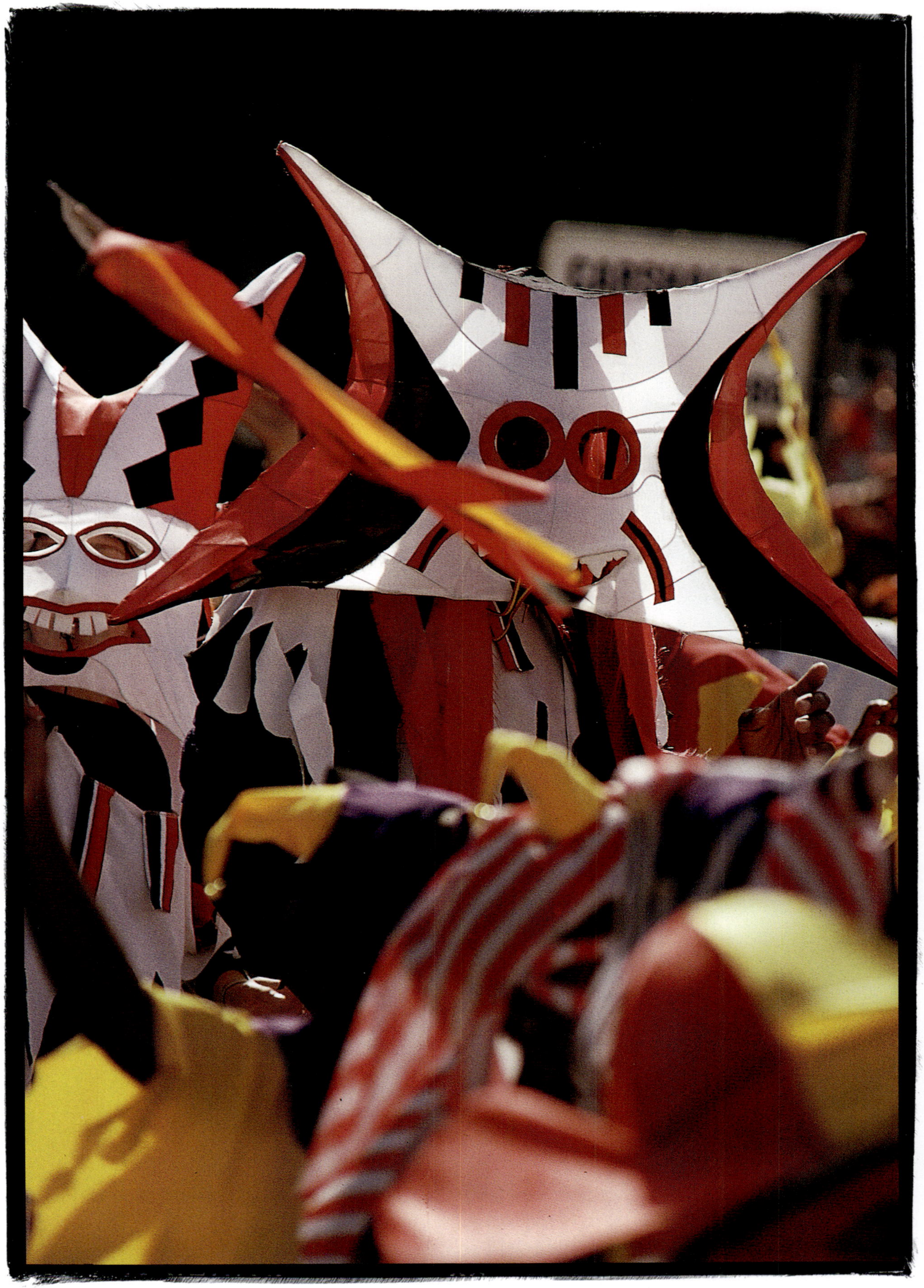

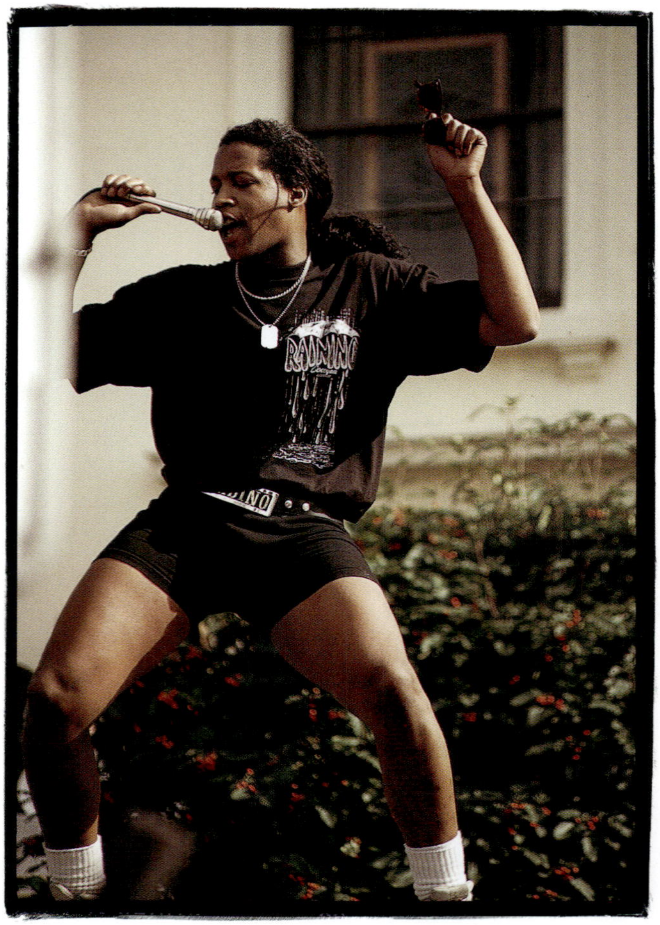

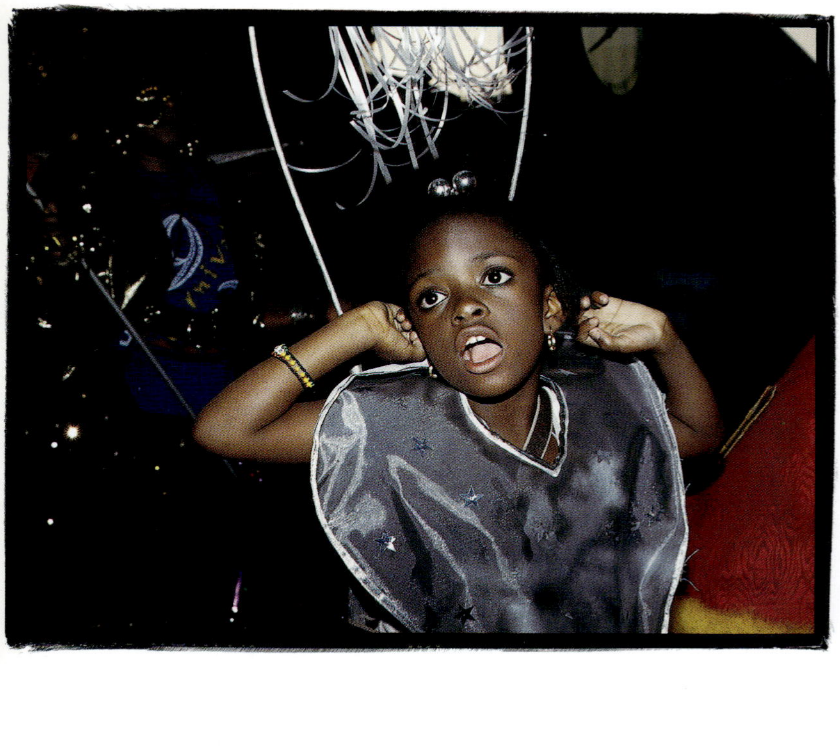

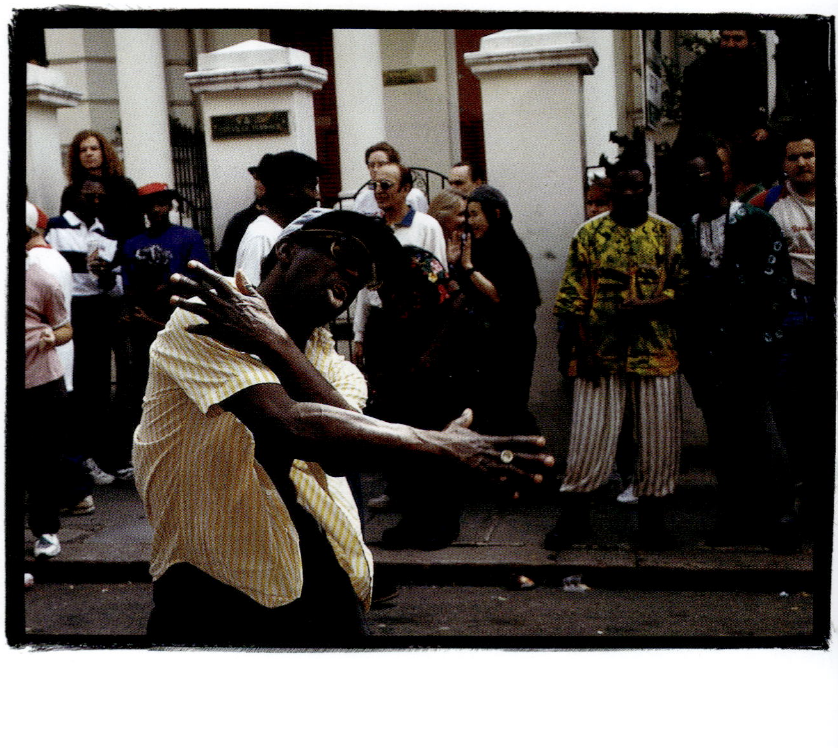

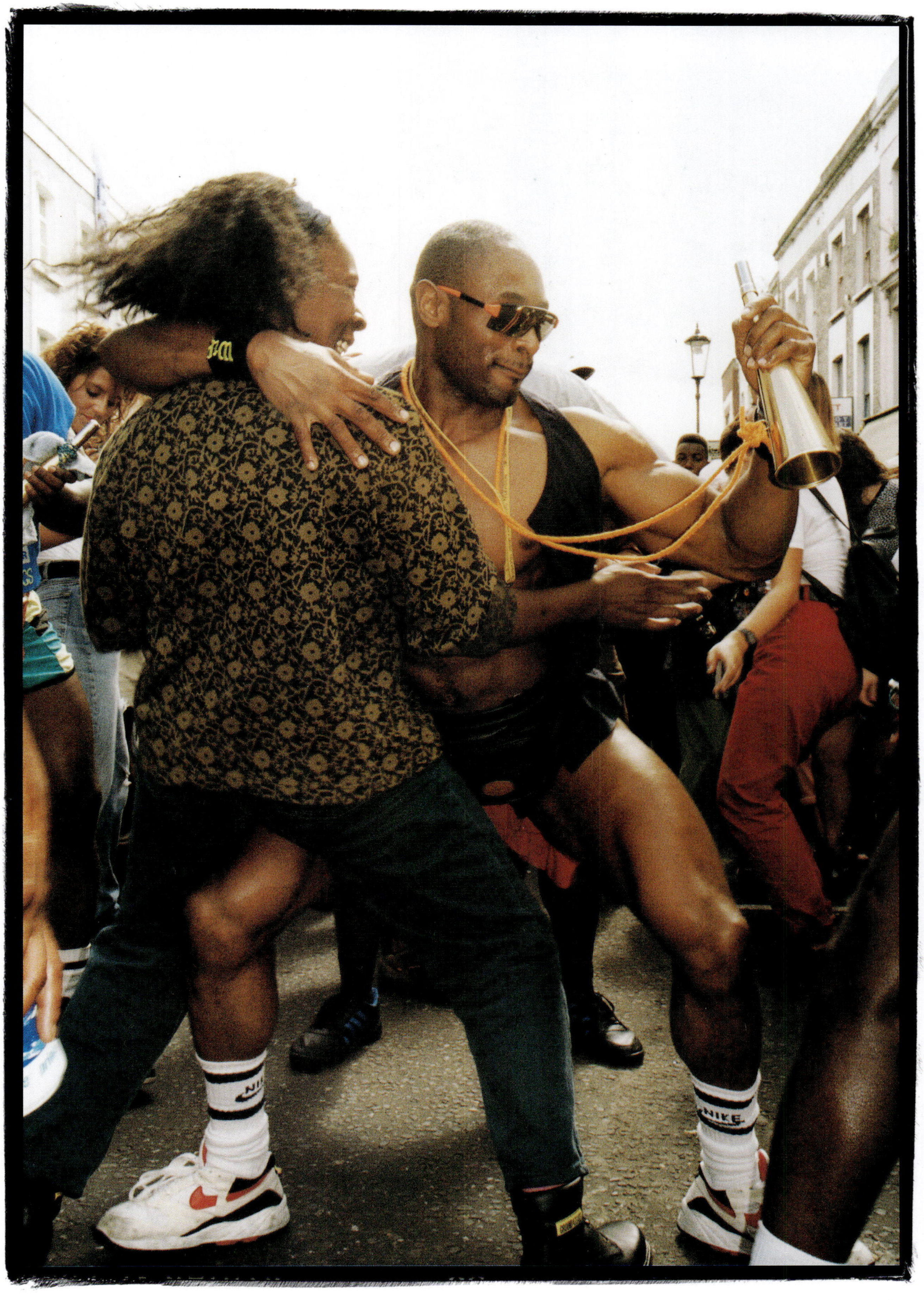
NIKE

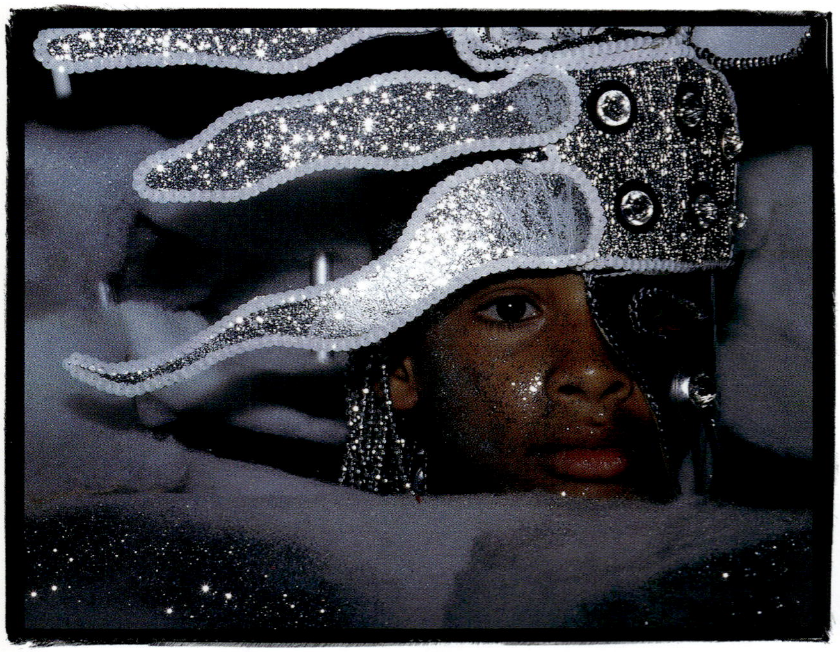

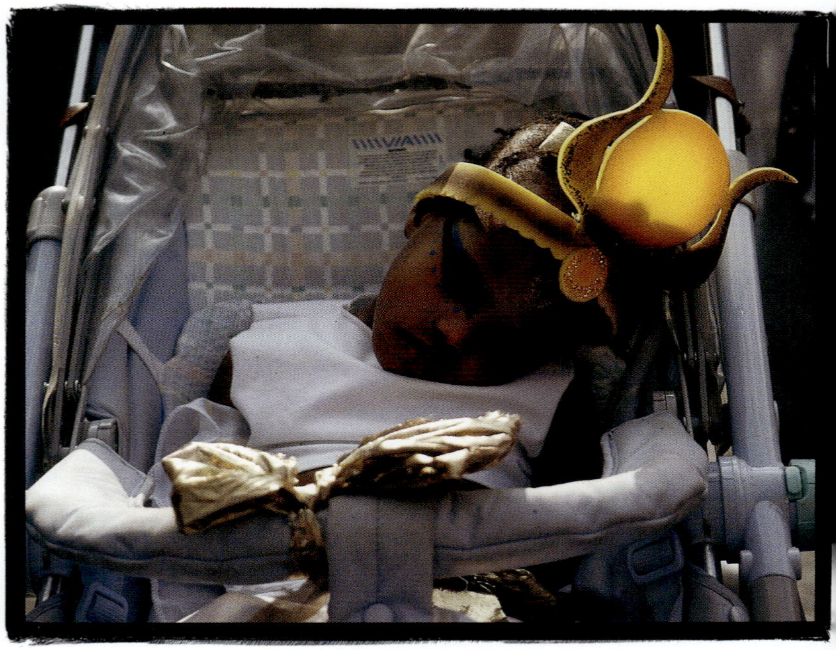

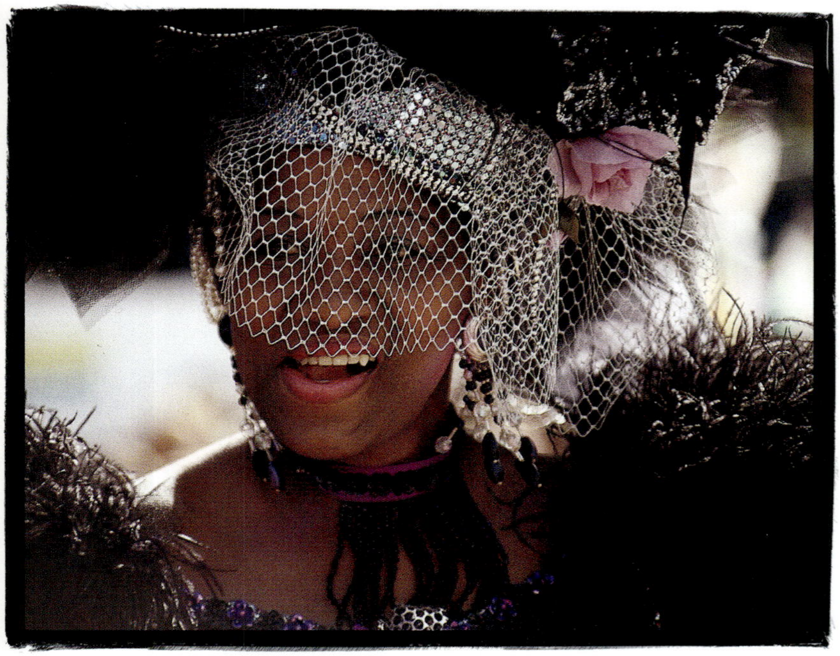

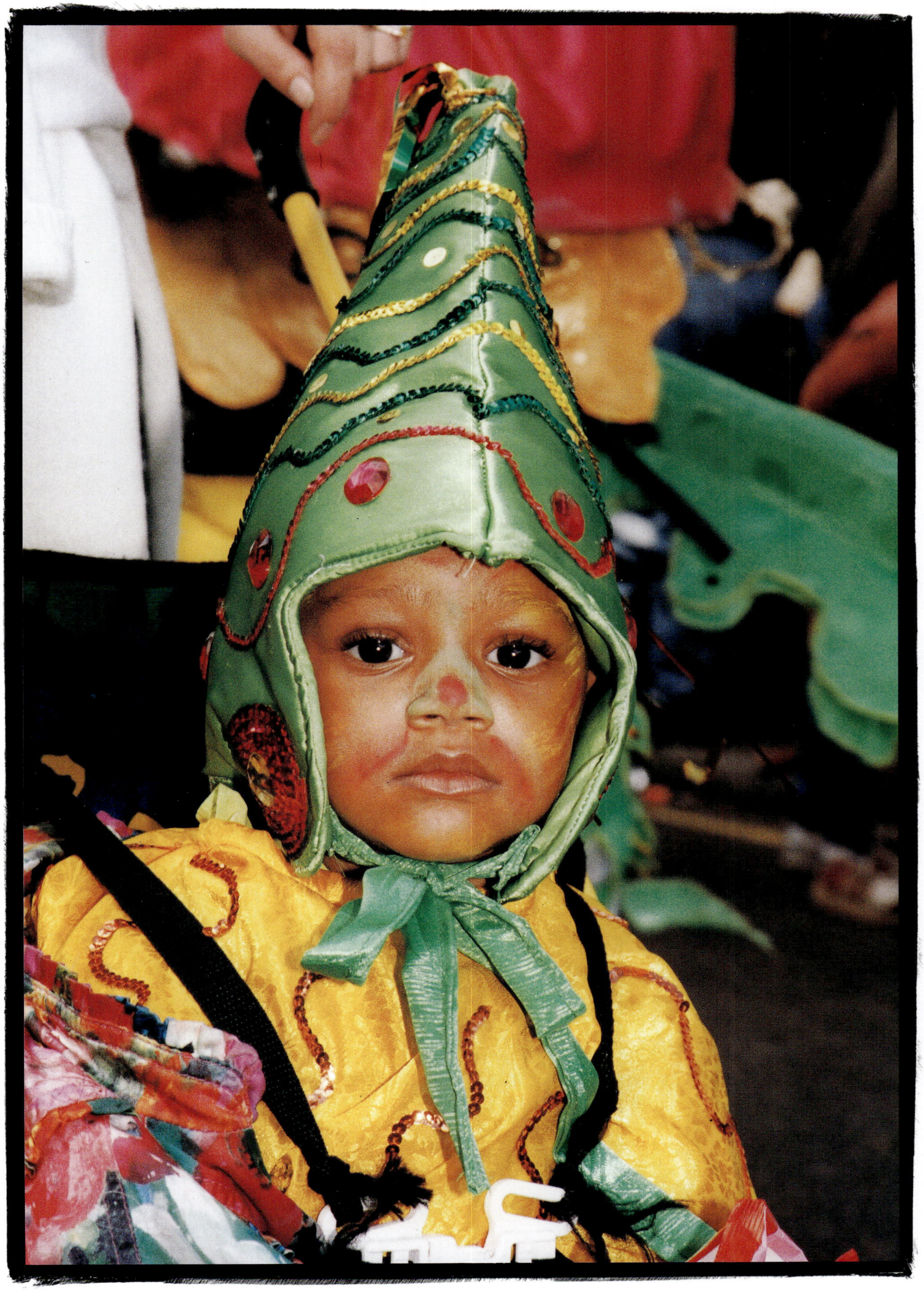

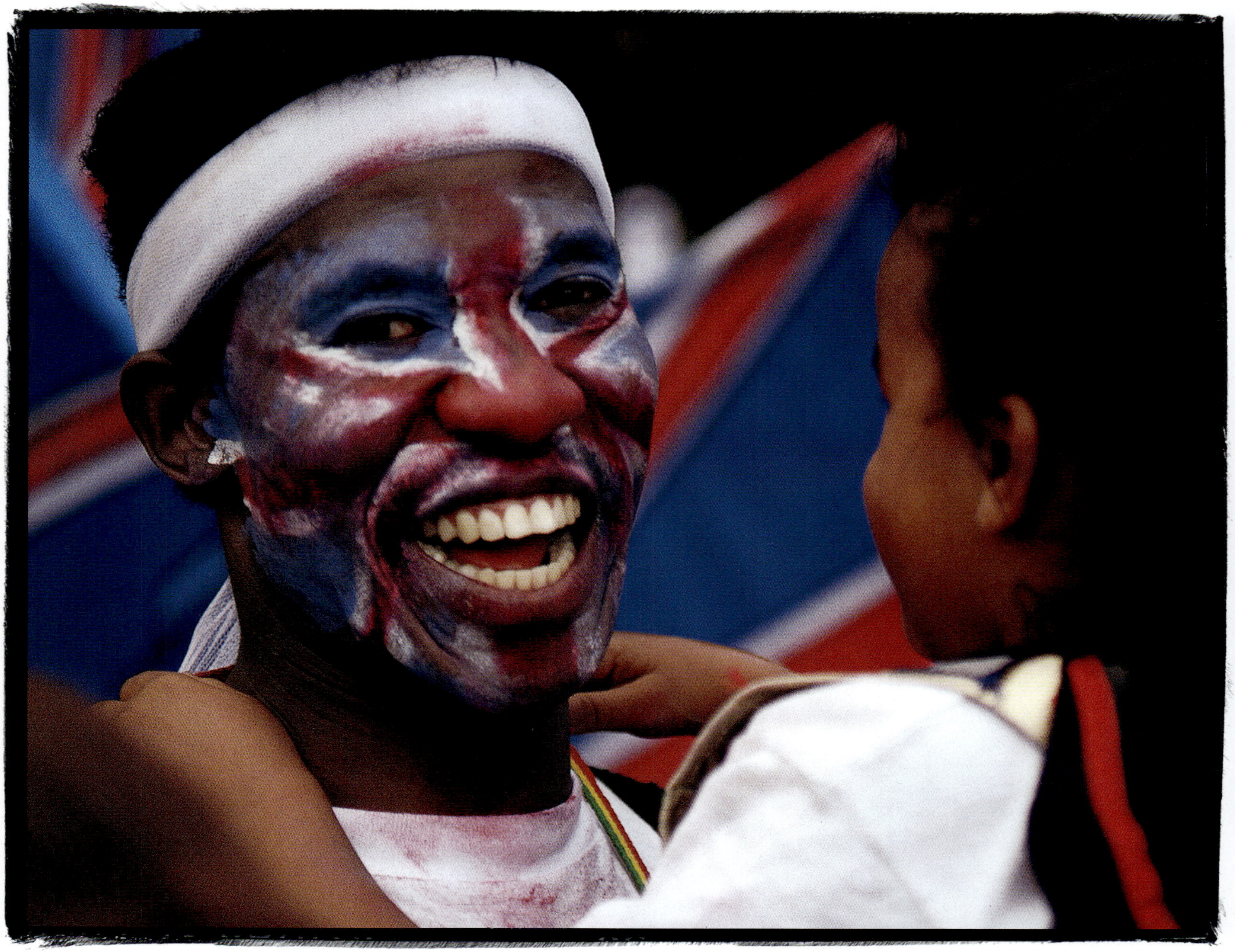

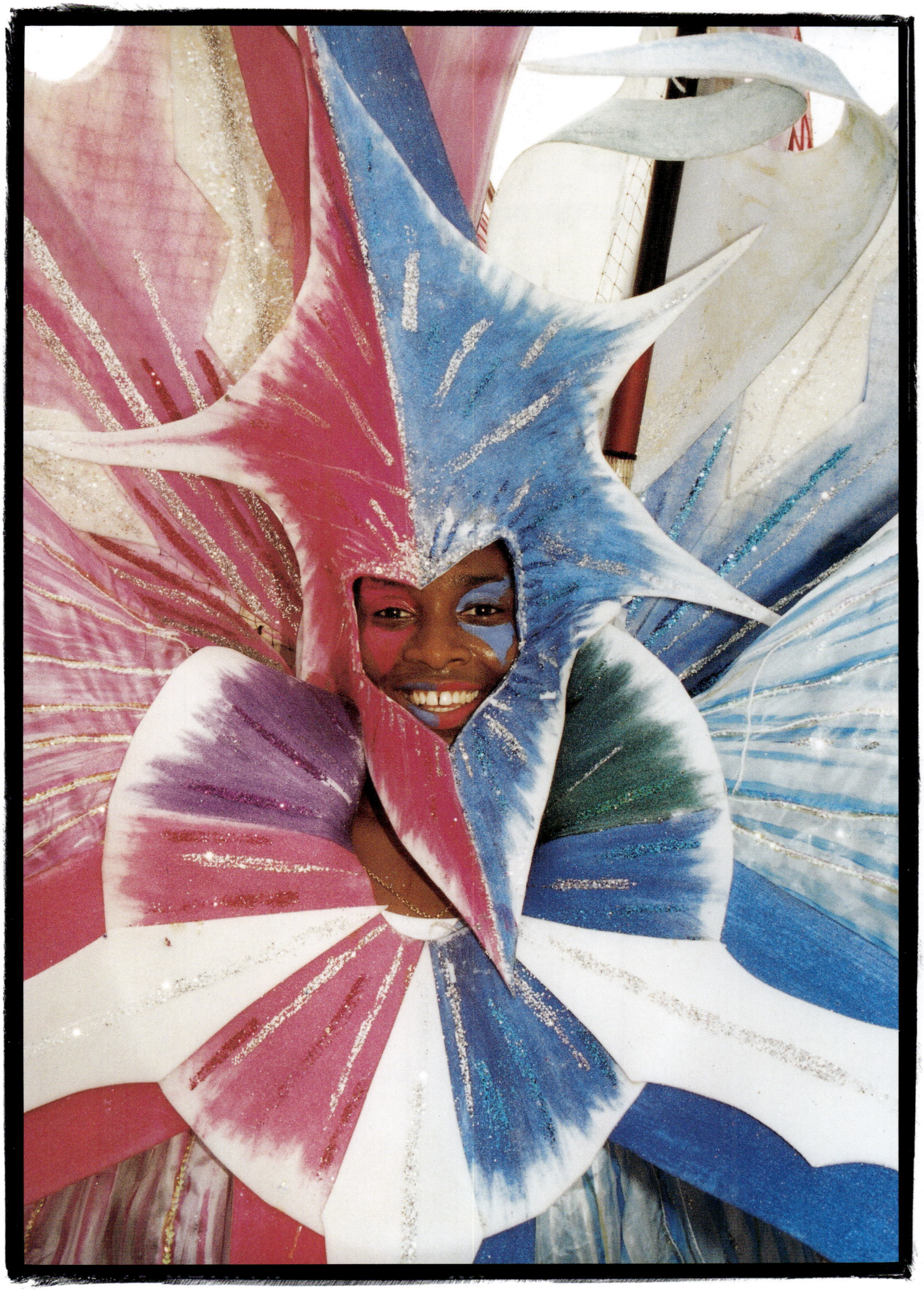

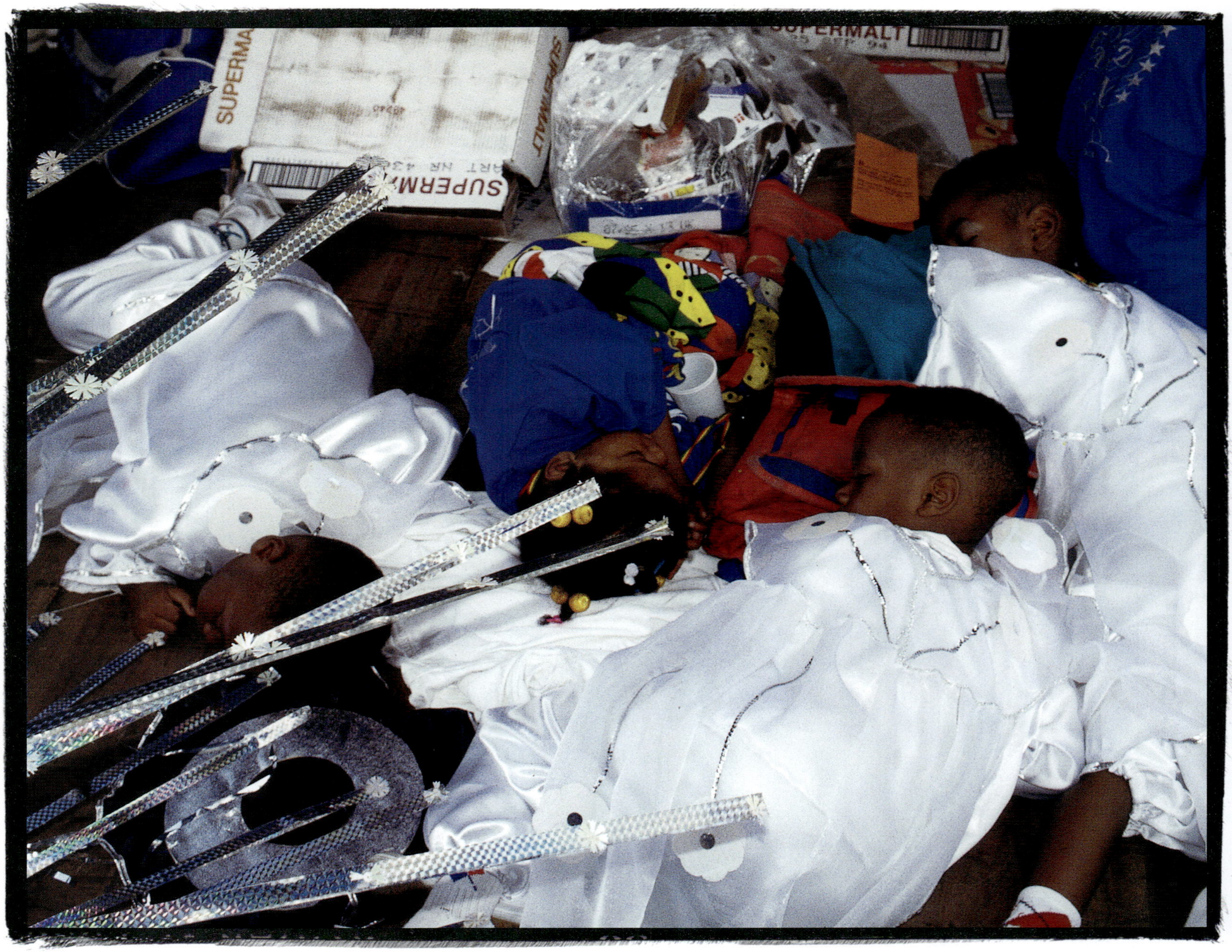
SUPERMALT

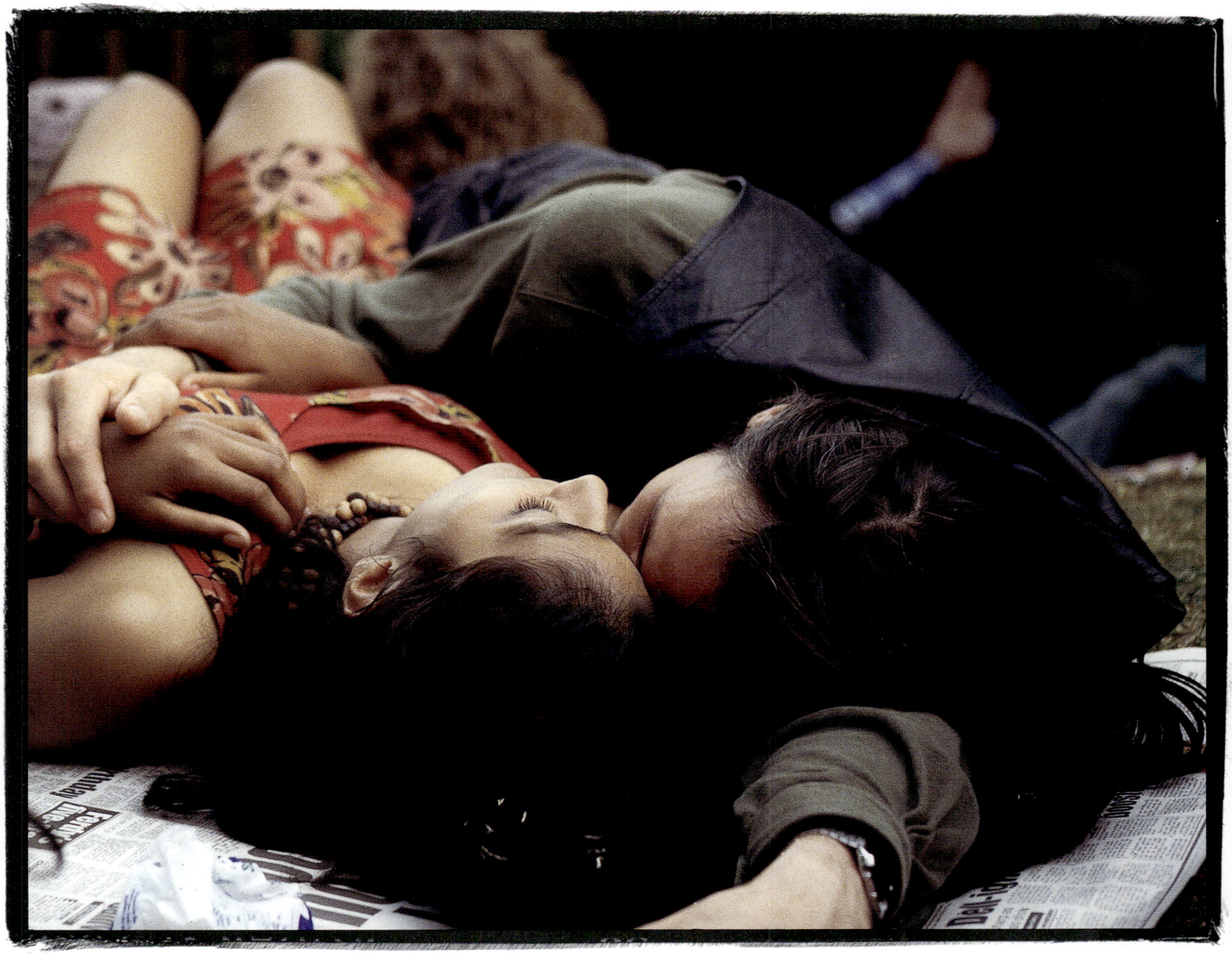

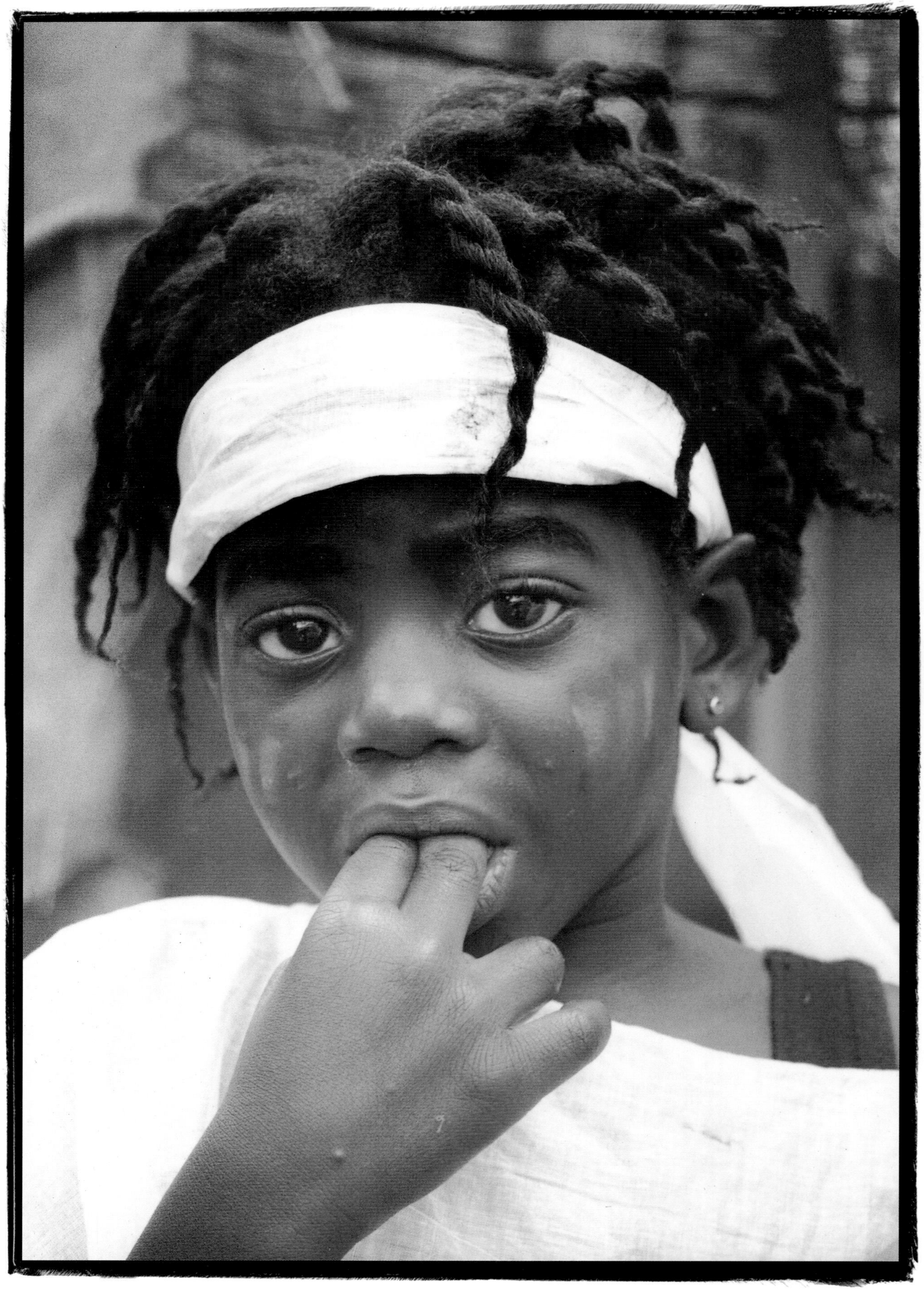

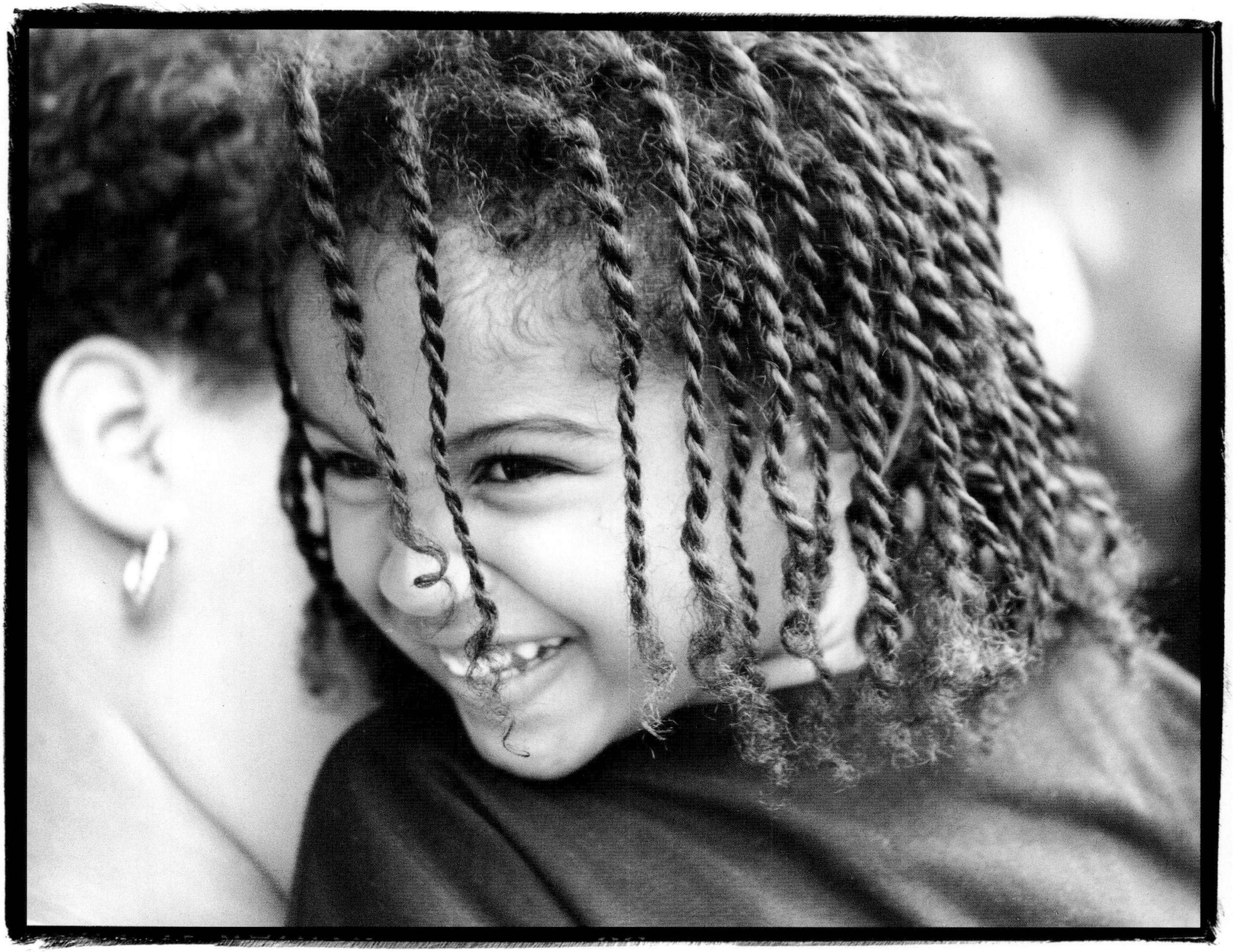

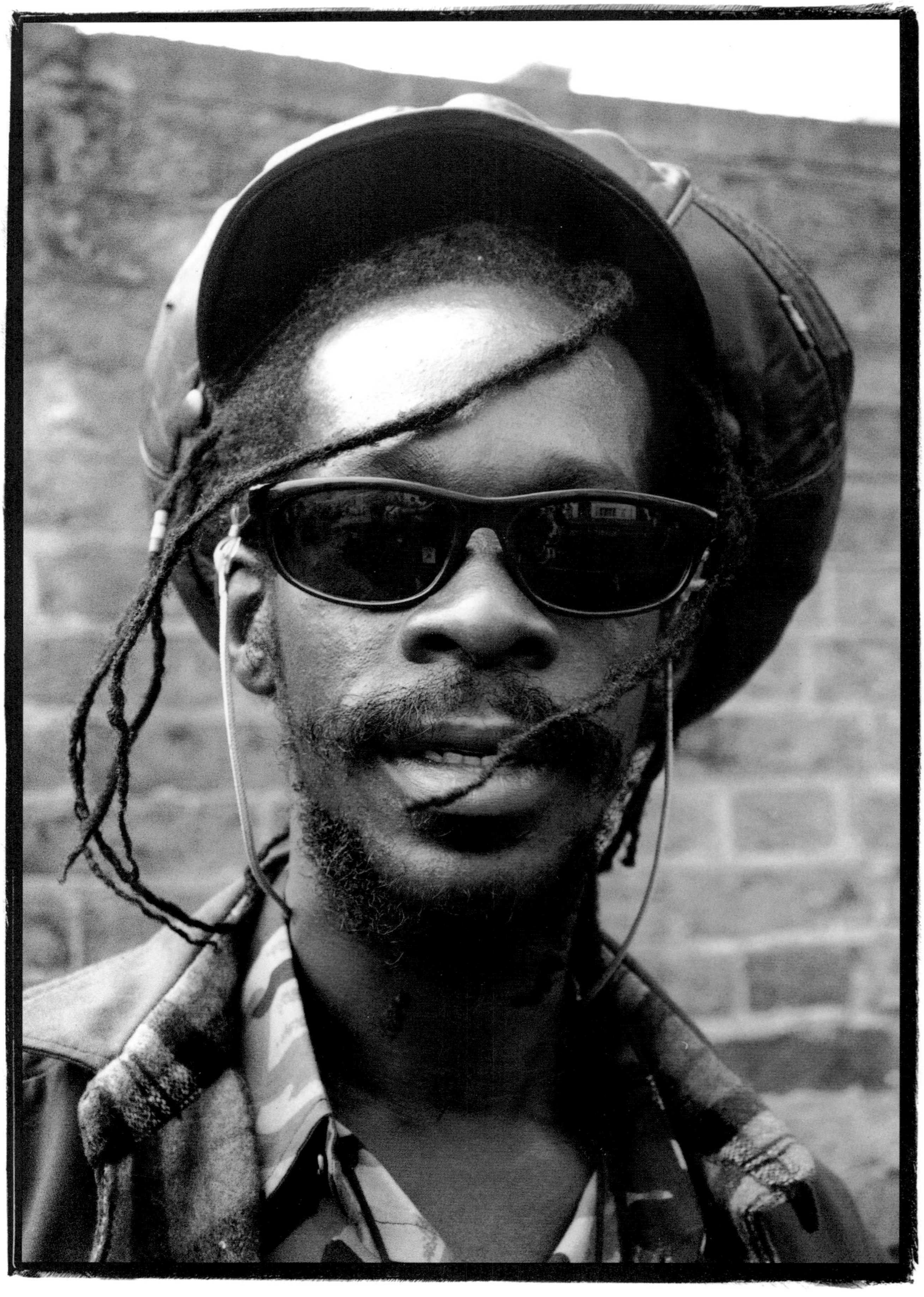

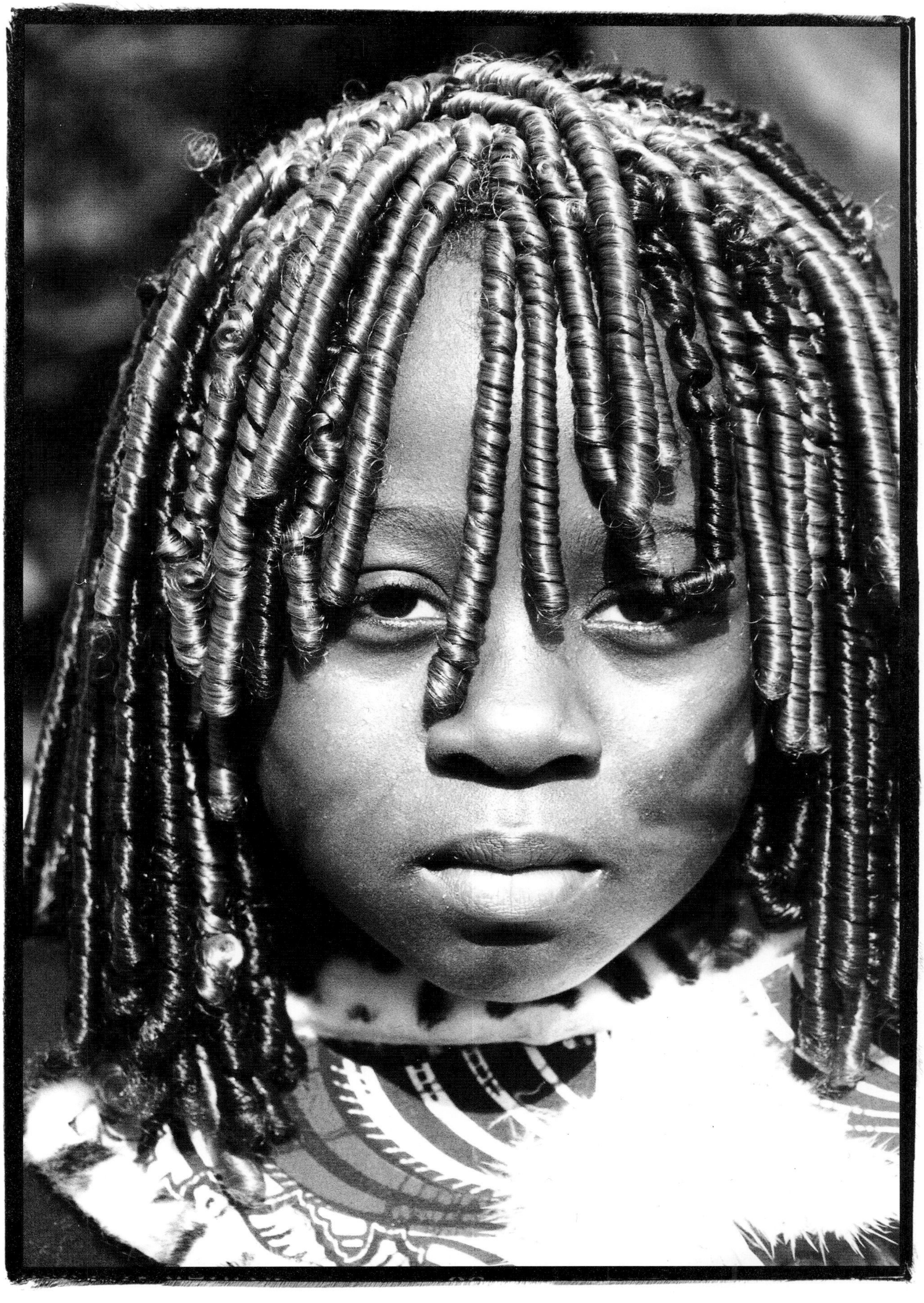

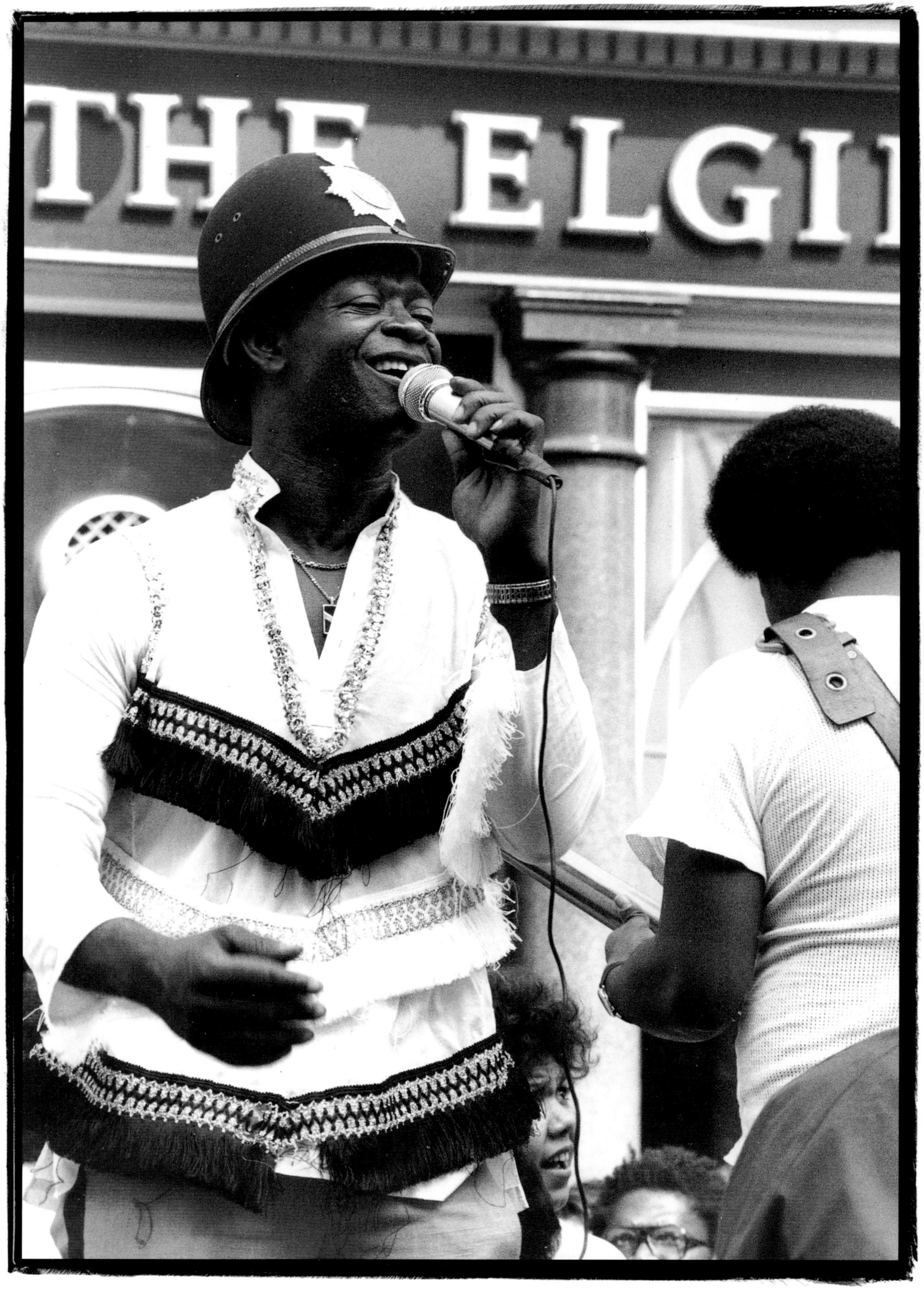
THE ELGI

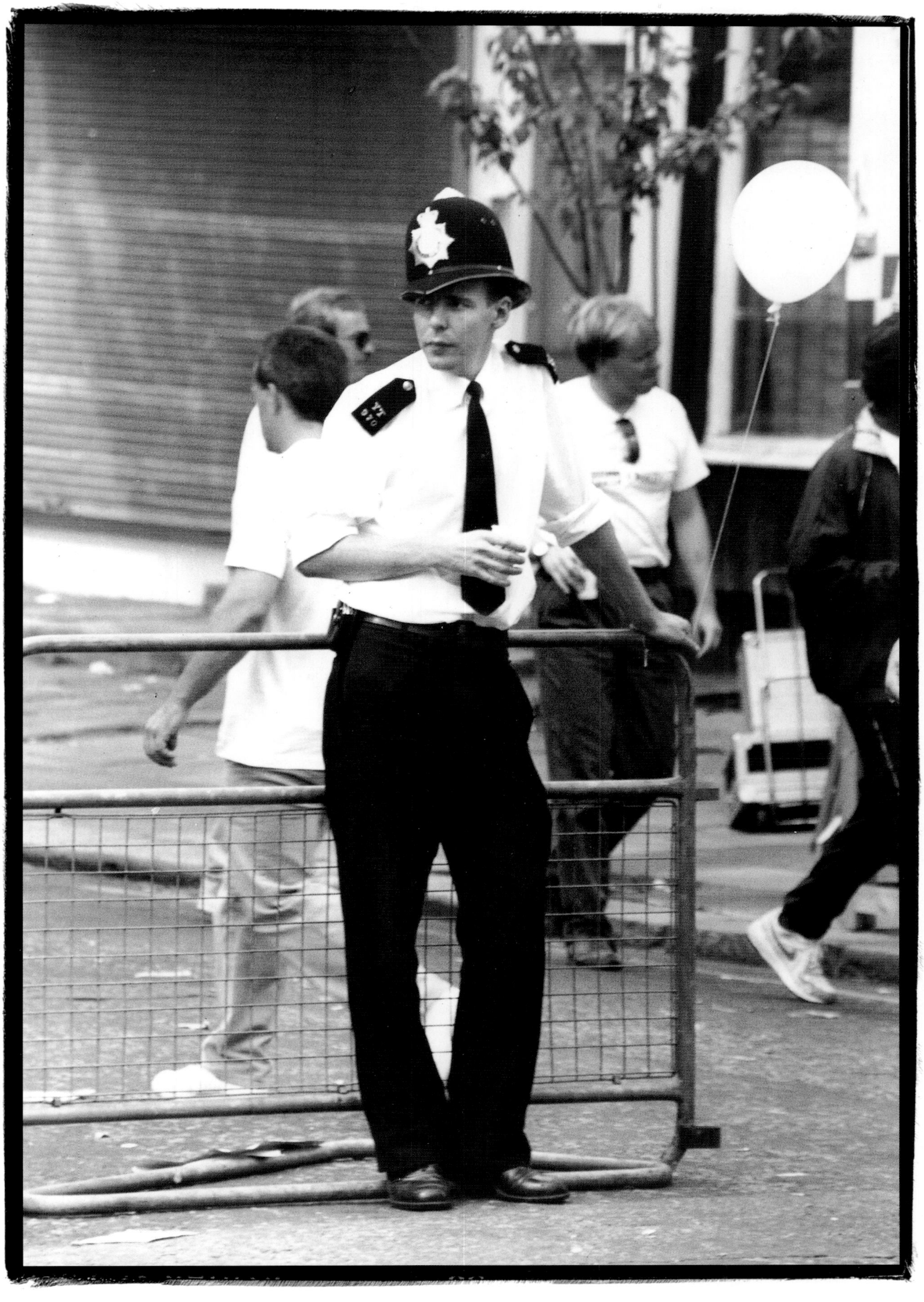

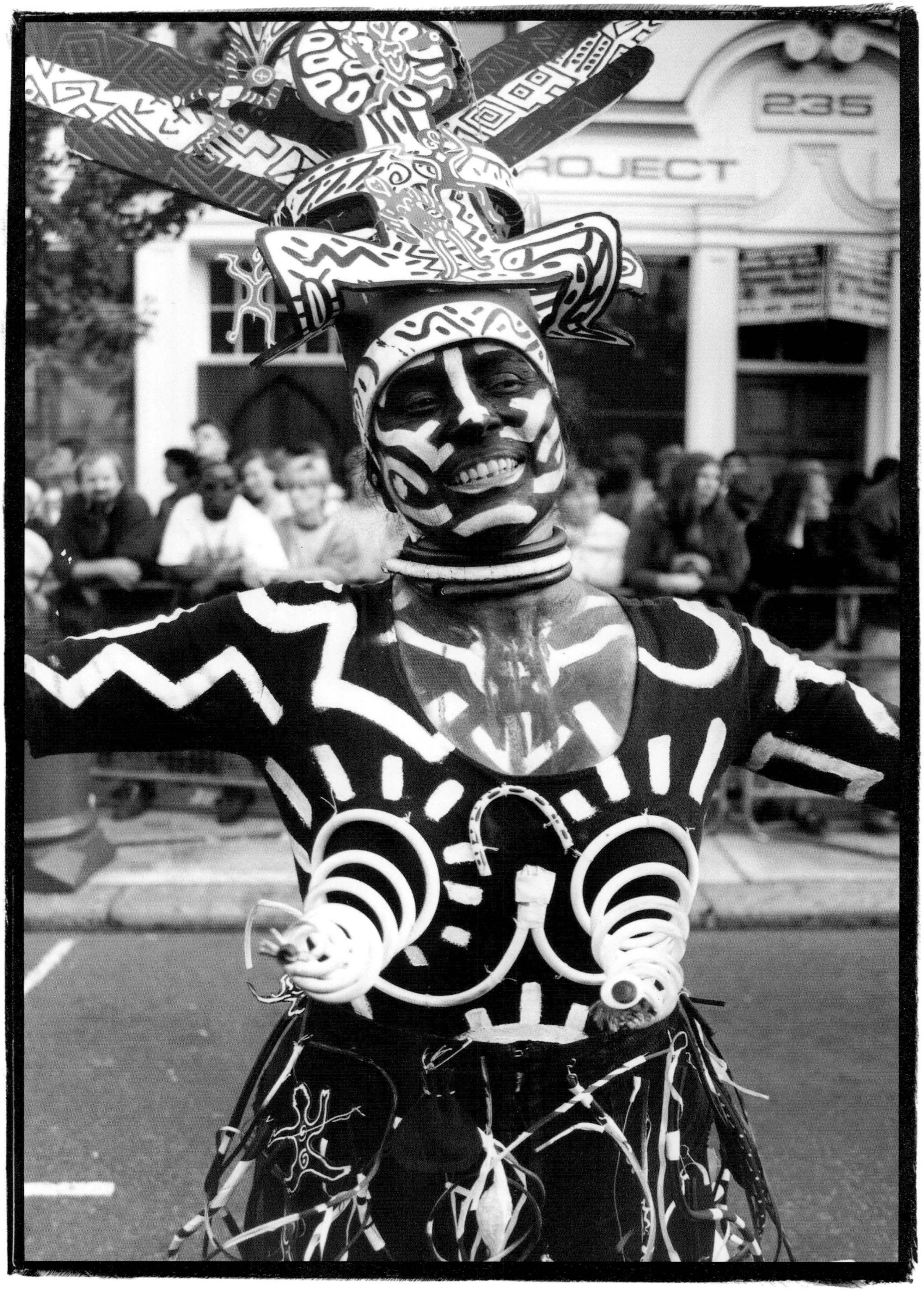
235
ROJECT

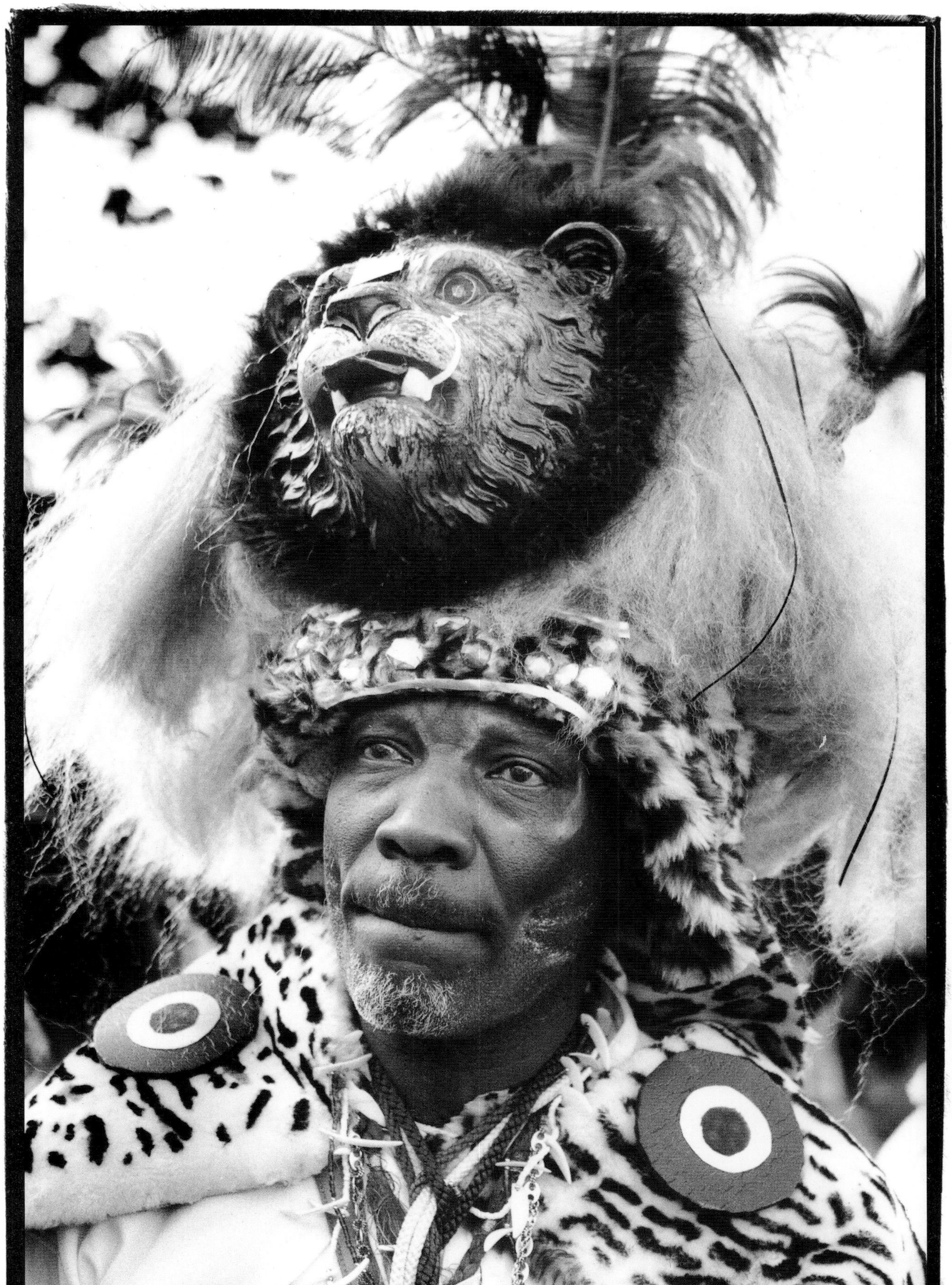

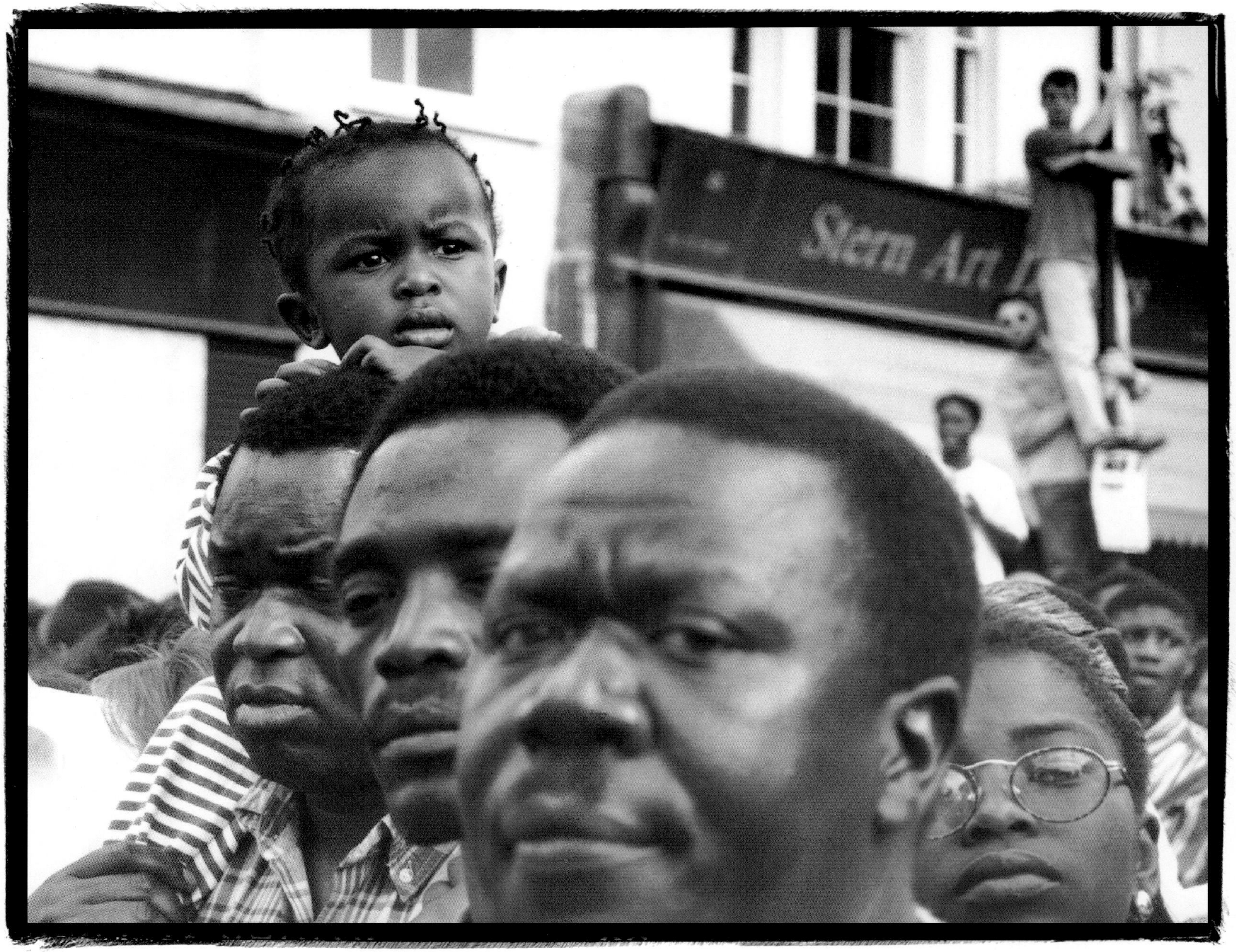
Stern Art

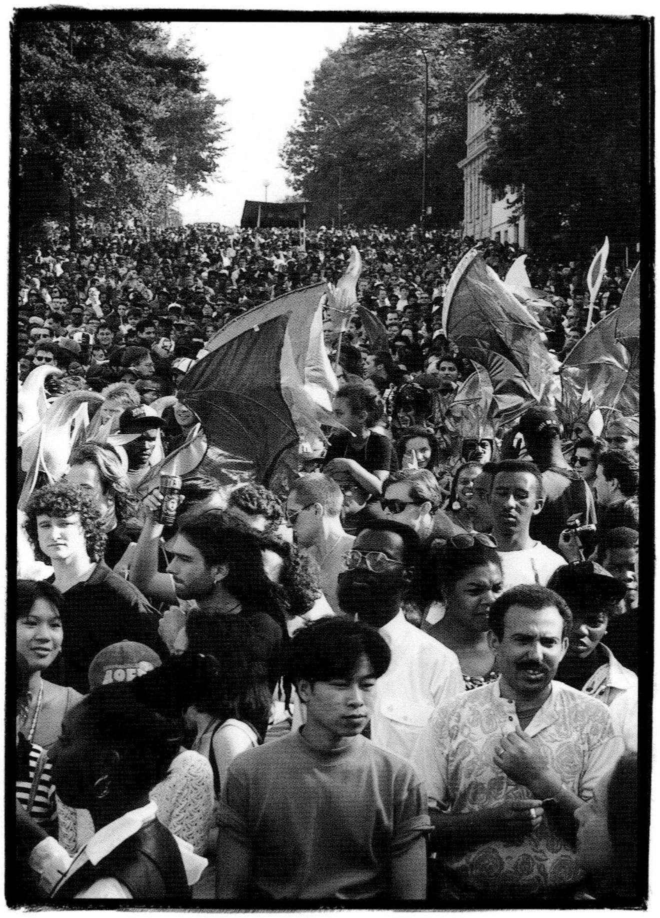

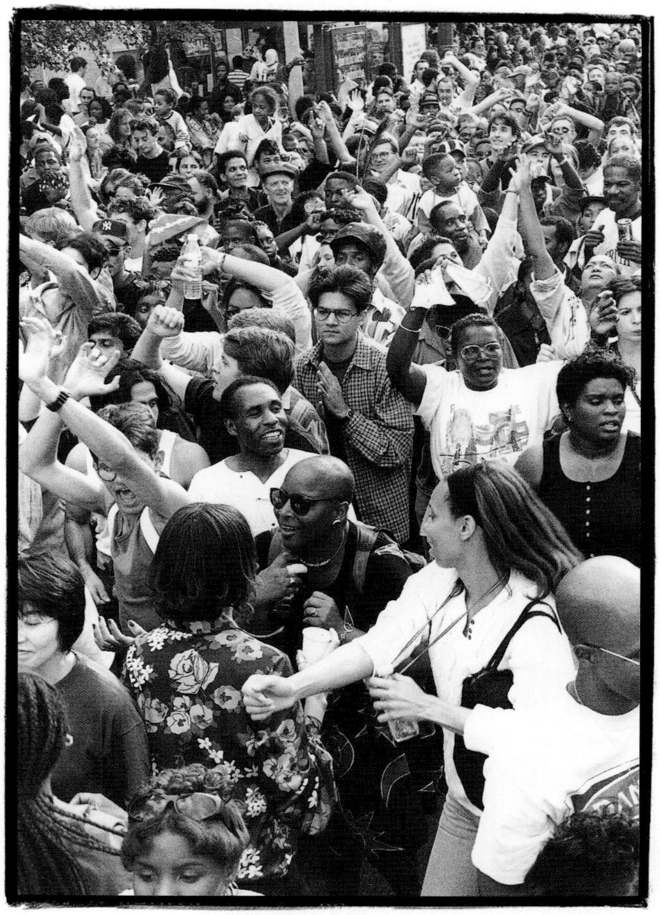

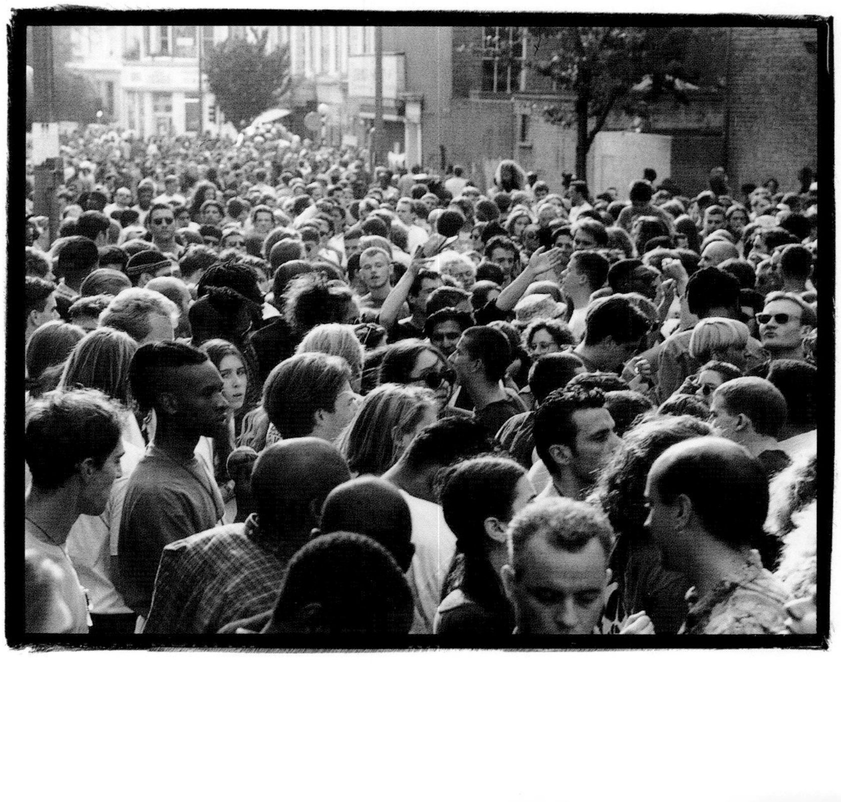

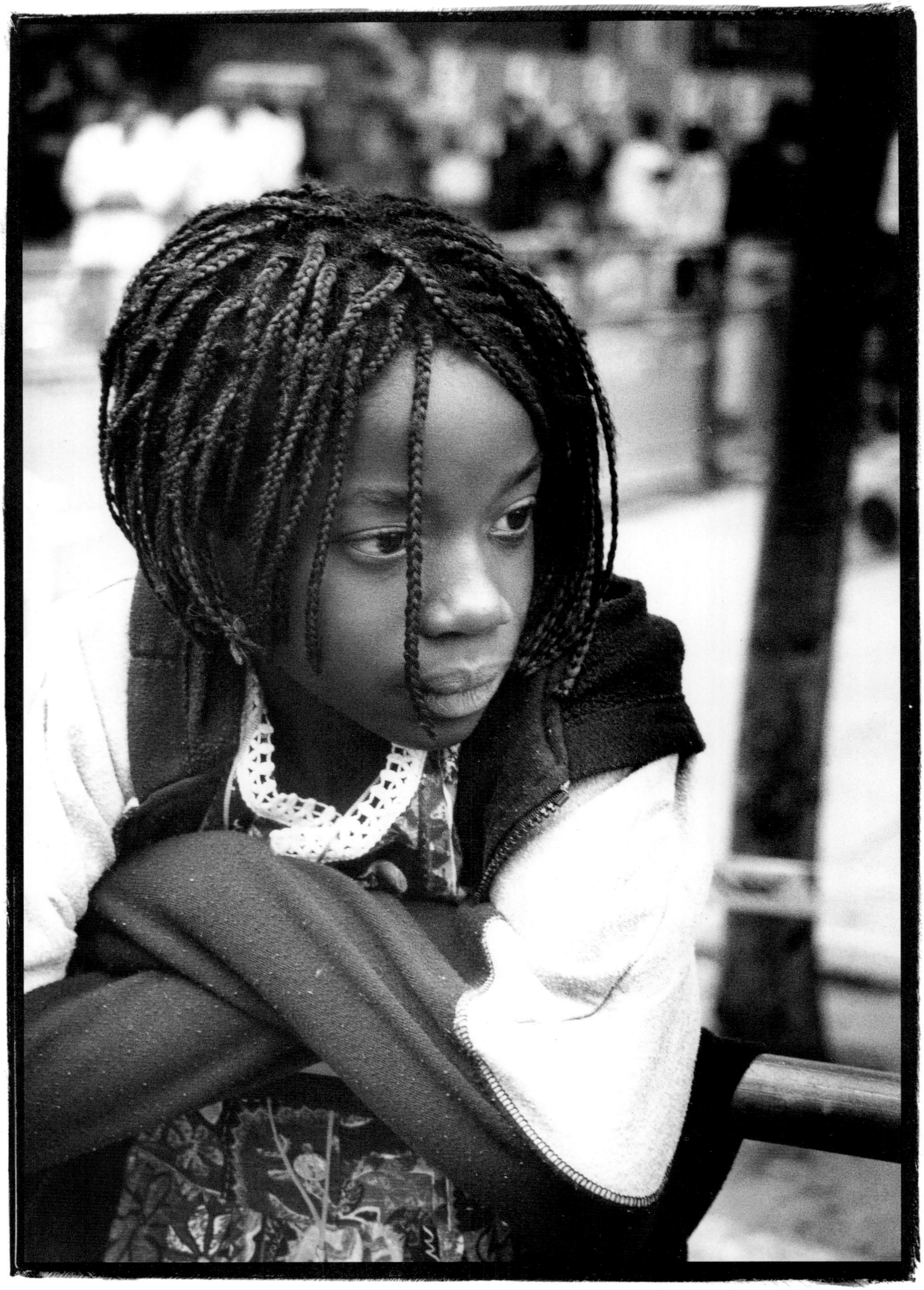

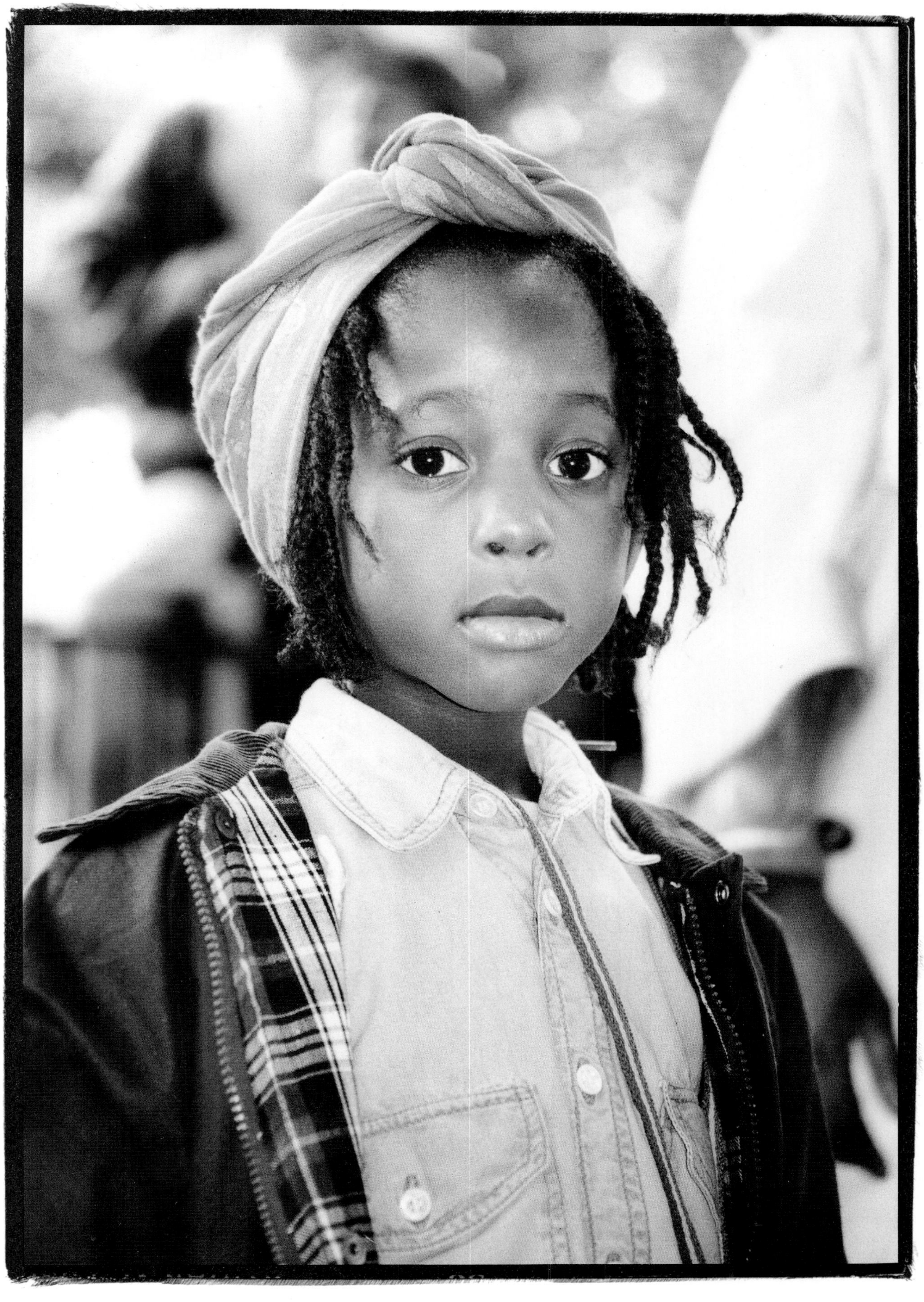

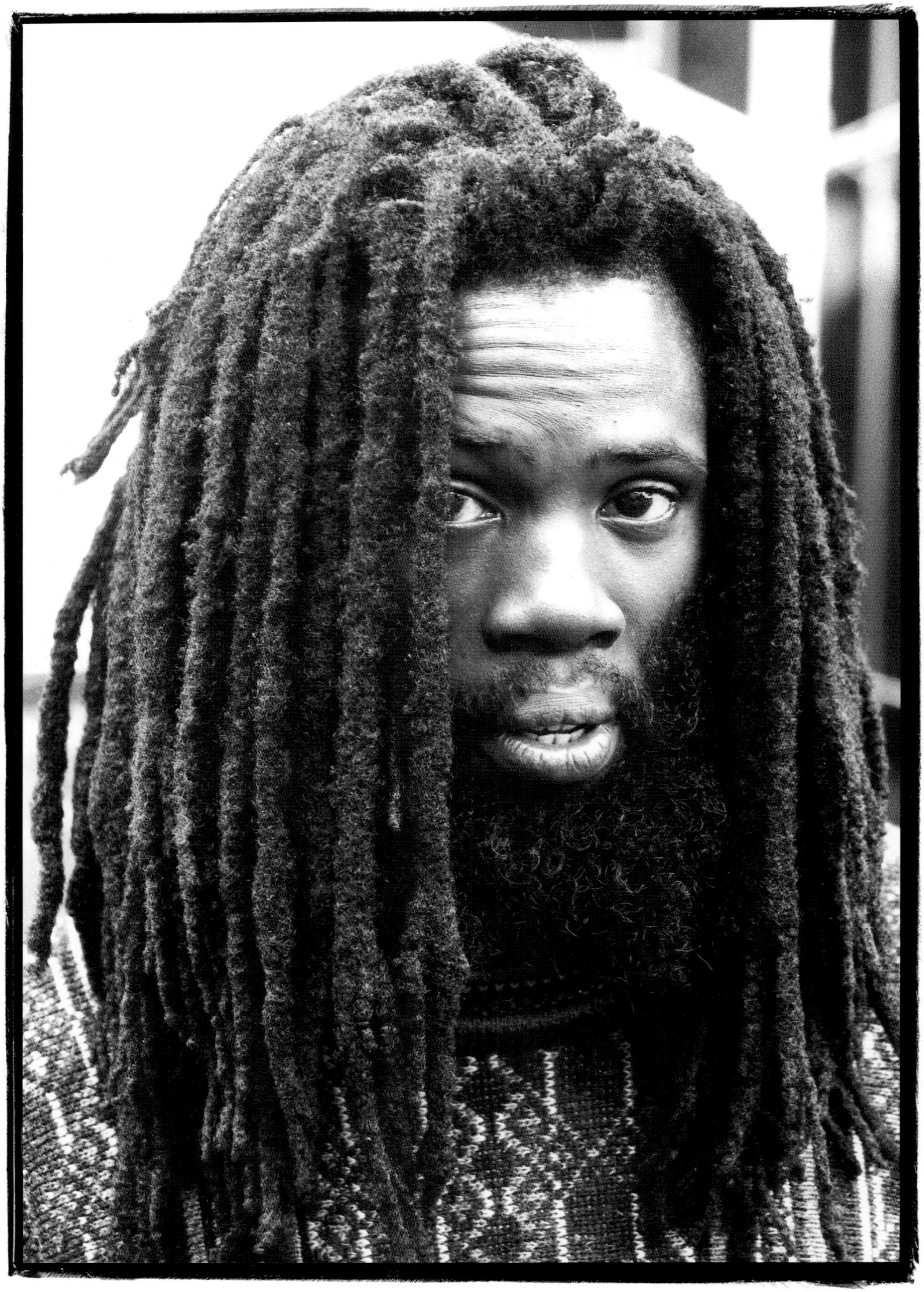

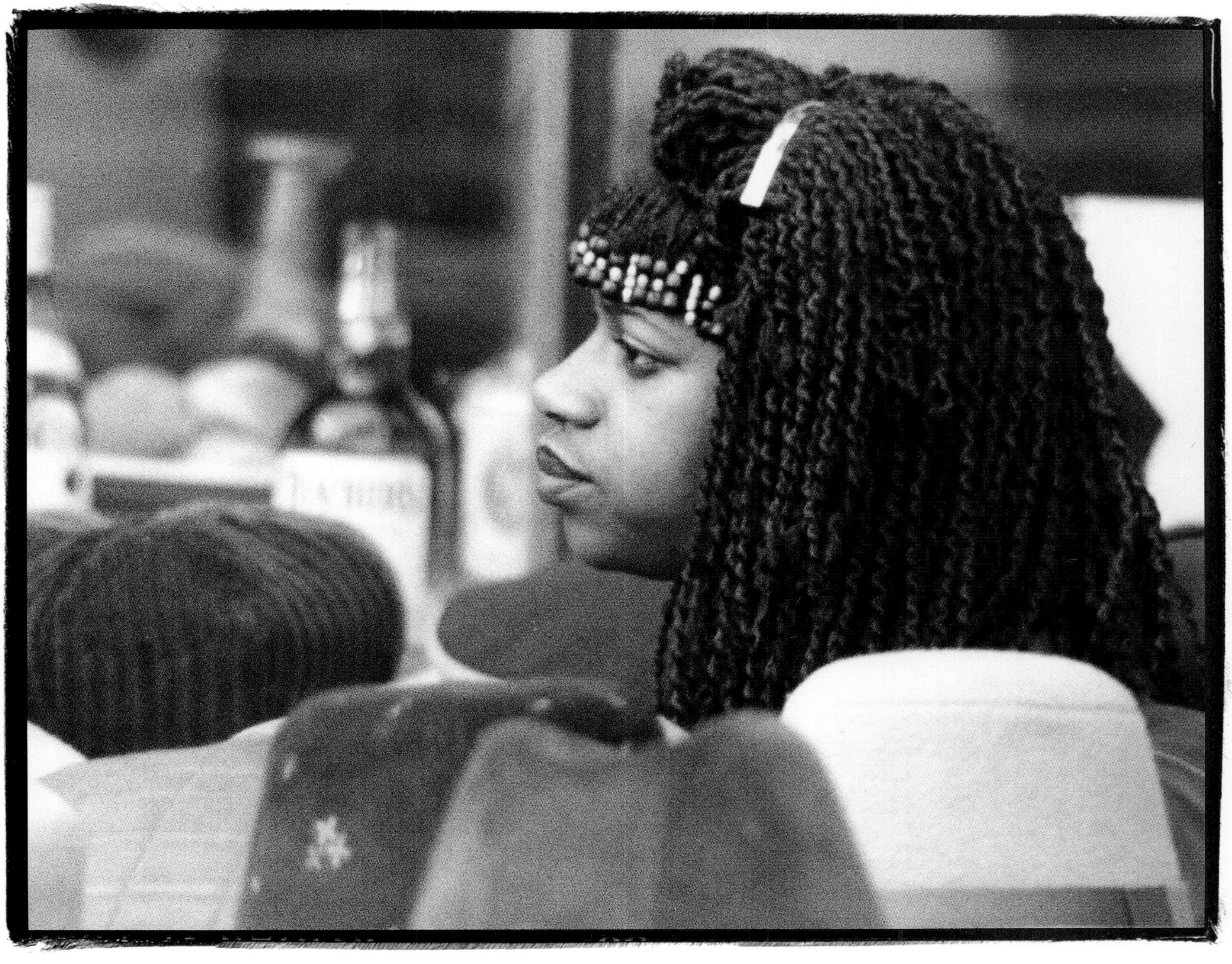

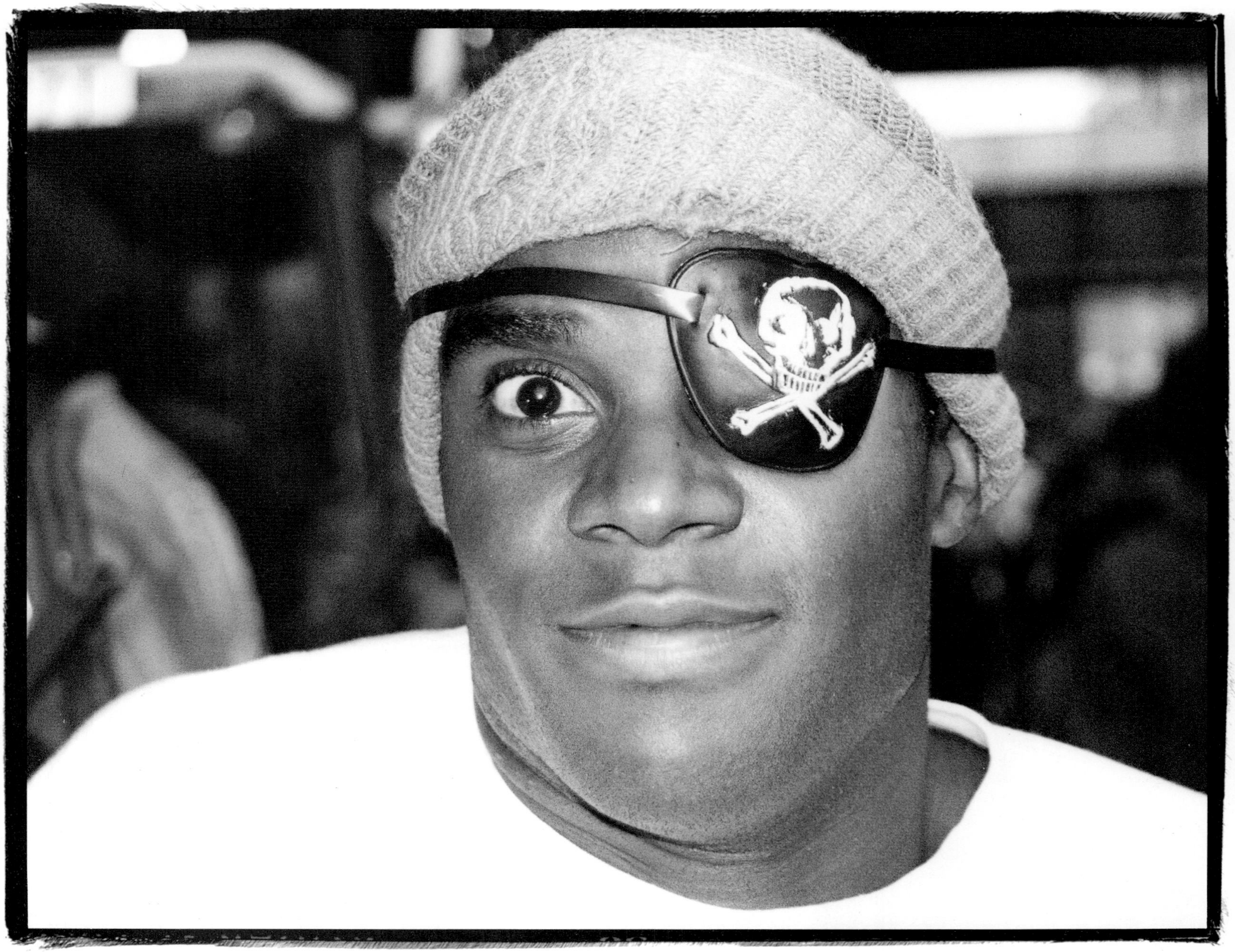

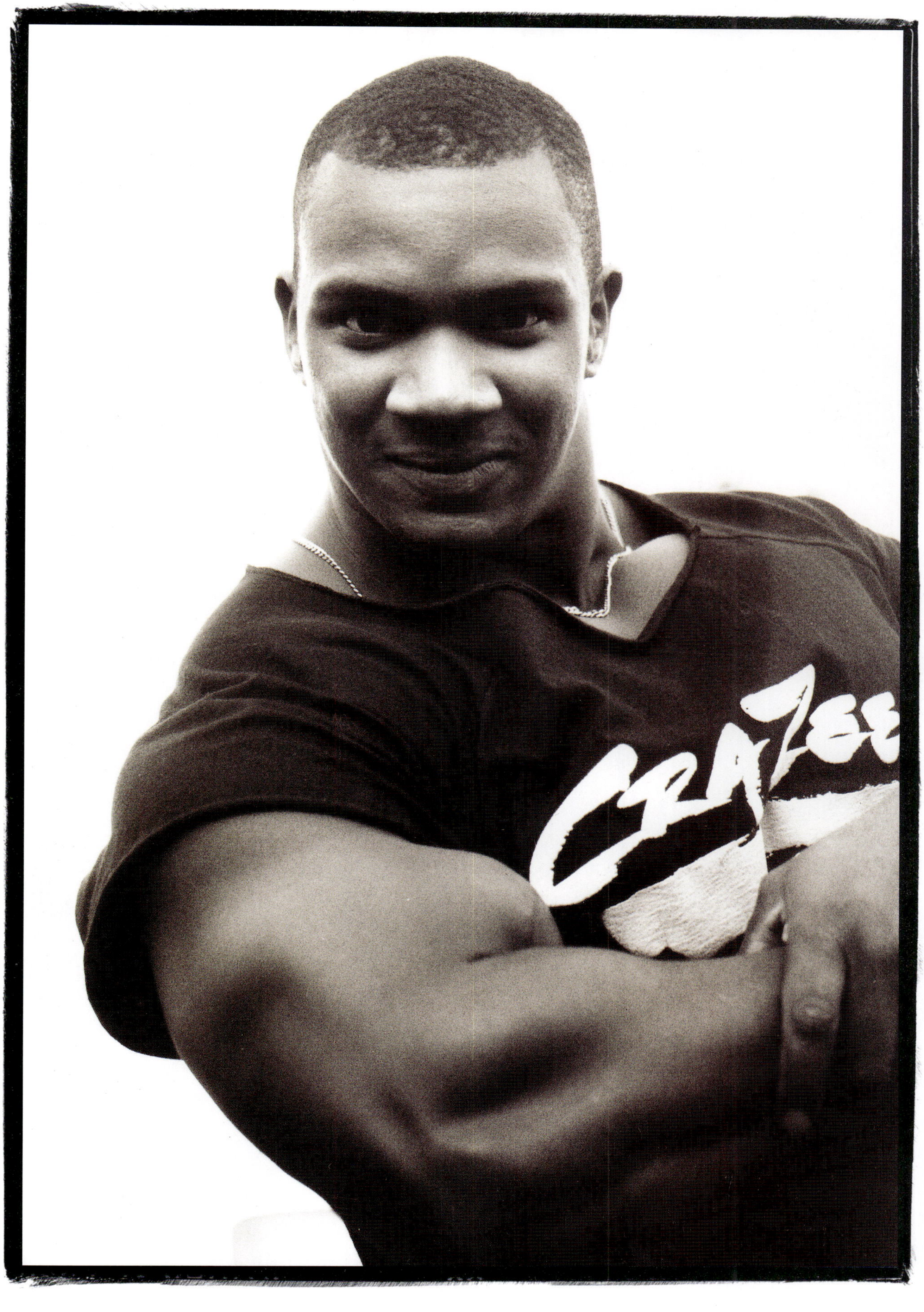

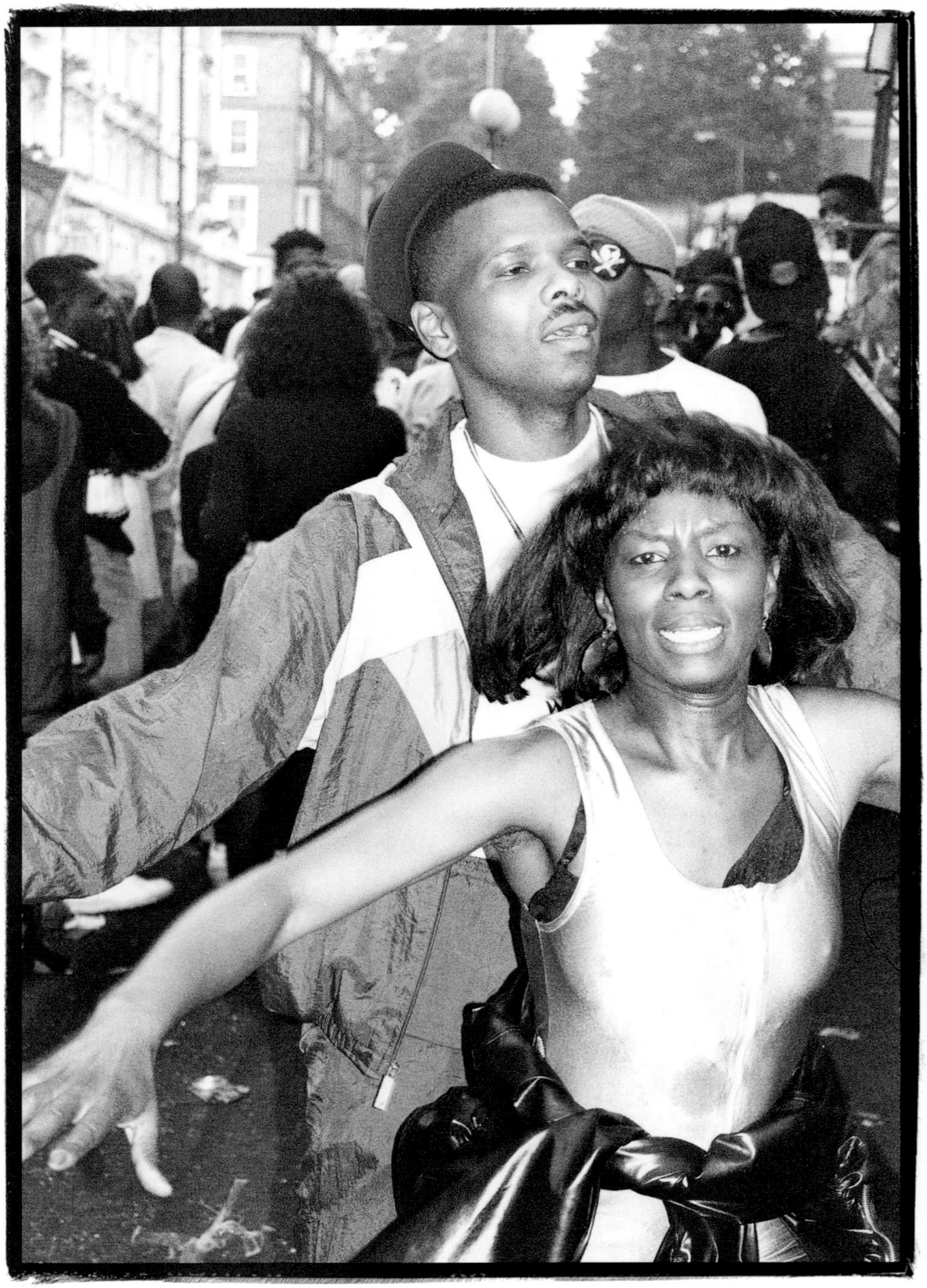

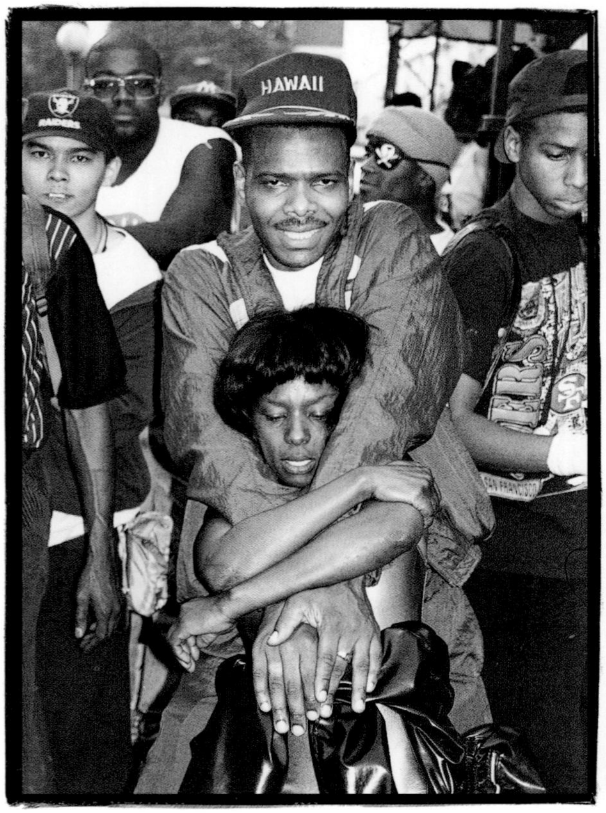
RAIDERS
HAWAII

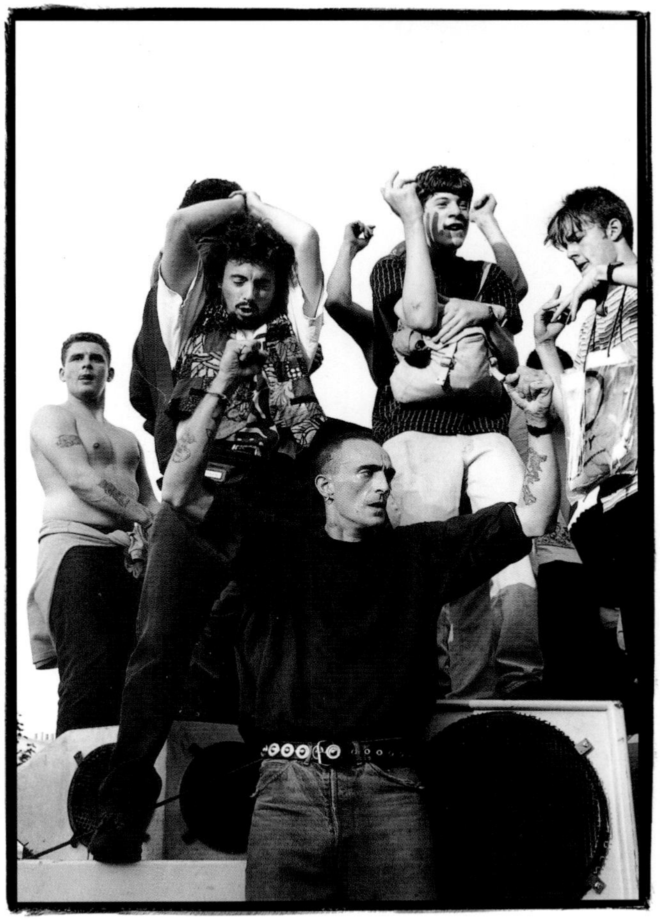

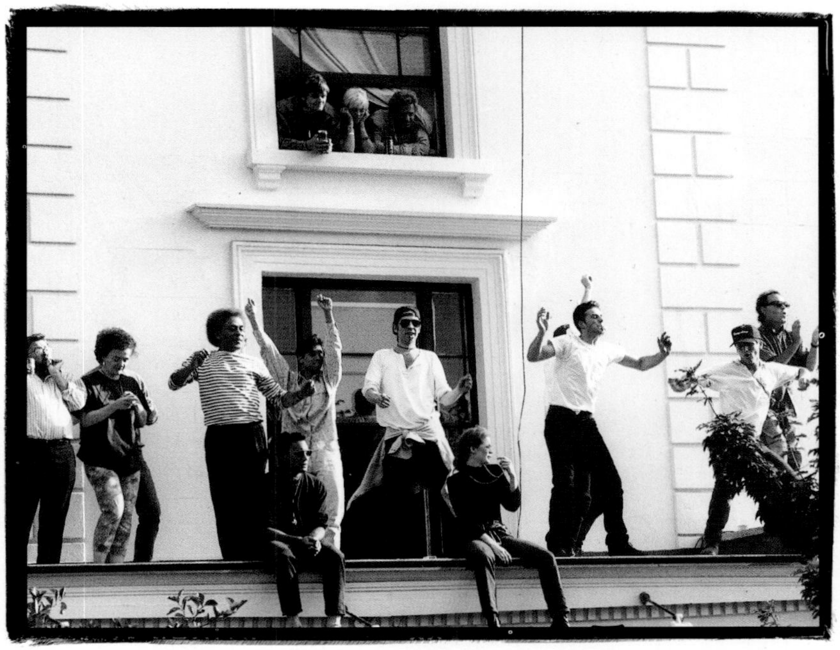

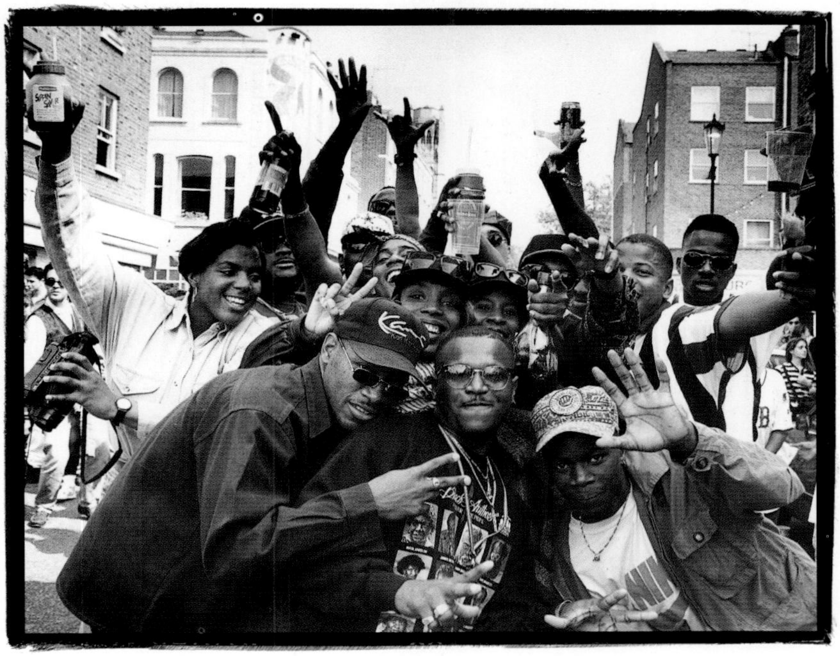

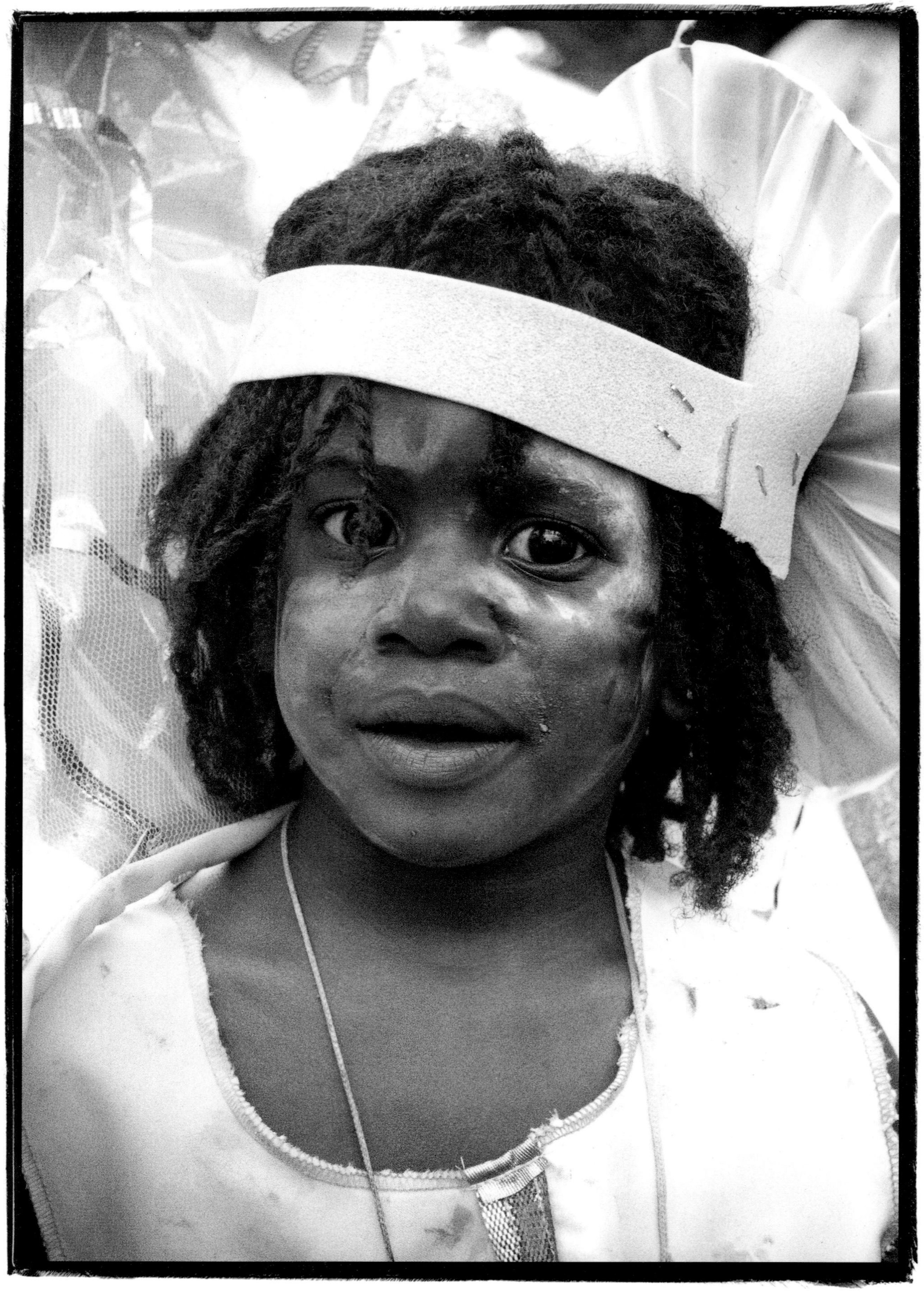

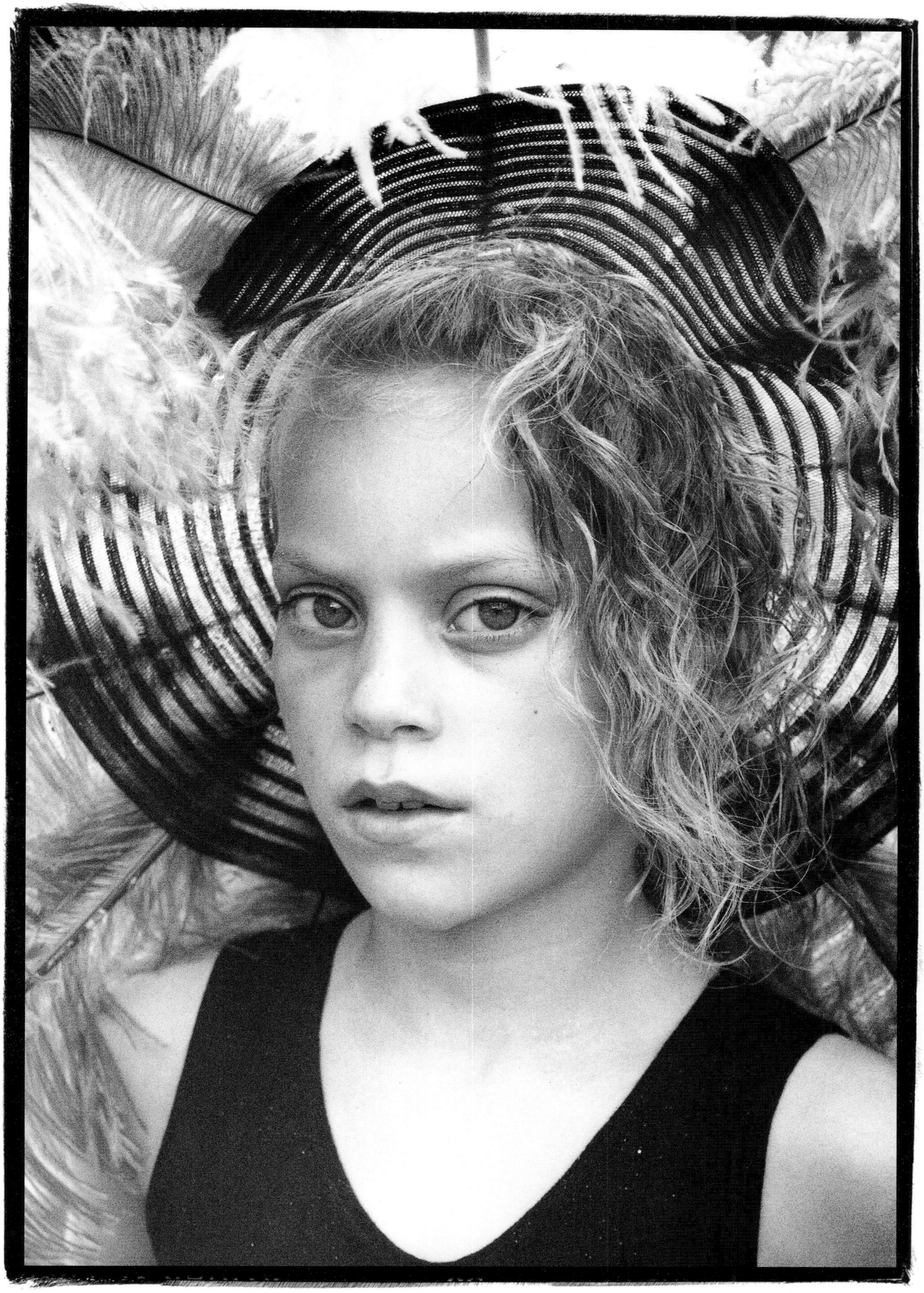

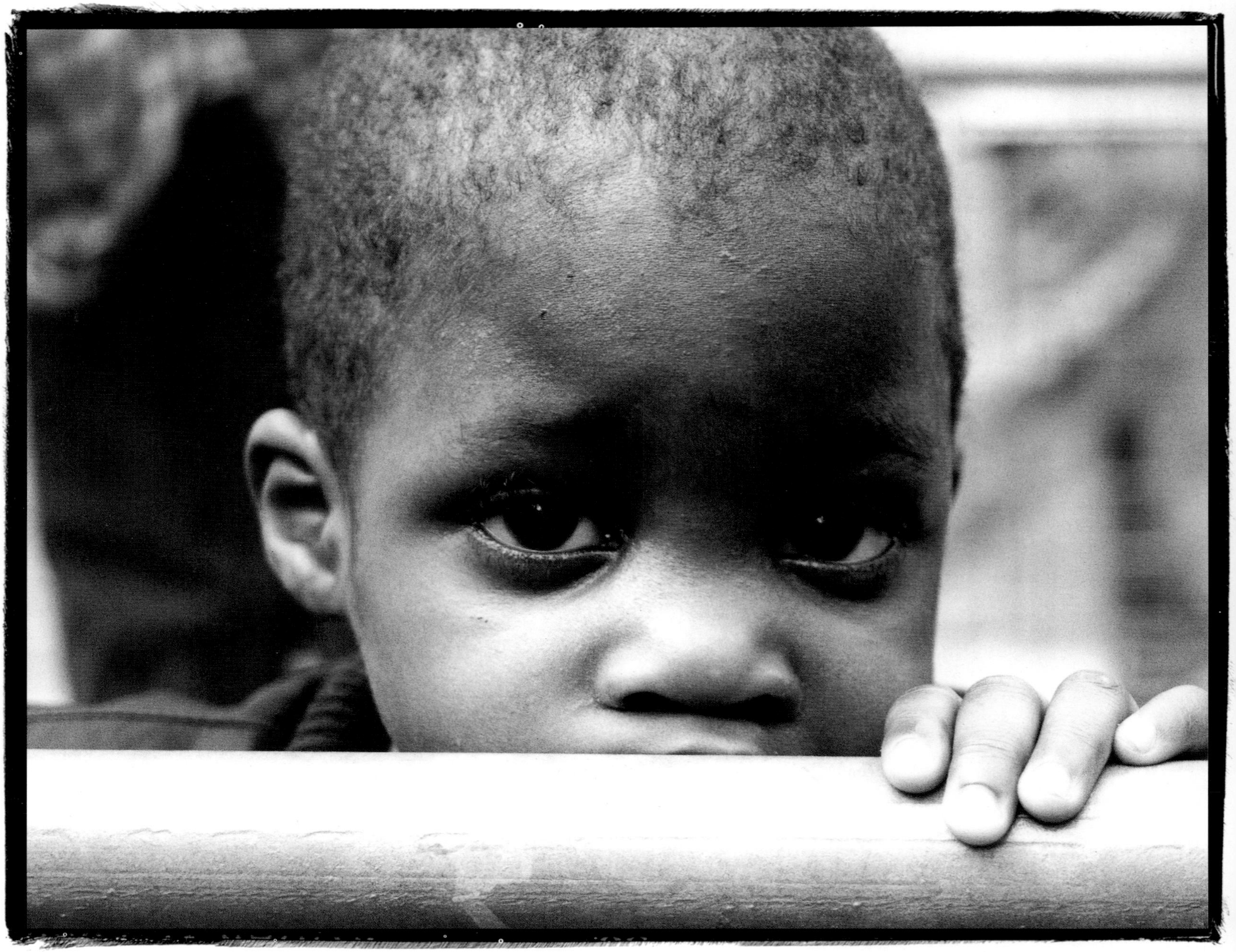

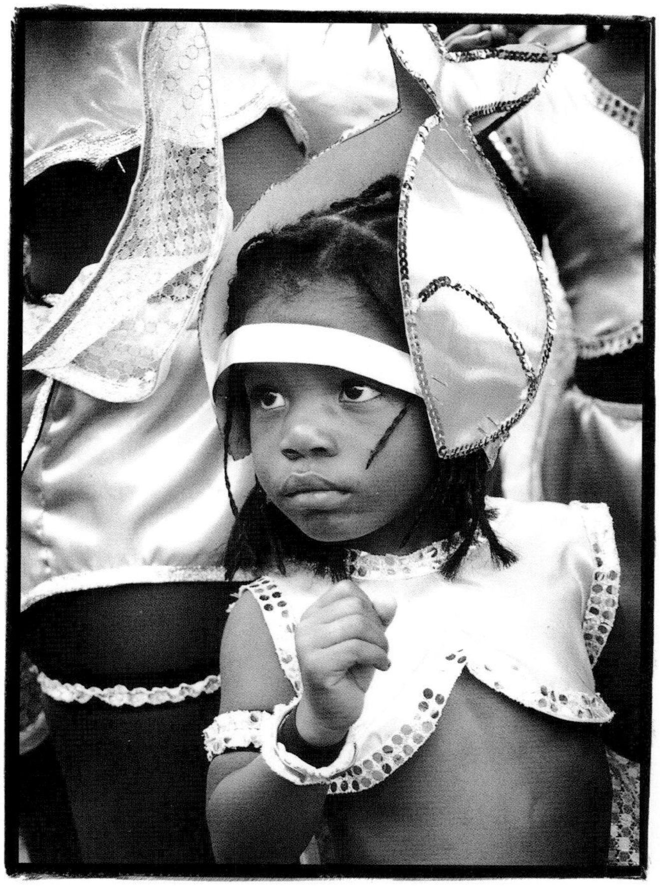

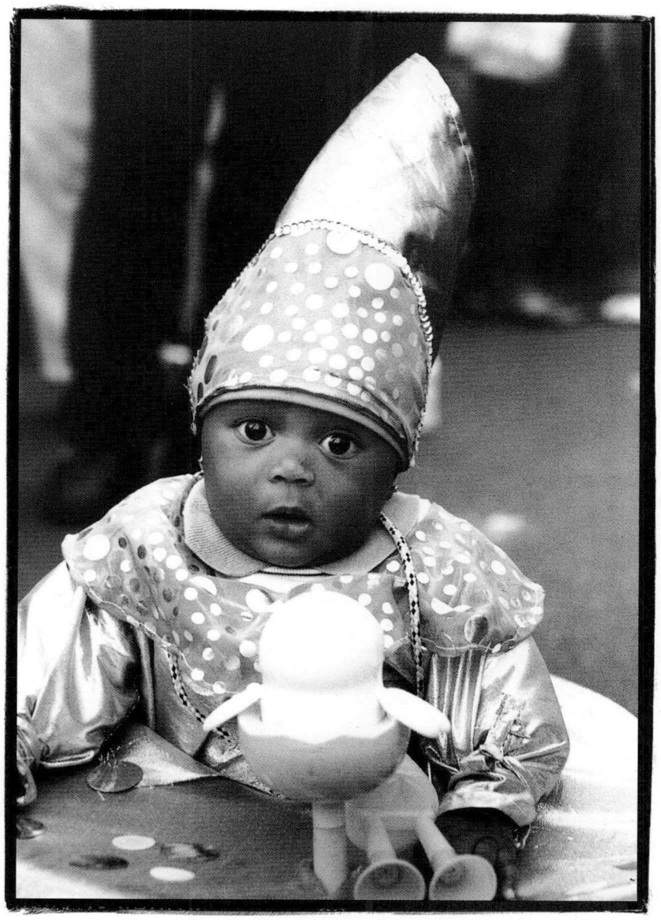

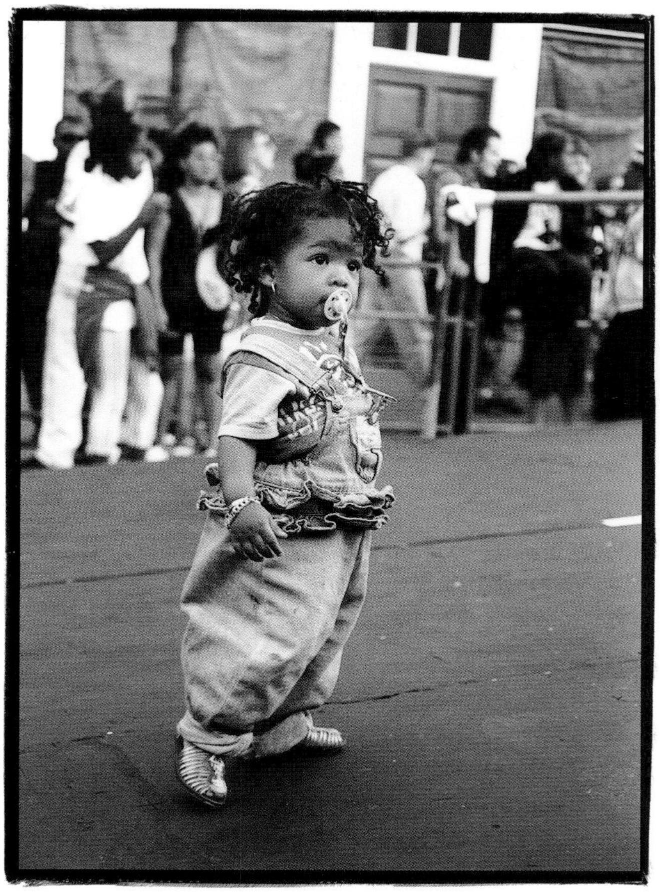

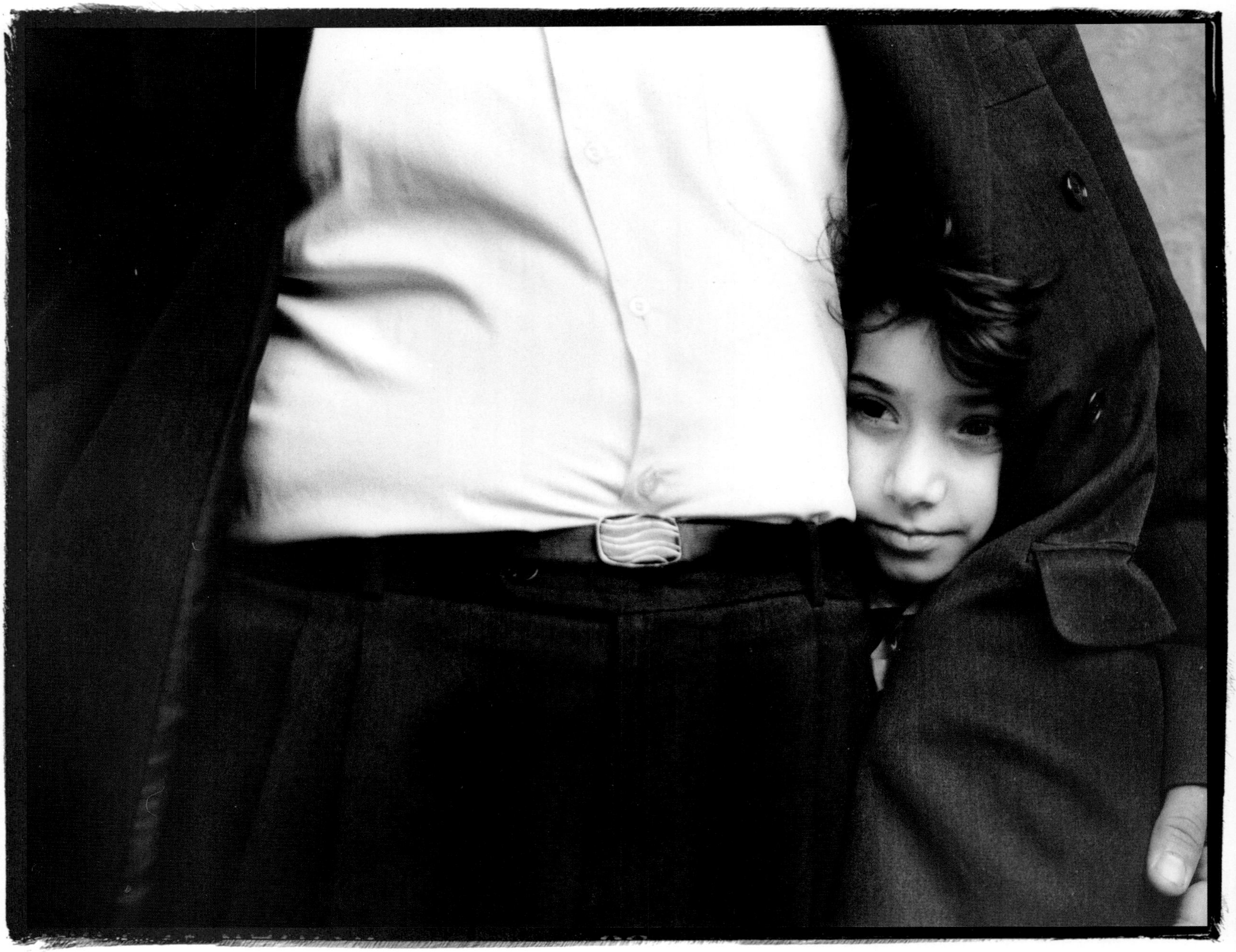

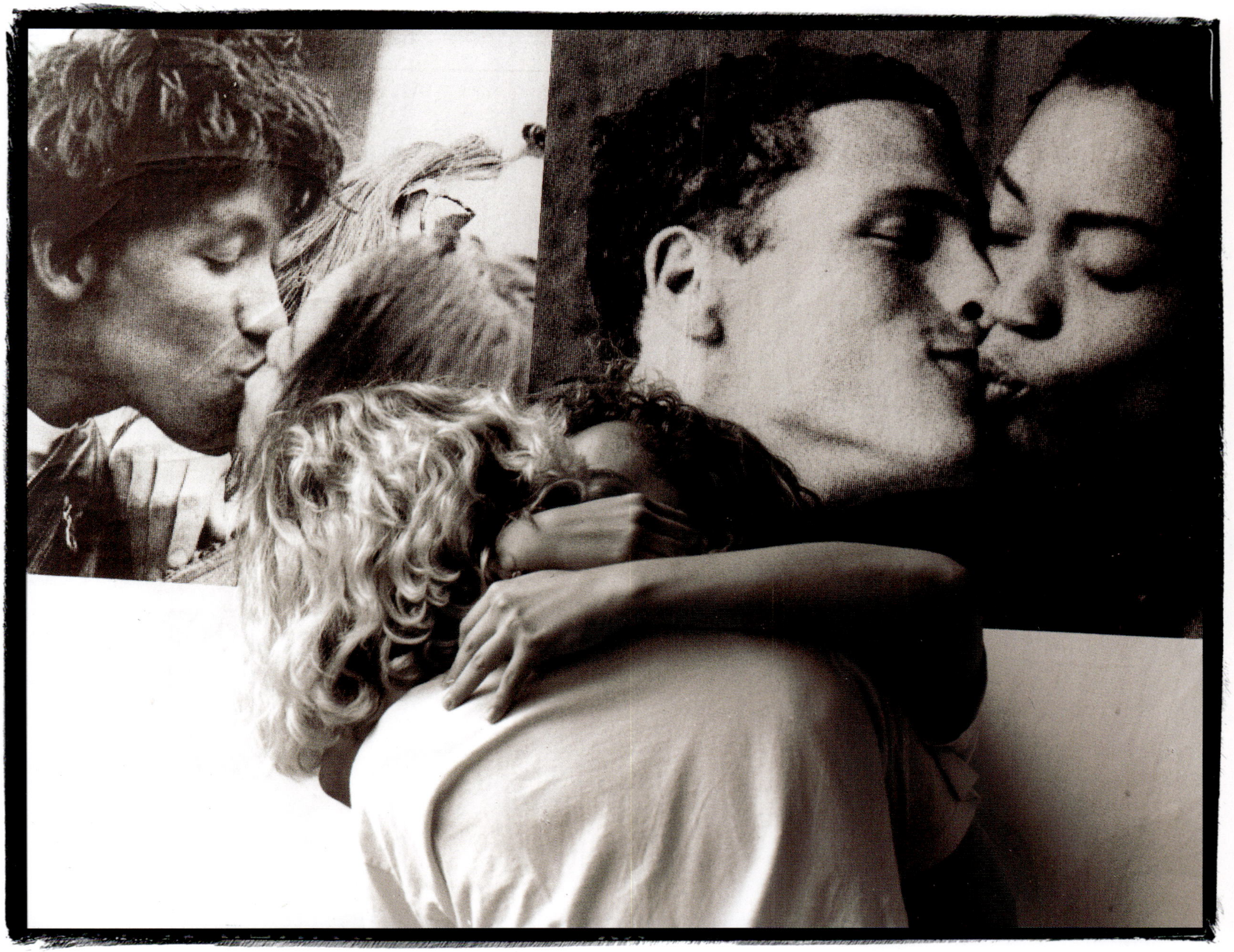

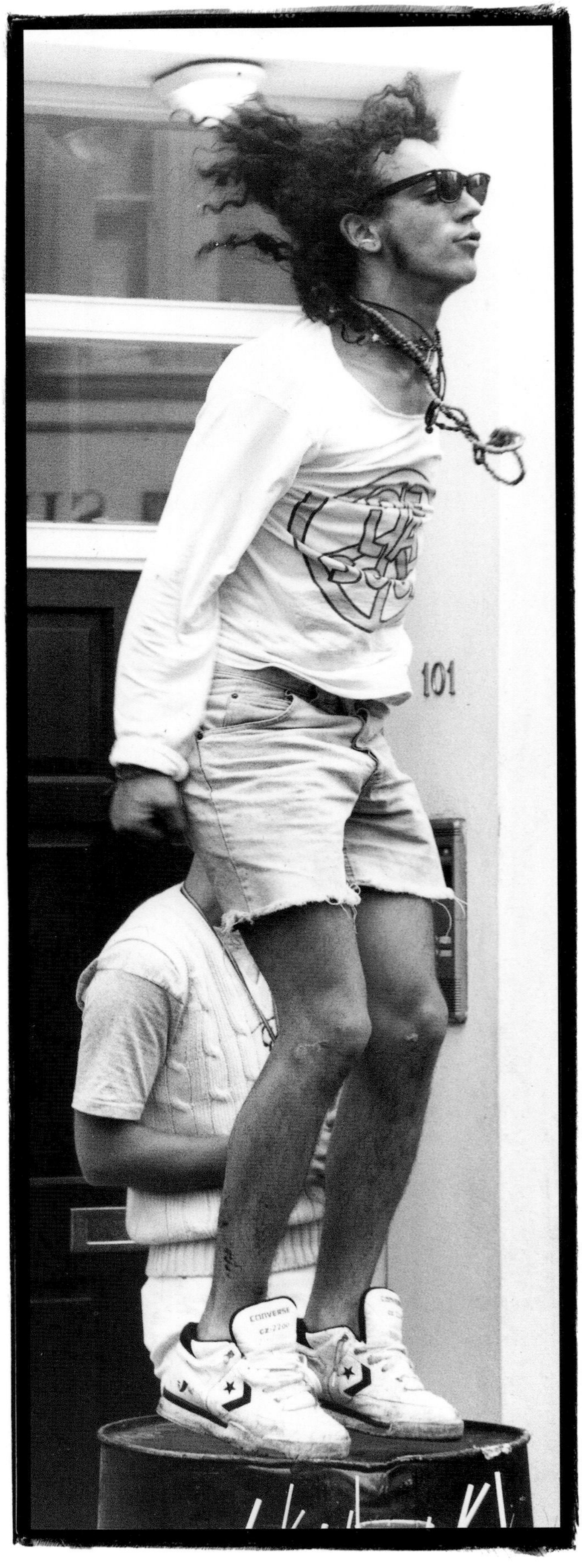
101
CONVERSE

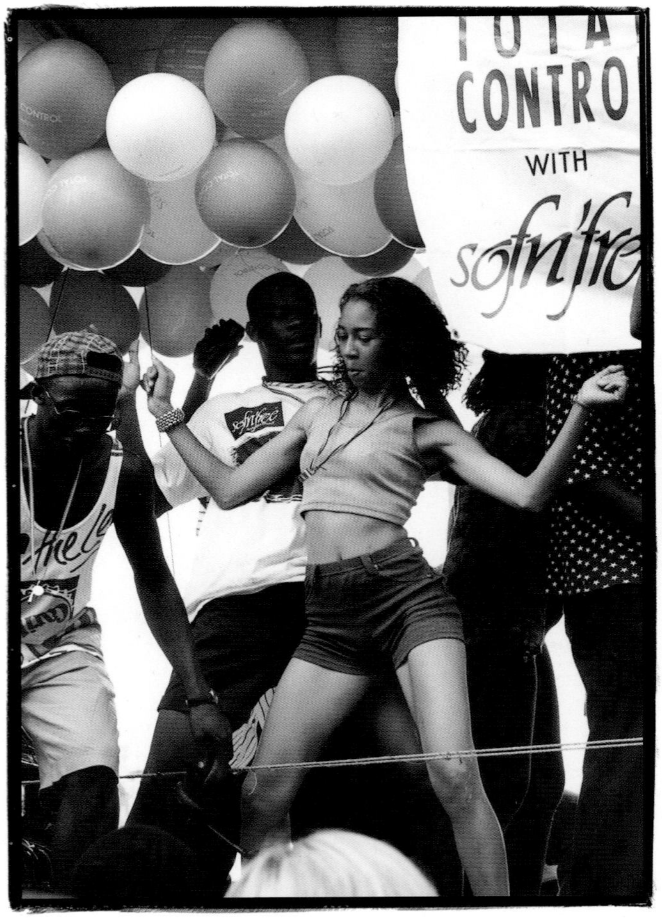
CONTRO
WITH

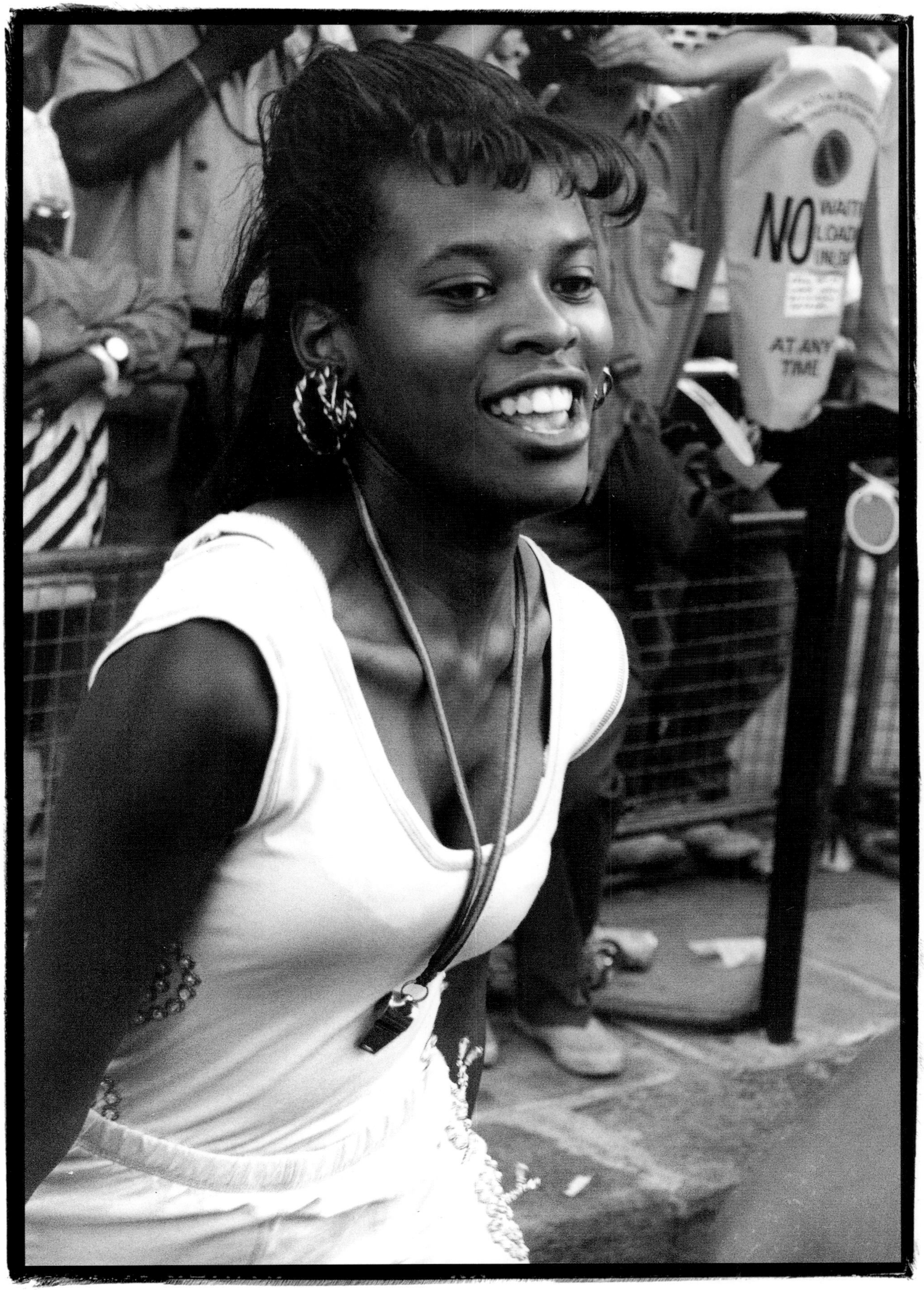
NO
AT ANY
TIME

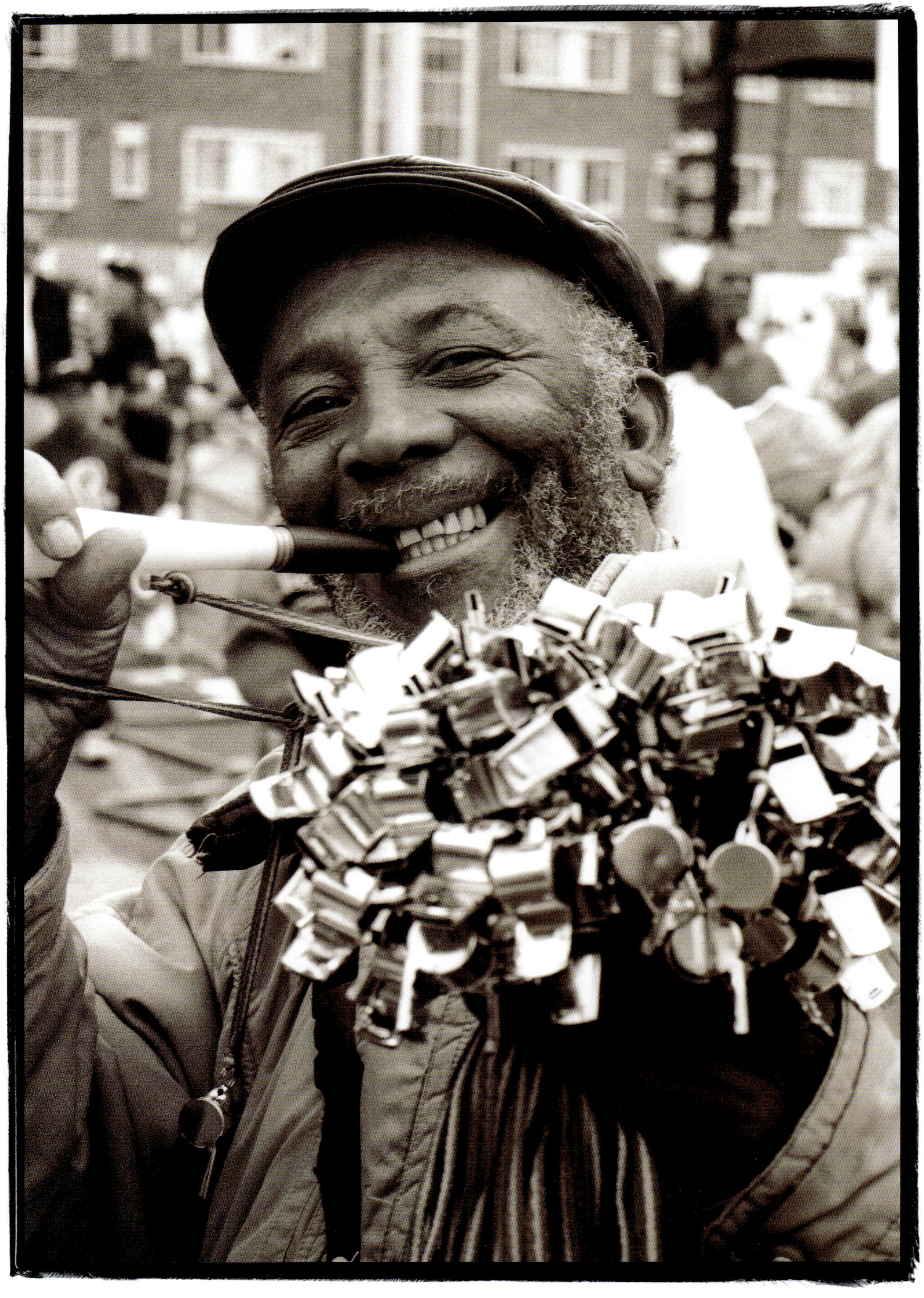

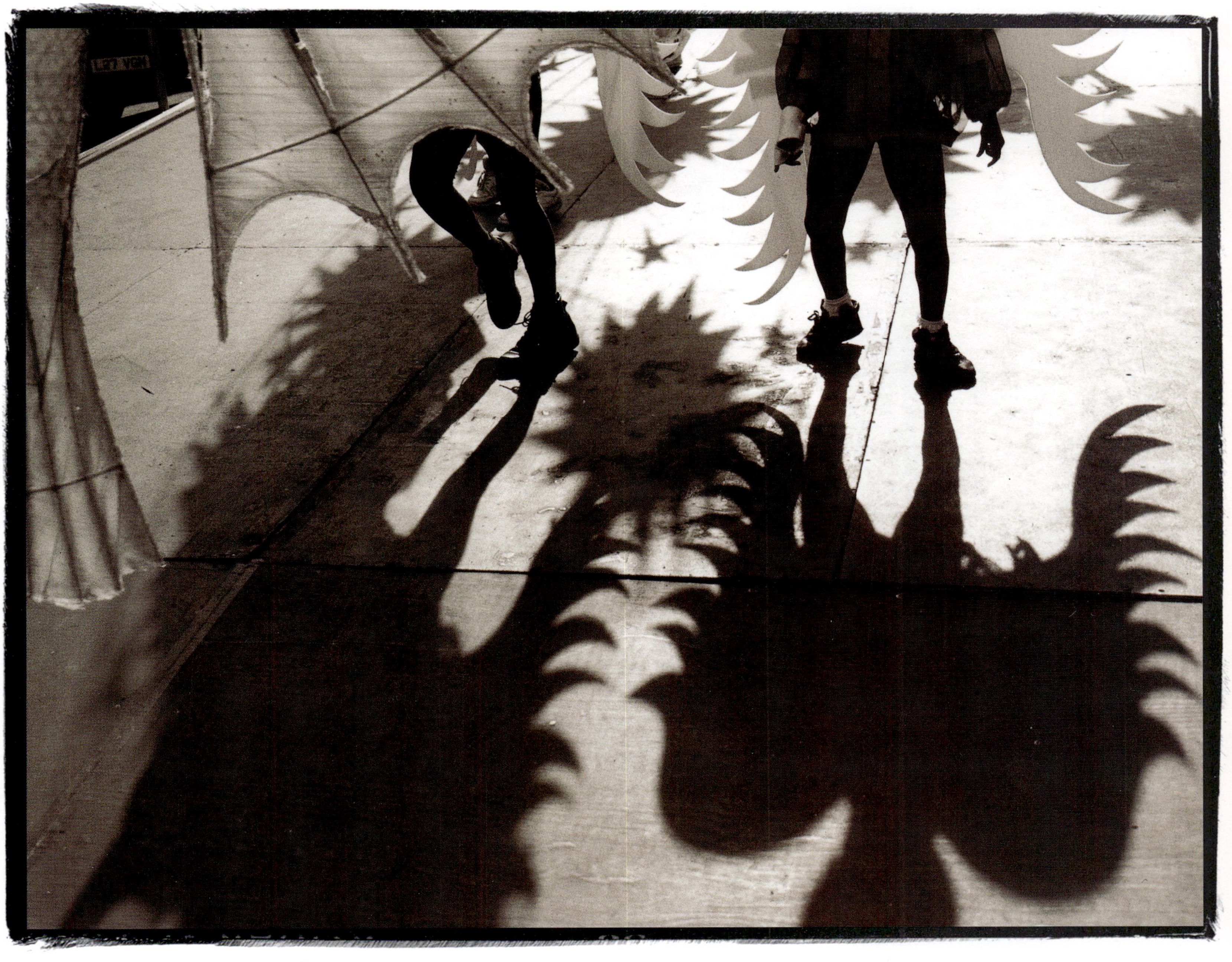

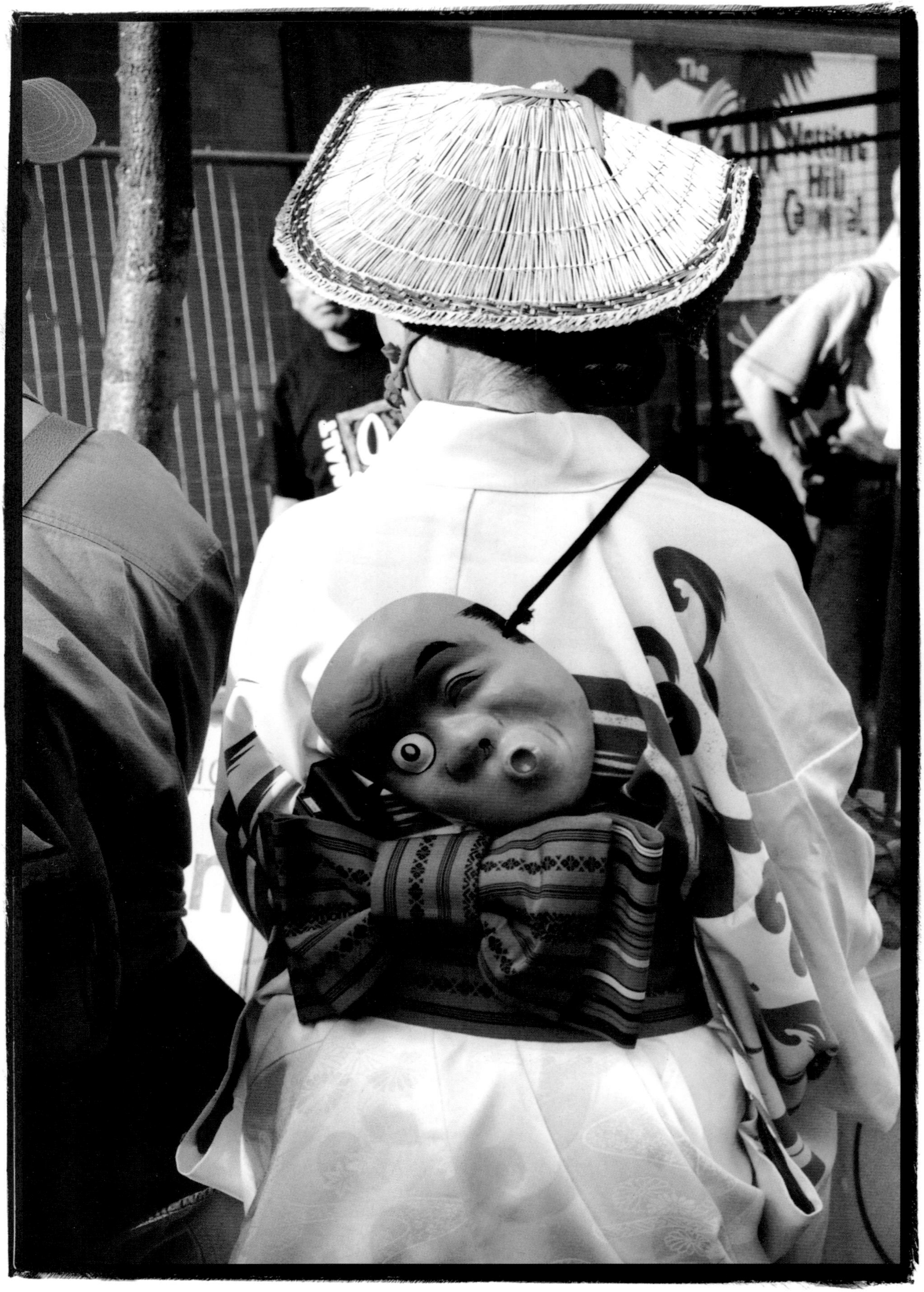
The
Hill

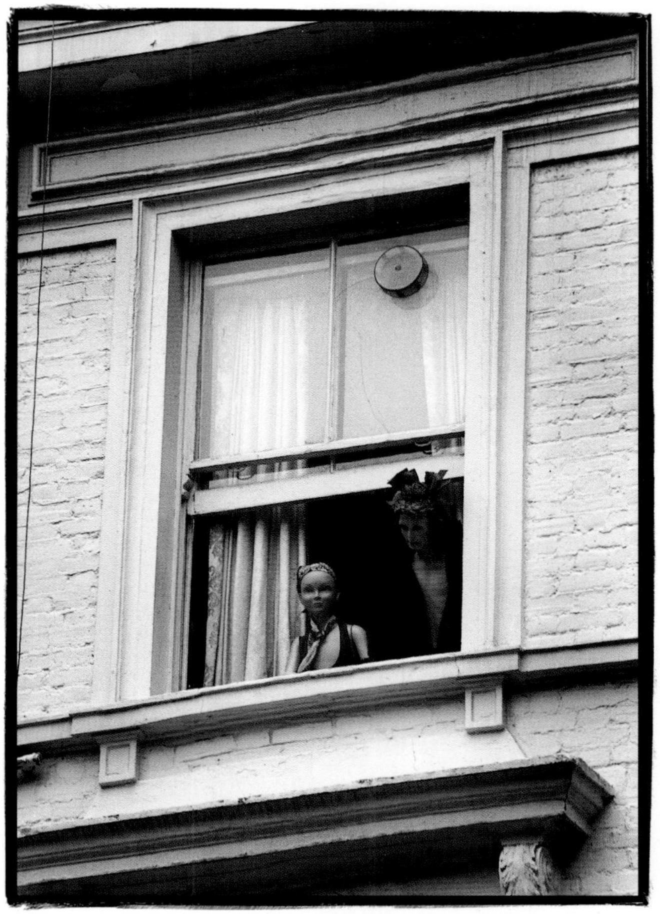

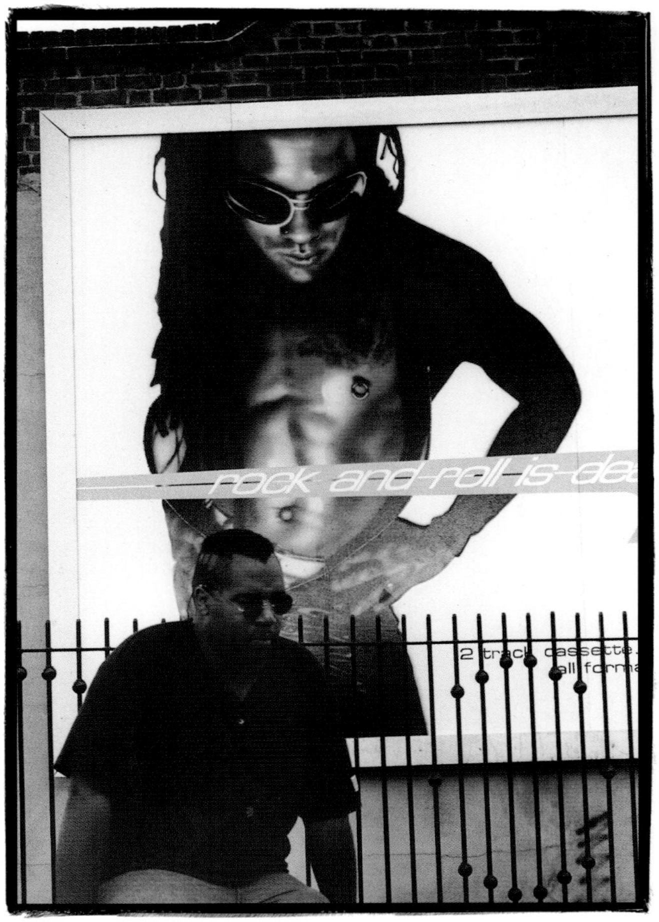
rock-and-roll-is-
2 track cassette.

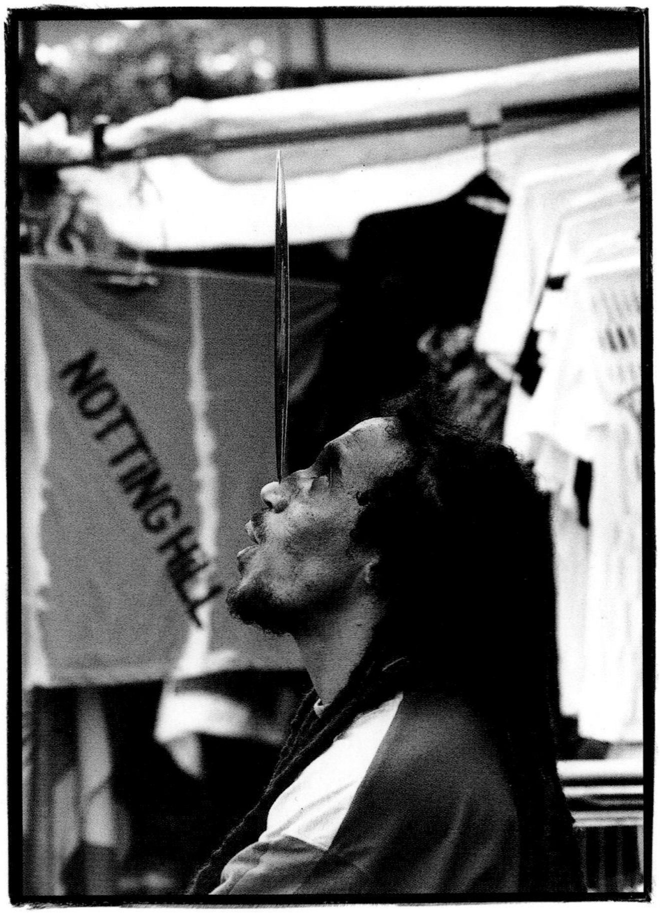
NOTTING HILL

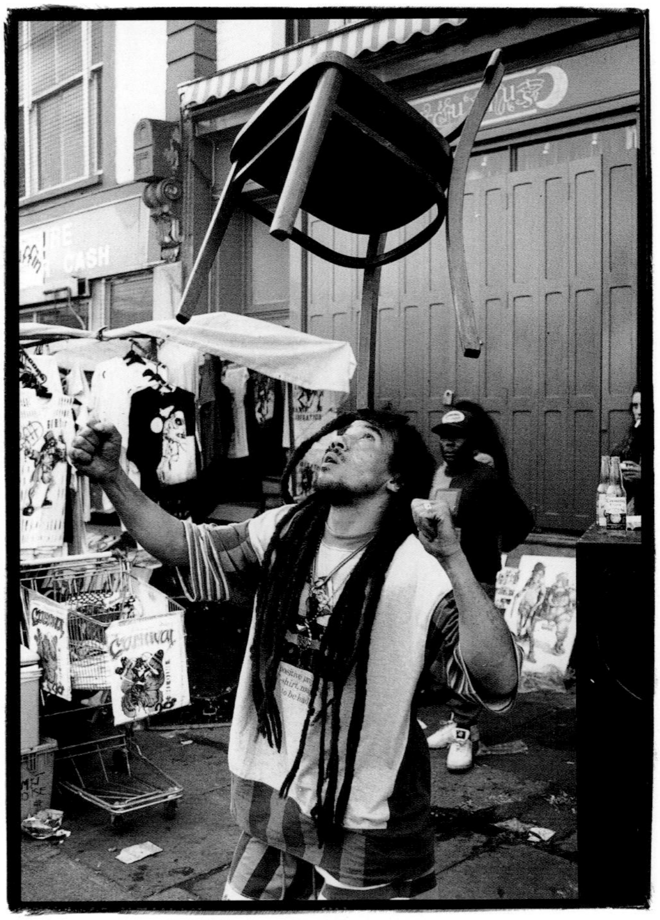
CASH

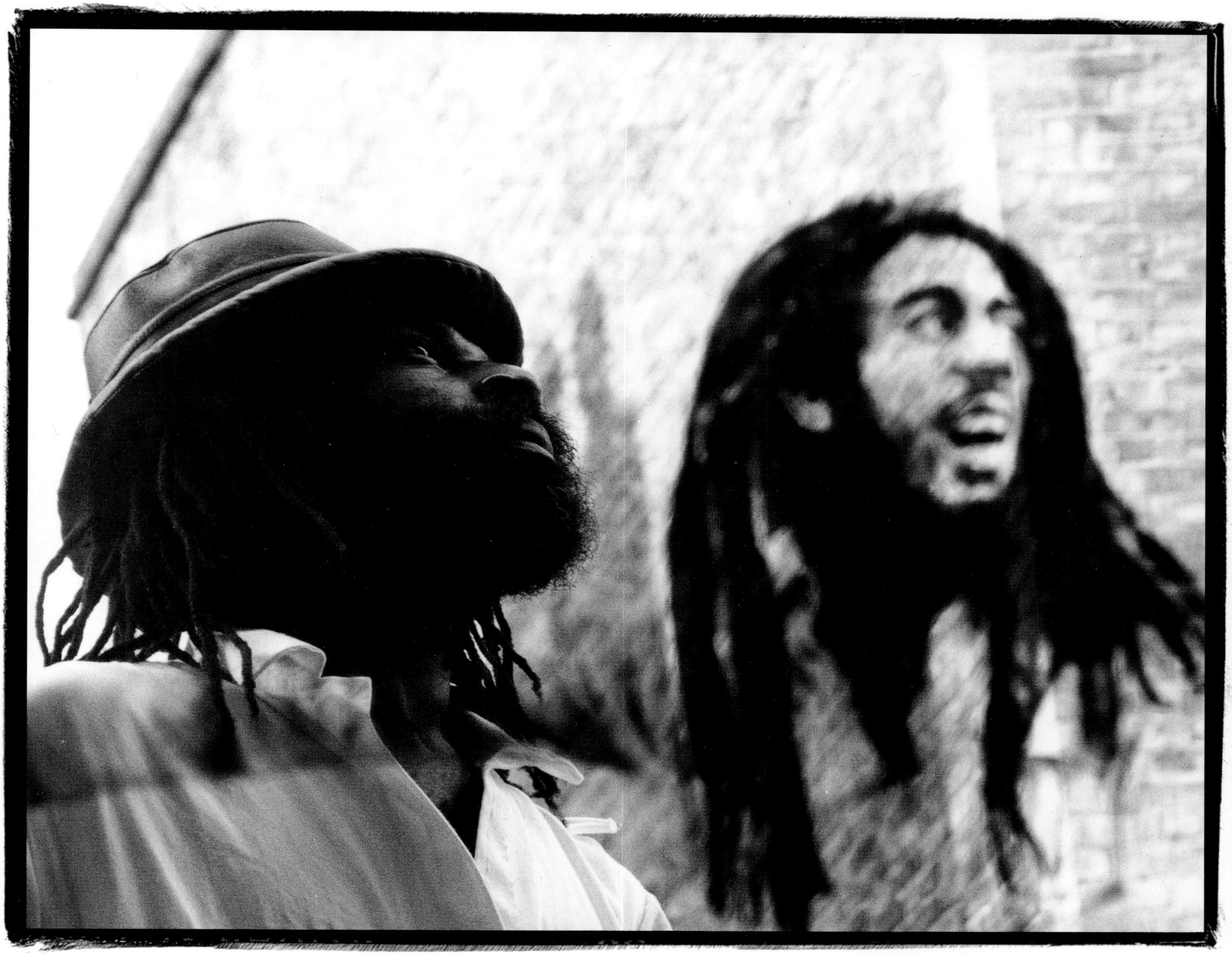

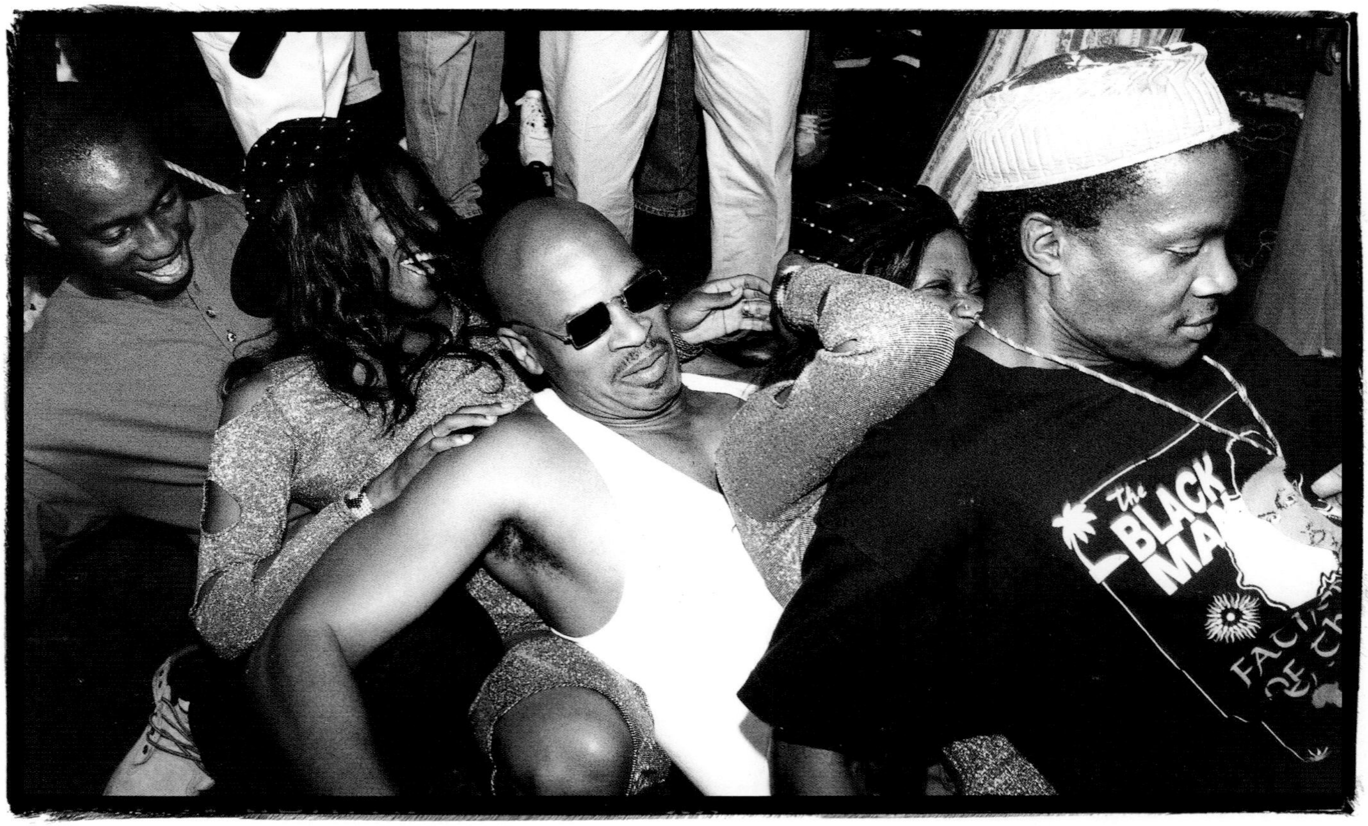
The
BLACK

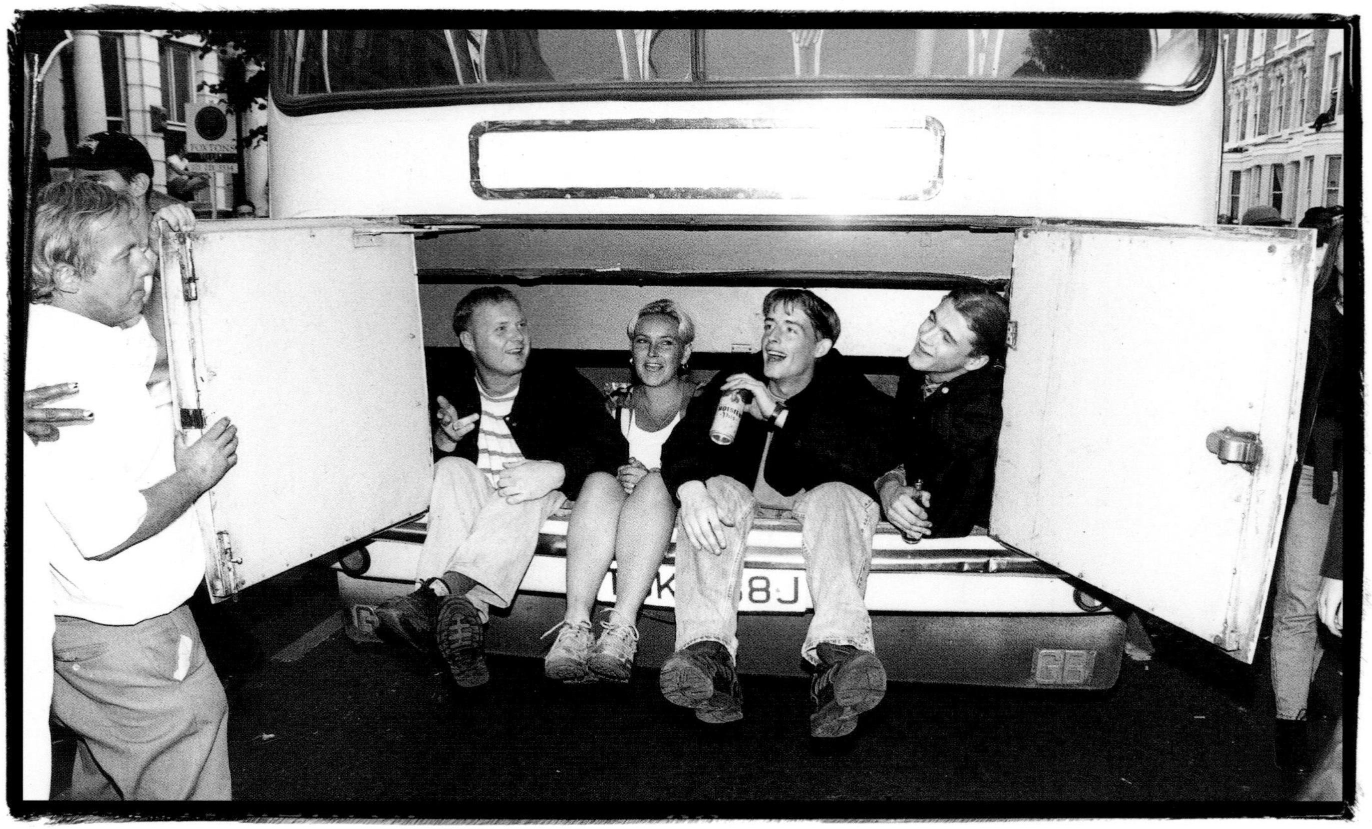
GB

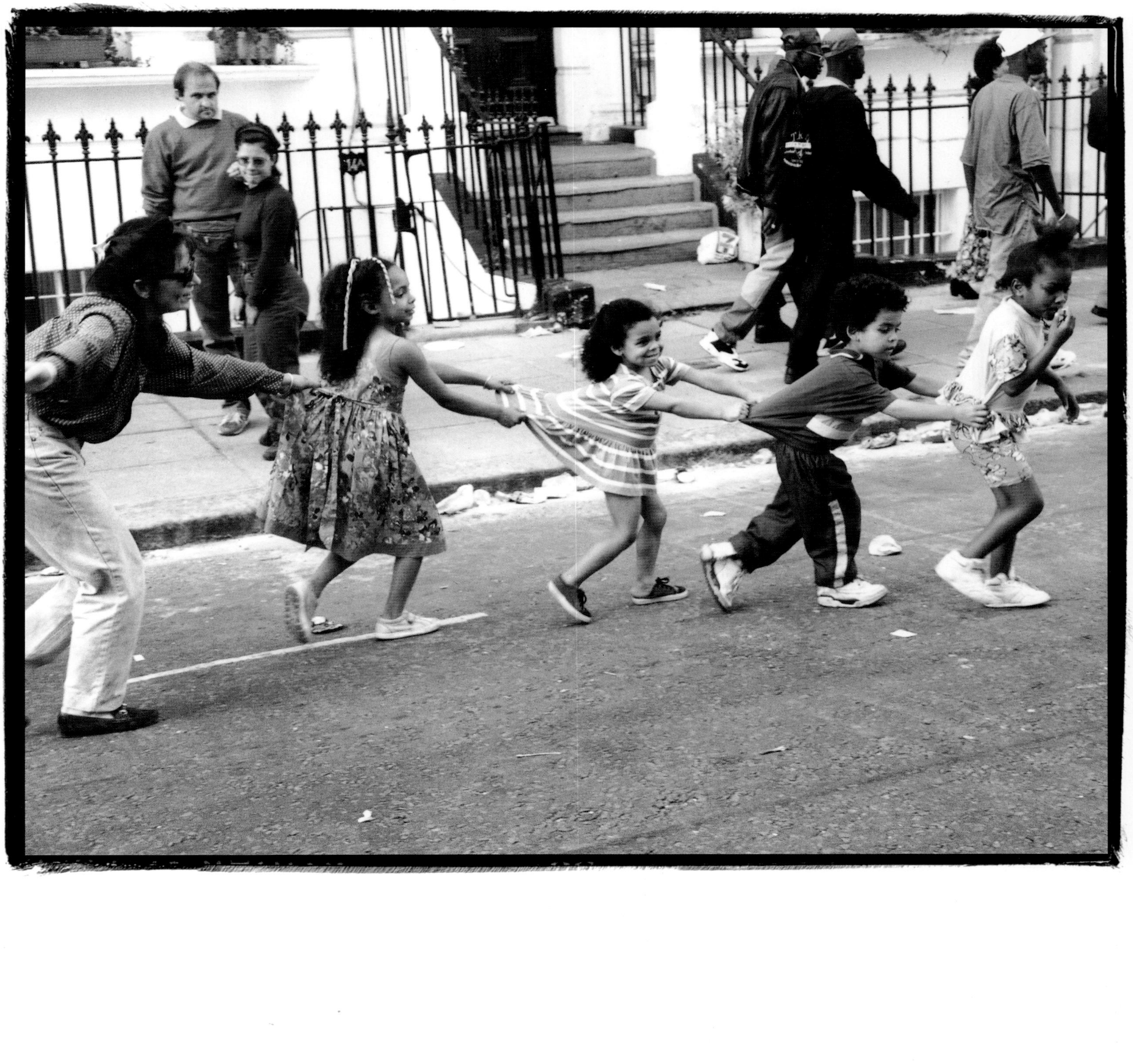

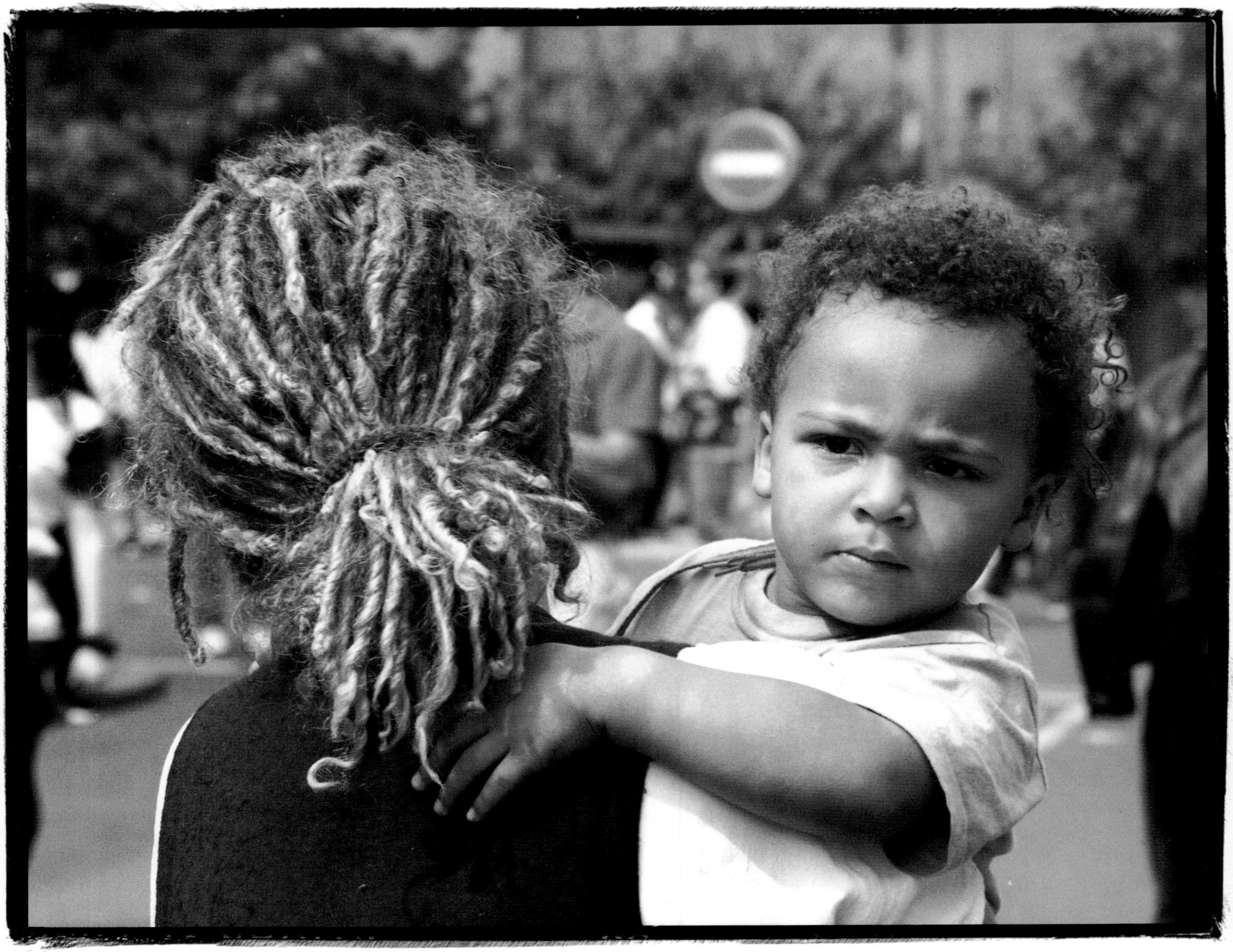

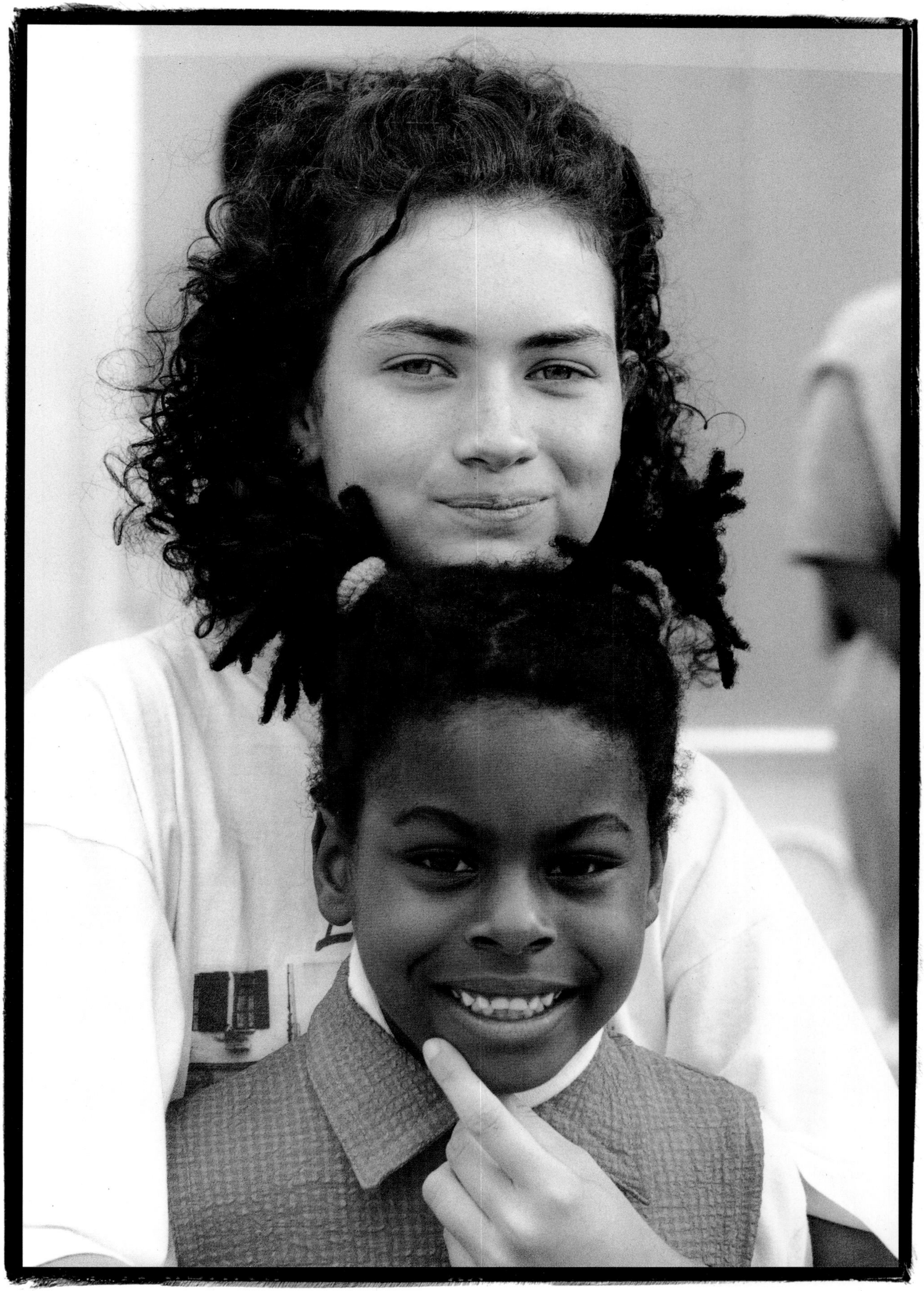

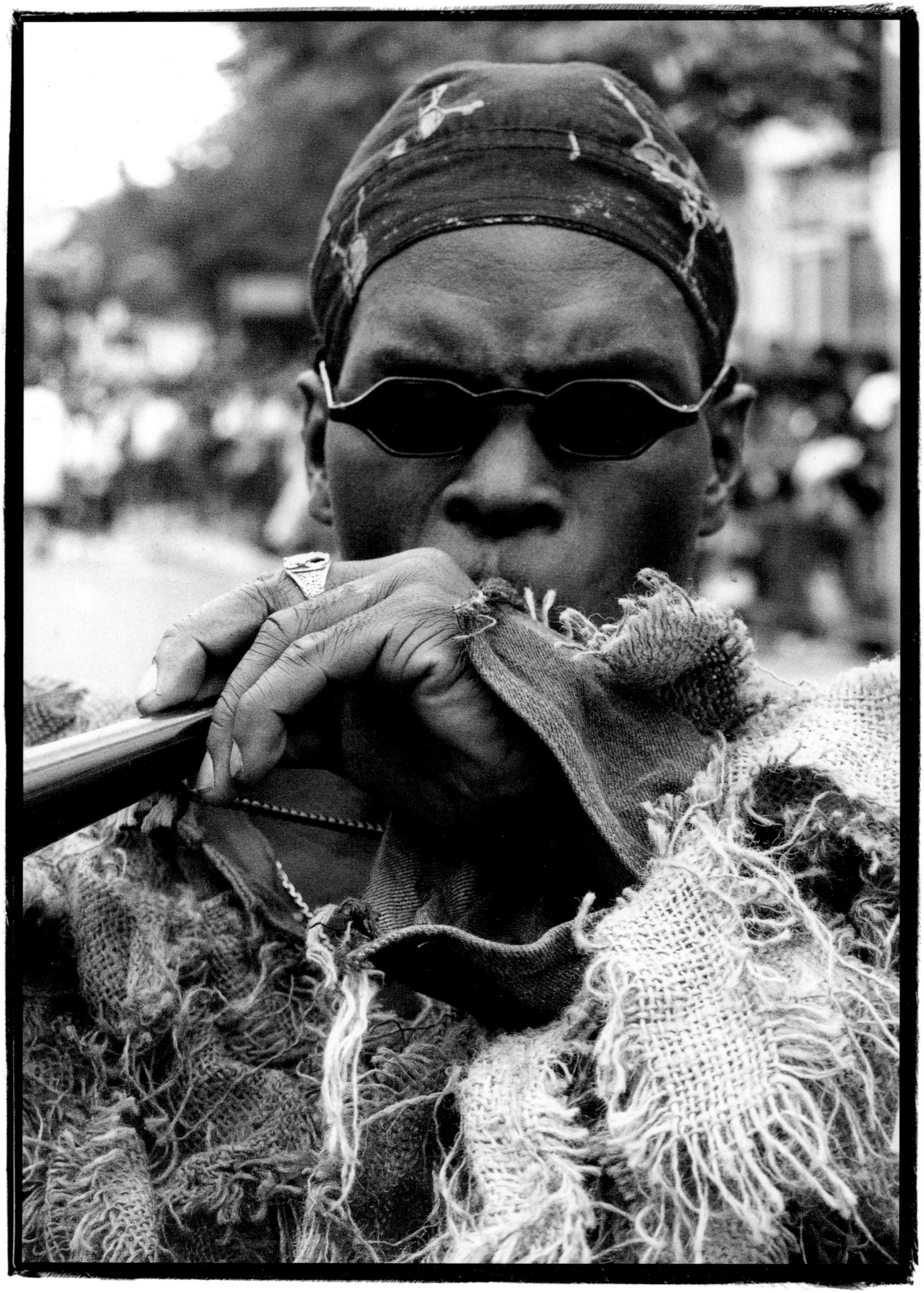